The Current Debate

Edited by Gail Chester & Julienne Dickey

Series Editor: Gail Chester

PRISM

Published in Great Britain 1988 by:
Prism Press 1988
2, South Street
Bridport, Dorset.

in collaboration with Ultra Violet Enterprises
Series Editor: Gail Chester

Distributed in the USA by
AVERY PUBLISHING GROUP Inc
350 Thorens Ave
Garden City Park
New York 11040

ISBN 1 85327 022 9

Cover Design: Eleni Michael

Typeset by: Maggie Spooner Typesetting, London
Printed by: The Guernsey Press Ltd, Guernsey, Channel Islands

CONTENTS

Hallo Sister,
Do you remember me?
I've called to collect
My skin.
I'm the one you slaughtered
Last week
During that discussion
We were in.
You know you kept your head
Down
As you handled
The knife
So you never saw
My face
Or wanted to know about
My life.
You sat across the circle
From me
Acting you were all
Sorted out
But you needed me there
Somehow
Me, with all my doubts.
So yes Sister
You're right
I'm not as good
As you say you are
I'm classist, ageist, racist
And more disablist
Than you.
Though not necessarily in that
Order
And thank goodness my dad
Was a jew
But can I have
My skin back now
I need it to wear
Down the street
When I'm facing men
You know, the enemy,
It's essential
I try to feel complete.

Berta Freistadt
Dec 86, Camden Lesbian Day

INTRODUCTION

Julienne Dickey and Gail Chester

Why is the problem of censorship important to us as feminists? Should feminists have a different perspective on censorship from other groups of radical people? What, indeed, do we mean by censorship? For some women this pertains to state censorship alone; for some it denotes the silencing of oppositional voices in a variety of ways; for others it represents an acceptable method of controlling material that is offensive, degrading and possibly dangerous. For all, it is a question riven with dilemmas and potential conflict.

A balance has always to be struck between state power and the rights of the individuals. In this case we have to weigh the fact that, as feminists, we must protect our freedom to put views which are often antithetical to a patriarchal state against a need to protect the interests of those who have relatively little power in society — in this instance, women. We rely on being free to communicate our ideas for our movement to survive and grow. In the area of sexuality, feminists demand freedom of expression and representation to prevent women's enforced return to asexuality and the invisibility and persecution of lesbianism. At the same time, most feminists feel strongly that the freedom enjoyed by pornographers and others to perpetrate their sexist and offensive images of sexuality at the least undermines our struggle for freedom in other spheres, and is possibly even a significant cause of our oppression.

Feminist opinion currently ranges from the belief that pornography is central to women's oppression and must be subject to state controls, through the understanding that it is against women's interests and must be campaigned against, to an assertion that pornography is merely representation and, unlike acts, cannot cause oppression: sexist, racist, heterosexist, disablist, ageist behaviour — economic insecurity — these cause oppression. Indeed, they claim, pornography may even be liberating.

Are we seeking some kind of unity of opinion? Should we be? Can we assume that women have a commonality of interest? Is there one position which is more 'rational', more 'liberated', than another? Or should we be seeking a way to accommodate our differences? The women's movement has never managed to resolve the problem of what to do with fundamental disagreements, which raises the issue of whether there can be such a thing as 'a feminist perspective'. Certainly, there may be a perspective, a rhetoric, fashionable in certain quarters, or at a certain time, and fear of being attacked for not being sufficiently 'right-on' may stifle debate — but this simply perpetuates a false hegemony and leaves many women confused and unable to freely explore that confusion. It also leads to a 'party line' mentality, which in turn leads to a lack of original thinking and rigorous analysis.

A further dilemma for feminists around the issue of pornography is how far to form coalitions in order to achieve the goal of the elimination of offensive material, if that is desired. Do we work alongside men in mixed organisations to bring about changes in the media? Do we form alliances with those who also abhor pornography, but whose politics we abhor — can we reconcile within ourselves that on this issue we may share a common moral purpose?

Of course, a feminist analysis of the imbalance of power portrayed in offensive material has little to do with Tory championing of bigotry, masquerading as moral rectitude — opposing in one breath permissiveness, abortion rights, homosexuality, obscenity, pornography and all the other things that 'threaten family life', (thus providing a convenient smokescreen for all the things that *actually* threaten 'family life': unemployment, cuts in the health service, welfare provisions, childcare and education . . .) But where does political analysis leave off and the championing of moral rectitude begin? Are we always clear about the difference? How far do we want to confer upon the state the status of guardian of the nation's morals?

Some feminists argue that the introduction of civil legislation to control pornography sidesteps the issue of criminalisation of sexual expression and censorship, and puts the power of control into the hands of women rather than the state. It becomes a matter of challenging sex discrimination. But, aside from the question of how many women would actually bring prosecutions — a time-consuming and expensive business — it would be the agents of the state who decided on the outcome of the prosecution, not women;

and the powers of injunction would, in any case, amount to censorship.

The call for civil legislation is based on the ordinances drawn up in the United States by feminists Andrea Dworkin and Catharine MacKinnon. There is a sense in which this reflects the fact that the British women's movement is affected by American cultural imperialism; we are attempting to apply a model which may not be relevant to our particular circumstances. It is true that it is North American thinking which tends to be most readily available to us, but we seldom look to the experience of countries in Europe, Africa or elsewhere — some of whom have introduced forms of legislation to control sexist media content and pornography. (It is also true that, despite our efforts, there is a complete dearth of such information in this book.) We have included a number of articles on the North American experience, because the ordinances are being cited by many here as a possible model for us to emulate. Some of the articles illustrate the machinations of the right, and their use of the feminist cause for their own ends in perverting objective appraisal of the issues.

There are many feminists who agonise eternally about balancing the rights and wrongs of statutory or other controls of sexist material, yet who accept unquestioningly that racist and fascist material ought to be controlled. Most white feminists would probably agree that racist material incites race hatred, and that black people are entitled to inhabit a society free of racist insults and abuse. So are the qualms of such white women about censoring material which may similarly incite hatred of women, and whose insulting messages surround us daily, indicative of the fact that we take our oppression as women less seriously than that of black people? Or that few white women would dare to challenge openly censorship of racist material, whatever their views on censorship in principle? There is, of course, also no unity of opinion among black feminists on these questions — though they are in a better position to understand just how ineffective race relations legislation has been in controlling racist representation.

In spite of this ineffectiveness, there are some feminists who look to race relations legislation as a model for possible legislation against pornography. Sona Osman and Pratibha Parmar in this book argue that this is mistaken. Yet it does pose a dilemma: would we be better off without such legislation altogether, or would strengthening it provide a better deal for black people? In other words, just because the race relations legislation doesn't work at present, does that mean you don't attempt any kind of control?

Underlying the whole debate is the unresolved question of proving the connection between the images that people see and their behaviour; specifically, does viewing pornography and other sexist material cause men to behave violently or abusively towards women? Studies have tended to adopt one of two approaches: trying to find correlations between what men report that they have watched/read, and their behaviour; and laboratory experiments where men are exposed to certain material, and then the immediate effects observed, either in terms of behaviour, or through attitudinal tests. The former kinds of studies are riven with procedural problems, the major one being that just because there is a correlation between, for example, a man's consumption of pornography and his raping a woman, it doesn't mean that there is a causal relationship. In other words, all it may prove is that a man who is likely to rape is also likely to read pornography. Removing the pornography may not remove his propensity to rape. (And of course, rape and other abuse of women pre-dates mass pornography by many centuries: furthermore, abuse of women is common in countries where pornography is outlawed.)

Studies of the second kind, based on controlled laboratory conditions, have yielded inconclusive results — and in any case are only capable of proving that some men act in a particular way in a laboratory setting, not that they would necessarily act this way in the outside world, with all its attendant restrictive influences. Furthermore, experiments such as these that have done follow-up studies have almost always shown that there is little or no long-term effect of the laboratory experiments on the men's behaviour.

There are other problems with trying to establish causal relationships. Why do we assume that we, as feminists, can distinguish between fantasy and reality in pornography, but men can't? Is this not similar to the assumption by the moral right that it is only 'other people' who are adversely affected by such material, while they remain pure? Also, if pornography is supposed to explain so much violence and sexual harassment of women, why does it not explain the huge incidence of child sexual abuse? The amount of 'kiddie porn' in this country is proportionally tiny, and never seen by the vast majority of child molesters.

We are not saying that being surrounded by negative images of women has no effect on men's behaviour, nor that it is impossible that someone could devise a test of sufficient scientific rigour that its results would be beyond rebuke — it's just that nobody has done it yet. So, if we are to use this argument as a reason for censorship of offensive material, we need to be quite clear that there is little *scientific* evidence. We have to use other, *feminist* arguments, especially when it is clearly possible for the results, such as they are, to be manipulated to back up different and opposed political/moral positions. Alice Henry and Carole Vance discuss this in their articles.

The political climate of the eighties both exacerbates these dilemmas and provides us with new ones. Increasing state censorship abounds, both of material that is politically contro- versial (*Spycatcher*, *Real Lives*, *Secret Society*, the Local Government Act, the extension of the Prevention of Terrorism Act) and of material deemed obscene (for example, the Video Recordings Act, the extension of the provisions of the Obscene Publications Act to television, through the new Broadcasting Act). Section 28 of the Local Government Act 1988 is a salutory reminder of this govern- ment's attitude to representations of homosexuality, and should give anyone pause for thought before bestowing yet more powers upon it.

The frightening pace of moral retrenchment goes hand in hand with the politics of despair. As we see the hopes of the sixties and seventies fade and as we lose more and more ground, it becomes increasingly difficult to maintain our fervour. The weakening of the campaigning strength of the women's movement leads some feminists, in desperation, to seek assistance from the state, while it leads others to a 'post-feminist' liberalisation of attitude, manifest- ing itself, for example, in an increase in the availability and acceptability of lesbian pornography. Others simply give up caring and retire to the country with their cats and a good book.

There are some feminists who look ahead to better times by believing that we should be drawing up model legislation in preparation for, say, a future Labour government. There are certainly members of the Labour Party committed to media reform, including the elimination of media sexism and pornography (as discussed by Teresa Stratford). But would this produce any better results than legislation under a Tory government? Who would draft the legislation and who would enforce it? Legislation will remain in the control of white, unreconstructed, 'establishment' men. The question is fundamental: can we ever count on sufficient of these men to be our allies and to exercise their control in our interests?

As we set out to edit this book it became clear the extent to which pornography has come to dominate the debate about censorship. To some extent this ignores the more all-pervasive effects of media sexism in general. To an even greater extent it leads feminists to neglect to speak out against other censorship legislation. Freedom of expression *in itself* is a feminist issue — you cannot campaign for women's rights or lesbian and gay rights, still less their liberation, without it. Failing to make vital connections is a significant cause of the fragmentation and disintegration of the progressive movement.

It also became clear that there is a prevailing lack of awareness among feminists about how the media industry operates. Yet any discussion of the subject of representation needs to be set within the context of the ownership, structure and control of the media. The ownership of all forms of media is becoming increasingly concentrated in the hands of a few multinational corporations, which either own or have substantial shares in many different forms of media, from newspaper and book publishing to television and film companies — as well as other forms of leisure activities. These corporations are needless to say controlled by rich upper- and middle-class white men. The management and senior staff of all mainstream media concerns are also from this background. Thus the flow of information (including 'entertainment', which also informs us about our world) is controlled by patriarchal capitalism. This is reflected not only in the profits made by the media industry, but also in their entrenched, institutionalised sexism, racism and other oppressive attitudes and practices. It ensures that women do not have equal work opportunities in any branch of the media, certainly not at decision-making level; and consequently there is little possibility of overturning this state of affairs.

Therefore, what we have at present is in-built censorship on a massive scale — against women, against black people, against lesbians and gay men, against the working class, against anyone whose interests do not coincide with that privileged minority who control the media. Of course, this is not always a deliberate conspiracy, but the structures are so powerful that they militate against ideas and pressures that might lead to any significant transformation.

We are talking about a huge denial of civil rights: the right to communicate and to have access to correct, unbiased information

— or at least to information reflecting a wide variety of well-informed perspectives, since true objectivity is an illusion. (Often when talking of censorship, we tend to think of it only in terms of banning what presently exists. But one might say that women's voices are censored *now*. This will continue as long as the current patterns of media ownership, employment and control are kept in place.)

For this reason some argue that by focussing on the current evils and devoting so much time to trying to eradicate them on a short-term, piecemeal basis, we are dissipating our energy, leaving the structures intact. Perhaps in the long-term, it is more effective to challenge such things as employment practices, support media union initiatives for equal opportunities, encourage the growth of independent, including feminist, media. To say nothing of working towards changes in our society that will give women greater power of self-determination and a better life.

All of these would provide alternatives to legislation as a means of influencing what appears on the news stands, on television and elsewhere. Even in terms of short-term strategies, there are other non-legislative options. It is true that the non-statutory bodies like the Press Council and the Advertising Standards Authority are by definition toothless, internally self-defensive organisations which are of little practical use to women. The government-appointed boards of the BBC and the IBA do not think or act in terms of anti-sexism. But these bodies could be replaced by more effective ones; this possibility is explored by Kate Holman and Wendy Moore. Let us not forget that in the current climate, they could also be replaced by *less* effective and probably more repressive ones. As we go to press, William Rees-Mogg, well-known supporter of the Church, 'the family', and Margaret Thatcher has been appointed to head the new Broadcasting Standards Commission. What prospects now, for censorship which defends women rather than the status quo?

Both the National Union of Journalists and the ACTT (the television and film technicians' union) have codes of practice concerning the portrayal of women (and other groups), which are manifestly largely ignored by their members. Attempts have been made to improve the situation within the NUJ by the formation of the Ethics Council, which has more of an educational than an admonitory approach. For codes of practice to work, the battle for the hearts and minds of media workers must be won, and this is bound to be a long process. This is the issue which Denise Searle addresses in her article.

We, the editors, are both members of the Campaign for Press and Broadcasting Freedom; this book is jointly published by it, and thus it is probably worth stating its position. The Campaign, as its name implies, upholds the principle of freedom of speech and expression. But it has never maintained that this freedom is absolute. It believes that there can be no real freedom without responsibility, that the rights of individuals and groups of people in some cases outweigh the rights of other individuals and groups to say what they like. Thus it supports, for example, restrictions on rape reporting in order to protect the identity and thus the freedom of the victim. It also supports restrictions on the publication of racist material that is inimical to the interests of black people, directly threatening their rights and their very lives.

The Campaign is also founded on the principles of media democracy and diversity, and thus recognises that restrictions must be placed on the 'freedom' of the rich and powerful to monopolise the media and thus control the flow of information for their own profit. It recognises that legislation may be necessary to ensure that all sections of society, including the largely disenfranchised, are also able to enjoy their right to disseminate information and imagery from their particular perspective. Such legislation would ensure the creation of mechanisms and structures designed to maximise diversity of media ownership and content.

(There are varying degrees of optimism within the Campaign as to the efficacy of these measures. In an ideal society, with such diverse and popular — in the true sense of the word — media, a range of perspectives on women would be widely available. But in an ideal society, there would be no entrenched sexist attitudes, so that people would make informed choices about which material to read or view, and would come to informed conclusions about the nature and role of women (whatever they might be.) In our society, sexist and other oppressive attitudes would militate against this, even if a greater diversity of progressive material were widely available. Would the greater availability of feminist material automatically lead to the elimination of sexist material? It would be cheering to believe that if all individuals were exposed to a steady diet of 'correct' information and images about women, sexist material would wither and die through lack of credibility and demand.)

In 1985 the Campaign's AGM endorsed a Code of Conduct on media sexism drawn up by the Women's Group. This Code was intended as a guide and a consciousness-raising tool for media workers and consumers, and an expression of the Campaign's disapproval of sexist material. In 1986 a resolution was passed at the AGM further condemning media sexism and suggesting that the campaign against it be accorded a high priority within the CPBF. Out of this, the Women's Group took on the task of assessing, through a questionnaire, both the extent of women's current understanding of what operates to control media content, and the range of opinion among women as to what else should be done.

(About the same time, two mainstream women's magazines — *Woman* and *Just Seventeen* — published the results of their own readers' surveys, the latter of which the CPBF Women's Group helped to devise. These showed widespread discontent about the treatment of women in the media and decisive support for Clare Short's Page 3 Bill.)

The results of the completed questionnaires we received reflected overwhelmingly the opinions of (professed) white middle-class women, and were thus not in any sense representative. However, they did indicate a general paucity of knowledge, and considerable confusion and uncertainty as to possible strategies. It is for this reason that we decided to compile this book. It is not comprehensive, but we have attempted to include as wide a range of opinions and experience as possible. Because of this, we asked many women to write from outside the Campaign, so it is important to state that not all the contributors subscribe to any or all of the policies of the Campaign for Press and Broadcasting Freedom.

As editors we are prone to all the dilemmas which we have outlined above. Throughout the course of editing this book we have swayed back and forth in our own views; controversy is stimulating, but uncertainty and confusion can be incapacitating. Section 28, however, did rescue us from such a fate — and probably tipped the balance for us into a more profound scepticism about the possibility of framing progressive legislation in such a reactionary political climate — and a more deeply-felt fear about how any legislation that controls representation of sexuality can be used against lesbians, as well as increasing our awareness of the vulnerability of all minorities and progressive people to political/state censorship. We still abhor pornography, but find it increasingly hard to support restrictive legislation as an appropriate strategy at this time.

We have been determined to provide a platform for widely differing views, provided that those views were not anti-feminist or containing personal attacks on individual women. We are aware of two things about this: firstly, we may well be attacked ourselves for giving space to some women with whom others disagree virulently. Secondly, by setting limits on what we were prepared to include we could be accused of censorship ourselves. The line between banning material that is offensive, and simply not including it on the grounds that there is wealth of material around (and we are actively seeking material that will further the interests of feminism) is a fine one. But we make no apology for our editorial policy; we believe that it is important on the one hand that an open and challenging debate takes place, and on the other hand that feminists treat one another with respect. This has not always been an easy position to maintain, for there are views expressed here with which we are individually or collectively uncomfortable, but we have persevered in the belief that they deserve to be heard. We admire all the contributors to this book for their bravery in nailing their colours to a particular mast; each has ensured that the voices of many do not remain silent.

A QUESTION OF ALLEGIANCE?

Ros Schwartz

I looked at my fellow jurors: nine men and two other women, a young Asian girl and a woman with very bleached blonde hair and a skirt slit up to her crotch. That sounds like an unkind stereotype, I know. I am talking about first impressions, and, unfortunately, there are some women who reinforce certain stereotypes by their dress and their behaviour. The defence had used twelve objections to ensure as large a proportion of men on the jury as possible. It was a pornography case, our task was to decide whether a certain number of publications seized in a raid on a Soho shop were 'likely to deprave and corrupt' persons unknown, and threaten the 'fabric of our society'. Before the trial could begin, we had to read the books — this meant spending a week locked up in a jury room, from ten until four, with a break for lunch, reading one 'sex' book after another. While the trial was going on, we were not supposed to discuss it or the contents of the reading matter with anybody outside.

This was in January 1982. Although I had been a feminist of sorts for a number of years, there were vast areas I had not addressed: pornography was one of them. It was something I had simply not really thought about. To me, pornography meant *Playboy*, 'blue movies', magazines with pictures of naked women, strip clubs — I found it distasteful but had an attitude of 'live and let live' towards such things. I did not feel personally threatened by it, it did not affect me, it was not a 'gut problem'. I even looked on the whole trial as a bit of a joke, certainly 'meatier' than a boring old burglary or restaurant brawl.

By the time I had read the first few pages of the first book, my complacency was shattered. By the end of the week, I was nearly a candidate for the Mary Whitehouse brigade. I had never imagined the existence of such material, or that the male mind was capable of inventing and consuming such fantasies. All the books except one — a gay love story and the only one that was not violent — were variations on a theme. That theme was the inextricable association of sex with brutality. Women got fucked, against their will, raped, always raped, repeatedly, screamed with pain and then said 'thank you' to their violator. The message was clear: when women say no, they mean yes, the more you hurt them, the more they'll love it. The men were all equipped with giant members, capable of screwing non-stop for days on end. Incest featured prominently, the settings varied, the most offensive being a concentration camp, and various accoutrements and instruments of torture were part and parcel of the sex act. This was presented as 'normal' — sex was never, ever, presented as an act of love or tenderness between two consenting beings, it was always indissociable from pain and degradation. These books were all united in their profound hatred of women and their urge to humiliate us. Interestingly, they were all imported from America. What made them all the more pernicious was the inclusion of an introduction, in pseudo-scientific language, by someone purporting to be an academic, presenting these books as 'normal' human behaviour. None of the books contained pictures.

'How could you sit there reading it?' women asked me. 'How could you bear it?' I read it, sick to the stomach, but I had to understand, make connections. Bells were ringing, tenuous links beginning to form. Worst of all, I did not know what my fellow jurors felt. A detail which made me feel uncomfortable, some of the men spent the week lying on their stomachs while they read — was this stuff giving them a hard-on? I was going to have to discuss these books with a bunch of men, some of whom might be the sort of people who buy such publications anyway, and one thing I wanted to do was collect my arguments together in order to speak coherently. That, I think, was one of the most unnerving aspects of that week, spending my days in this unreal world of horror, surrounded by strange men. Some of them said they found it boring and just skimmed through it. Perhaps that was their way of distancing themselves from the horror of it.

Over lunch, everybody was embarrassed and a little ill-at-ease. People tried to make small talk and the atmosphere was tense as everybody avoided discussing the books. My other women companions? The blonde liked to have a bit of a laugh with the lads, couldn't be bothered to read the books, but thought that 'queers were disgusting' and that the gay book ought to be banned. The Asian girl avoided the rest of the jury, slipping off at lunch time and, I feel ashamed to say, I did not make any special effort to talk to her, perhaps because my own feelings were in such a turmoil that I did not consider anybody else at the time. There was one particularly antipathetic man who kept complaining loudly that he ran his own business and was losing hundreds of pounds a day through doing jury service and would we please all hurry up so that he could get back to his desk. He also thought the obscenity law was badly worded and to express his dissatisfaction intended to abstain anyway and urged everybody else to do likewise. He was determined not to confront the issue and some of the other jury members seemed to be impressed by him because he made himself sound so busy and important and drove a Jaguar. I was concerned that they would be intimidated by him.

As the week wore on, I became aware of conflicting feelings. On the one hand, utter revulsion at the books I was reading and a powerful, vengeful desire to see the defendant — the book shop owner — behind bars for ever and his shop and all the others like it razed to the ground, while on the other, a nagging voice kept saying 'What about censorship? What about war films? Where do you draw the line?' A conflict between my emotions and my intellect: I was torn between my allegiance to women and my duty as a citizen to assess the books according to the rather ambiguous law. I also knew that banning such books would not eradicate the problem, prevent them being written or stem the demand — in fact it would probably increase it. At the same time as this tussle, on a more personal level, these books also brought up a lot of painful reminders of a destructive relationship I had had in the not so distant past. The man I had been involved with had been a sort of manifestation of a frightening self-destructive urge in me, the existence of which I had had to deal with and purge. Somehow, this man became synonymous with the characters in these books. I don't want to go into that at length here, suffice it to say that I was having difficulty untangling my emotions and confronting the facts of the case objectively. I also questioned whether it was possible, or essential, to be objective.

In the evenings, I went home and read Andrea Dworkin[1] and Susan Griffin[2] to try and gain a wider feminist perspective and help me resolve the conflict between dealing with the issue of pornography and being censorial. I began to define pornography as the association of sex with violence, the brutalisation and degradation of women. There is a world of difference between that and women being seen as sex objects as on Page 3 or at the Bunny Club. Although some women may feel this is degrading, there is the fact that the women concerned are consenting, and that they are seen as playthings in some sense rather than objects of hatred. Reams have been written on the subject, by people eminently more qualified than myself, and, for the purposes of this article, I am not interested in entering into academic debate. I am talking about how I came to define pornography in the specific context of this trial. I am talking about the evolution of my own thinking rather than trying to define pornography once and for all.

On a purely gut level, I felt threatened by these books. Threatened because they were degrading not only to women but to men as well. Men who read these books, who are only capable of enjoying sex vicariously through this medium, are degraded. The degradation of human beings makes fertile ground for fascism to take root. This, I think, is the most important thing that emerged for me. I understood on a visceral level what felt like a wide intellectual leap, the connection between pornography and fascism, the ultimate degradation of human beings. Pornography isolates — individuals locked away, reading in secret. This is why I came to the conclusion that it has to be confronted. Similarly, I believe that extreme right-wing organisations should not be granted free speech. Pornography, as I began defining it, threatens women in the same way as those organisations threaten ethnic and minority groups.

As the trial progressed, I grew more convinced of this, and my thinking was reinforced by the court room charade. The defence was represented by John Mortimer, who insisted on speaking to the jury as if we were idiots. I was struck how, for the prosecution and the defence, it was merely a question of ego, of winning the case, the issue mattered little, it was just a game of words, while I felt threatened as a human being by the sort of books I had spent the week reading. The jury was frequently reminded by the judge and pressurised by the defence to bear in mind the letter of the law and not let our personal feelings influence our decision. Although the law is ambiguous, I concluded that it was ridiculous to pretend to be objective when I and all women were being threatened by the spread of such material. I decided that I would fight for all I was worth to have people who make money out of it put behind bars for as long as possible. I knew this wouldn't prevent the minds that dream it up from producing more, or the people who are hooked on it from craving more. Nor will it make the world a better place for women. But if the penalties for selling such books are crippling, then maybe those bookshop owners will turn their hand to something else, or at least stop importing that particular brand of 'literature'.

What about censorship? One of the problems in the debate on censorship, it seems, is that we are not all talking about the same kind of book. I had never come across books like that before, and I wonder how many people who are so adamant about non-censorship have ever read one, or have any idea of the content. To be liberal about the sort of pornography with which I was confronted is as obscene as expecting a Black person to condone apartheid.

The jury was asked to return a unanimous verdict. Because the man I mentioned earlier and another one insisted on abstaining, this was impossible, and after several hours, the judge agreed to accept a majority verdict.

Most of the jury were very conscientious about not allowing their personal revulsion (if indeed they did feel revulsion) to interfere with their judgement, given the vagueness of the law. I and another juror argued passionately for the defendant to be found guilty on the basis that such material does indeed threaten the fabric of our society, which is the family. A slightly dubious argument for a feminist to be putting forward, but I felt that all means were justified and this one did seem to strike a note with my fellow jurors. Besides, I really do believe that anyone who reads this kind of material, particularly young boys with no experience of sex as an act of tenderness, *is* likely to be 'depraved and corrupted'. They could end up with a very sick idea of what women are about, what sex is about and what they themselves are about, when such material claims to present 'normality'.

The defendant was found guilty on all counts except one, which was the gay book, a sort of gay Mills and Boon and the only one which did not feature torture and degradation. It was interesting that the jury, some of whom had expressed distinctly homophobic sentiments at various times, were unanimous in agreeing that this book was not offensive. He received a massive fine and a prison sentence. The following week, there was a series of raids on Soho bookshops, many of which have since closed down.

I have not resolved the general problem of censorship to my satisfaction. But, to my mind, there is no doubt whatsoever concerning those books. Nothing I can say here can convey the horror of the contents. To me, as a woman, they felt life-threatening. I would never have imagined they existed if I had not been obliged to read them. In the light of my experience, it seems to me that for any debate on censorship to be meaningful, the first thing is to ensure that we are all using the term 'pornography' in the same way.

The case of the gay book in the trial is an example of the sort of thing that worries me. There are undoubtedly many people who favour censorship who would classify such books pornographic, and indeed, the series of raids on *Gay's the Word* Bookshop might have been part of such a crackdown. It shows how easily any form of censorship can lead to abuse, particularly where minority groups are concerned, and there is no doubt that the gay community is particularly vulnerable at the moment. I am unclear how we could censor the kind of vile pornography with which I was confronted, without providing the Right with ammunition to use against us. Perhaps the key lies in the inevitable linking of sex with violence.

Interestingly, one of the largest collections of pornography is in the British Library. Let people go there and ask for it if they want to read it, rather than have porn barons making money from it. Somehow, it is the men who grow rich on this sort of thing that make it all the more obscene.

Footnotes

1 *Pornography: Men Possessing Women*, The Women's Press, 1981.
2 *Pornography and Silence*, The Women's Press, 1981.

BOOKS FOR BAD WOMEN: A FEMINIST LOOKS AT CENSORSHIP

Sigrid Nielsen

When I first began to call myself a feminist, in 1971, I took it for granted that I was opposed to censorship. We all did; it was easy. Censorship, we probably would have said, if we had ever talked about it, was a relic of a dying age. 'That's censorship!', we would occasionally say to someone; meaning, 'You can't get away with that.'

We weren't entirely ignorant. We read books like Kate Millett's *Sexual Politics*, with its graphic quotations from DH Lawrence and Henry Miller, and vaguely realised that, long, long ago, Millett's book would have been banned. But that long-dead past was so hard to imagine that it seemed like a joke, and a weak joke at that. There was even a rock and roll song about a girl whose walk was 'banned in Boston and censored in Cleveland'. Ha-ha.

By the early eighties, a great deal had changed, but censorship seemed further away than ever. Some feminists — and I was one — began to question whether, as an issue, it was relevant to women at all. Books like Andrea Dworkin's *Pornography* and Susan Griffin' *Pornography and Silence* gave rise to a kind of thinking which implied that 'censorship' had been invented by male civil libertarians. What they called censorship was just a scare-word for obscenity law, which might have done women a favour by limiting the growth of the pornography industry. Perhaps a few 'good' books had been suppressed, but they were mainly the work of male authors with the same sexist message as Lawrence and Miller. At least, so we assumed: Dworkin and Griffin made no reference to the history of obscenity law, and I, at least, knew no more about it than I had done in 1971.

In 1984, I began to think very differently.

On 10 April, 1984, Gay's the Word Bookshop in Marchmont St, London was raided by officers of HM Customs and Excise. They held some of the staff for hours, (allegedly) denied them access to solicitors, raided their homes and seized personal property, and drove off with a third of the shop's stock. Later they officially seized 144 titles, including *The Book of the City of Ladies*, by Christine de Pisan, a fifteenth-century writer; *Contemporary Feminist Thought*, by Hester Eisenstein; and *Annie On My Mind*, by prizewinning novelist Nancy Garden, a book about two eighteen-year-old girls who fall in love with each other. One woman who shared a flat with one of the shop's workers told me how she had asked the Customs officers to leave her a half-used video cassette when they impounded all the rest in the flat. The officers sat there watching the entire contents of the half-used video, apparently certain they would find something obscene.

The most surprising part of the story was that everything Customs had done was legal. They had seized only imported books, which were not covered by the Obscene Publications Act of 1959 — the law which, at least in England, had given us the security we took so completely for granted. Under the 1959 Act, books with literary, scientific, artistic or educational importance were exempt from conviction for obscenity. Penguin Books had tested the law in 1960 by publishing Lawrence's much-banned *Lady Chatterley's Lover* — and won their case. As far as Gay's the Word were concerned, however, the 1959 Act might never have happened. They were being charged under The Customs Consolidation Act 1876, which provided no grounds for defence and no definition of 'indecent or obscene' — which could mean whatever a magistrate or a jury thought they meant. Later that year, Gay's the Word's directors and staff were formally charged with conspiracy to import prohibited books. If convicted, they could have faced unlimited fines, prison sentences of up to three years, and legal costs they estimated at £50,000, even though British editions of some of the books in dispute were freely available in this country.

It's complicated to describe the kind of shock I felt — as a lesbian, as a feminist, as a bookseller. I imagine many other people who had grown up in the same climate of thought as I had were just as shocked. I had known that obscenity law might be a threat, but I had never pictured such total and arbitrary power to disrupt everyday life — for an offence which no one could define, which many people saw as a joke, and which could not have been prevented (since no one knew whether the books were obscene until the court decided). Even before Gay's the Word had been charged with a crime, the sense of threat left by the raid changed everything. It spread an unreal and insecure feeling: like the physical uncertainty of walking in fog or on an uneven surface in the dark. This, I realise now, is the real power of censorship.

I decided it was time I found out more about obscenity law; unfortunately this paper only gives me room for a brief and sketchy survey of what I learnt. My sources are all secondary (they are listed at the end of the paper) and I can't make any claim to completeness or legal expertise. I'm not so much hoping to provide answers as to raise questions about what censorship is and how it works — and to inspire other women to look for the answers and think through the problems in detail. Even these few facts, however, give a very strong indication that censorship is thoroughly tied up with the forces which discourage freedom of action and equality in our society, particularly for women. Feminism itself does not exist in a vacuum; it is dependent on certain attitudes toward knowledge and information. Censorship not only implies different attitudes: it works by means of vagueness and arbitrariness, establishing them as a normal state of affairs. In the past women may only have been indirectly affected by this kind of law, but the effects may have been much deeper than we think.

* * *

Censorship is probably as old as society. The *Analects* of Confucius were burnt in ancient China; the *Index Librorum Prohitorum* was first drawn up by the Roman Catholic Church in 1557 in order to forbid its members to read certain books (about 4000 in the most recent list). How far back the history of opposition to censorship goes is not usually considered.

By comparison, English obscenity law is a newcomer; it dates from the eighteenth century. But it has grown from a long tradition of political censorship. Starting in 1557 (again), printing presses had to be licensed (like radio and television stations today), and all printing was forbidden outside London, Oxford, and Cambridge. Books had to be cleared with the authorities before publication. This system was allowed to lapse in 1695, and obscenity law began to appear some years later.

Obscenity law was, and still is, largely made and changed in the courts. At first, 'publishing an obscene libel', as it is technically known, was a minor offence. Authors like Chaucer and Shakespeare had always written fairly freely, and pornographic novels like *Fanny Hill* could be published without fear of any drastic penalties. (John Cleland, author of *Fanny Hill*, pleaded poverty when brought to trial and was granted a pension on condition that he turn to some other kind of writing.) But by the end of the century, the situation had begun to change: the idea of respectable writing, completely free of sexual references, had appeared.

The reasons for the change are mysterious. There had always been those who were in favour of strict obscenity laws; an early version of the Obscene Publications Act was drafted in 1580, shortly after political censorship had set in. But two hundred years were to pass before this current of opinion had much effect on law or taste. The reasons for the delay might be revealing if the right questions were asked from a feminist viewpoint.

For instance: what did the rise of obscenity law have to do with the creation of a mass female readership? In the eighteenth century, the first novels were being published — and unlike earlier literature, they were clearly aimed at women as well as men. *Pamela*, one of the most influential, followed a virtuous (and literate) servant who fended off the amorous advances of her master. Was literature being made safe for women? And when writers and publishers refused to cooperate, was it felt (by respectable men) that the courts should step in?

Another question: how much did evangelism and the anti-vice societies have to do with the development of censorship? Religious revivalism, and groups such as the Society for the Suppression of Vice, had their roots in the eighteenth century. (But they went on, and on, and on, while new versions arose, down to the Festival of Light in our own time.) They clamoured for the suppression of 'obscene' books: how far had they also discovered the uses of publicity, realising that a suppression campaign, successful or not, would circulate their names to tens of thousands of potential converts? Nor did the benefits stop there: a well-publicised prosecution could extend their influence as well as their numbers.

It is clear that their influence did grow through the early years of the nineteenth century; by 1850, the novelist William Thackeray was complaining that no writer was permitted 'to depict, to his utmost power, a MAN'. And in the speeches around the proposal of the first bill devoted entirely to obscenity, echoes of the evangelists' rhetoric can be heard. The bill, said its sponsor, Lord Campbell, was meant to counter 'a trade more deadly than prussic acid, arsenic, or strychnine.' He referred to the pornography industry, which had begun to flourish at about the same time as evangelism. Only those 'whose purpose in writing was to corrupt the morals of youth', Campbell promised, would feel the force of the law, which became the Obscene Publications Act of 1857. The Act provided no definition of obscenity, but eleven years later, one was created in court: a catch-all definition which had it that obscene material has 'a tendency to deprave and corrupt those whose minds are open to immoral influences'.

This definition was, as an Arts Council working party put it in 1969, 'a virtual vacuum waiting to be filled'. Over 120 years there has been no lack of people waiting to fill it, often for purposes which had little to do with the books in question.

The first test case came in 1877. When a medical pamphlet on sex and contraception, in print for forty years, was condemned, feminist Annie Besant and Charles Bradlaugh, a leading radical, re-published the pamphlet and were arrested, tried, and found guilty. (They were later acquitted on a technicality.) Around the same time a Holborn bookseller was prosecuted by the Society for the Suppression of Vice for selling *Moral Philosophy*, a pamphlet by Robert Dale Owen, the well-known labour organiser. He was convicted and sentenced to four months in prison with hard labour, even though he was nearly seventy.

In 1898 the police used the Obscene Publications Act to suppress a group they disliked. The Legitimation League agitated for legal status for 'illigitimate' children; it also dealt with other sexual questions and had raised adverse comment in the press. The League's secretary ran a bookstall at meetings, and after a raid, he found himself charged with the sale of an obscene book, Havelock Ellis' *Sexual Inversion* (about homosexuality). He was tried and pleaded guilty; the book was condemned and the League collapsed. In an autobiography, the detective in charge of the case congratulated himself on his destruction of 'a Frankenstein monster wrecking the marriage laws of our country'.

There were many other trials. They could be set in train by the police, the Director of Public Prosecutions, HM Customs and Excise (covered by their own obscenity law, used against Gay's the Word, the Customs Consolidation Act of 1876), or a private individual or a group. Radclyffe Hall's lesbian novel, *The Well of Loneliness*, was banned and publically burned in 1928. A *Daily Express* columnist, probably hoping to build circulation, had declared that he would rather 'put a phial of prussic acid into the hands of a healthy boy or girl' than *The Well*; the rest of Fleet Street had taken up the cry, and after a complicated series of events, there had been a raid and a trial. The Home Secretary, Sir William Joynson-Hicks, Treasurer of the Zenana Bible Society, and the Director of Public Prosecutions, Sir Archibald Bodkin, a zealous anti-obscenity crusader, set the tone of this period, which also saw the suppression of works by DH Lawrence and James Joyce. When accessible sex manuals began to appear in the thirties and forties, they also came under attack; three were the subject of trials, two were condemned, and one publisher went to prison in 1943. Dr Eustace Chesser, author of *Love Without Fear*, went on trial in 1942 and was taken to task for mentioning oral sex and lesbianism, but was finally acquitted.

These stories arouse fear and indignation; but, in some ways, they conceal the real scope of censorship of the past. For every book on trial, several more were probably suppressed through threats of prosecution. A few publishers, like Allen and Unwin (who refused to withdraw Edward Carpenter's *The Intermediate Sex* in 1915) had the courage to resist. Most did not. Booksellers were even more vulnerable; to deal with them, the police had a form known as a 'destruction order'. Once they had obtained a magistrate's approval, the police could present this form to any bookseller; once he had signed, they had permission to remove whatever books they saw fit to take. These orders were used year after year, all over the country. They probably had a predictable effect on booksellers' stocking policies. Bookselling is not a lucrative business — a shop often generates as little as 1% net profit — and few could afford frequent losses without compensation. At his trial, Dr Eustace Chesser had described the appalling sexual ignorance of his patients (and the men's views of their wives as 'conveniences'); a good, straight-forward book, he thought, could do something about that. He obviously knew nothing about obscenity law.

Though they were rarer than destruction orders, obscenity trials probably had further-reaching effects than generally realised. An obscenity trial is a public scapegoating — a serious threat and a harrowing experience. Few were eager to face it a second time. Research may someday reveal whether there is any relationship between the development of radical thinking about sexual politics and sexual freedom, and the growth of obscenity law. Such ideas were in favour before the Obscene Publications Act, at the time of

Mary Wollstonecraft and William Godwin; they went into eclipse at the time of the first obscenity trials in the 1870s, and only re-emerged after the law was reformed in the 1960s. Whatever the truth turns out to be, there is no doubt about the trials' effect on individuals. Radclyffe Hall's next novel was a religious work which she wrote 'as atonement'; she never wrote a controversial book or a bestseller again. Annie Besant was denied the right to visit her daughter as a result of her trial; she eventually embraced theosophy and celibacy. Havelock Ellis, though he went on to become an authority on sexuality, never forgot his experience in the dock; and all his works emphasised his support for marriage and female passivity. 'The curious thing about the Old Bailey dock is the feeling of overwhelming forces being ranged against you,' wrote one publisher who went on trial in 1954. 'The only touch of human sympathy you encounter is from a cheerful little cockney jailer.'

This trial was one of the five that finally led to obscenity law reform in 1959. A new crusading Home Secretary, Sir David Maxwell-Fyfe, had put five commercial publishers on trial for publishing the kind of novel which, then as now, lined the shelves at WH Smith. These trials — unlike earlier ones — were a clear threat to the everyday business of publishing. After a long campaign, a new law, the Obscene Publications Act of 1959, was passed; the next year, Penguin Books published *Lady Chatterley's Lover*, long banned, as a test case. They won. Obscenity trials now became rare, while destruction orders and private prosecutions for obscenity were eventually abolished. Little by little, as the sixties passed, the liberal publishing climate in which most of us later formed our ideas, and became feminists, grew up. It has lasted for nearly thirty years, but, given the age and strength of censorship tradition, it could hardly have gone unchallenged forever.

* * *

I wish I could end this paper on a calm — or even positive — note. So much writing on censorship revolves around threat and panic that the reader, after enough exposure, may be too exhausted to sympathise. This highly emotional tone is a particular feature of the new feminist debates on censorship in the eighties, which have caused bitter divisions in the American movement. The launch of a feminist campaign for antipornography legislation in this country may have a similar effect here. We, as a movement, need time to consider the issue of censorship dispassionately, to listen to a variety of opinions, and to think the issues through in detail.

Censorship is now at the centre of feminist campaigning strategy. Antipornography feminists such as Andrea Dworkin and Catharine MacKinnon appear to have decided that the individual power of men can best be opposed by using the power of the state. The Dworkin-MacKinnon anti-pornography ordinance, passed in two American cities but struck down later in the courts, would make 'degrading' images of women illegal and would give individuals or groups the power to sue writers, publishers, booksellers or any other supposed offenders. Similar legislation is being proposed in this country by a group of feminists called the Campaign Against Pornography.

All this activity has generated a considerable amount of writing, but none of it has much reference to obscenity law. Dworkin makes a point of emphasising that her ordinance uses an entirely new concept; that the issue is women's civil rights, not obscenity. I think that we, as feminists, should scrutinise this claim in detail. Even a very basic acquaintance with the facts puts it in some doubt.

The idea of leaving it up to individuals to take direct legal action, rather than giving the police and the courts more power, sounds like a radical departure from the past. But in fact it could easily create the same situation as England had to endure under the Obscene Publications Act of 1857. The initiative, and the advantage, lay with accusers. Because of the system of legal precedents, the application of the law became wider as time passed, while the legal definition of the offence remained as vague as ever. Dworkin and MacKinnon's definitions are not a great improvement on the present idea of 'depravity and corruption'. One clause refers to 'the depiction of women as vile whores', a phrase which, like the present definition, is a vacuum waiting to be filled. Anti-vice groups are now more legally sophisticated than ever; they will not miss their opportunity if Dworkin's ordinance becomes law.

We also need to ask ourselves about the wider effect of such a law on sexual information and sexual honesty. Feminists believe in choice for women, and choice requires knowledge. As we have already seen, legal censorship has frequently been used to suppress books of sexual information. A law based on Dworkin and MacKinnon's ordinance could easily be put to such use: a small bookshop could be forced to close by a legal suit, whether it won or lost, and large chains have shown themselves to be more than responsive to right-wing pressure. Feminist and left-wing book-shops, which are chronically short of money, would be among the most vulnerable.

These are only a few of the questions we should be asking ourselves about censorship; unfortunately, there is one whose answer is now obvious. A few years ago, it was still possible to wonder if there were groups with the will or the credibility to enforce sexual ignorance. Such groups now have considerable influence within governments on both sides of the Atlantic, just as they had in earlier eras. At their instigation, abortion rights are under direct attack; and a law proposed in California would make it a criminal offence for a pregnant woman to do anything which might harm her unborn child. Our right to sexual self-definition, one of the seven demands of the British women's movement, is deliberately being closed off. In the USA, both houses of Congress recently passed an amendment which would criminalise all lesbian and gay literature from *The Well of Loneliness* to Aids prevention leaflets. In Britain, an amendment to the Local Government bill, due to become law in June 1988, makes it illegal to use such material in school, or to give local government support to groups which 'promote' homosexuality.

In an ideal situation, we could consider the effects of censorship slowly and carefully. But as things are, I now honestly wonder how much time we have left. It is still difficult to imagine censorship used openly and directly against feminist ideas. However, I think that the effects of censorship — as a newly respectable concept — are already being felt in the women's movement. Censorship isolates; it makes us value ignorance and limits our ability to think independently; it strikes at the basis of all liberation movements, the belief in the power of shared experience to improve life. It is not a force that we, as feminists, can trifle with.

Sources

Books in the Dock by CH Rolph (London, Andre Deutsch, 1969).
The Banned Books of England and Other Countries by Alec Craig (London, Allen & Unwin, 1962).
The Obscenity Laws: A Report by the Working Party Convened by the Chairman of the Arts Council of Great Britain (London, Andre Deutsch, 1969).
Policing Desire: Pornography, Aids and the Media by Simon Watney (London, Methuen, 1987).
Our Three Selves: A Life of Radclyffe Hall by Michael Baker (London, GMP, 1985)
The Spinster and her Enemies: Feminism and Sexuality 1880–1930 by Sheila Jeffreys (London, Pandora, 1985).

PAGE 3 — AND THE CAMPAIGN AGAINST IT

Melissa Benn

> Down from the waist they are centaurs
> Though women all above;
> But to the girdle do the gods inherit,
> Beneath is all the fiend's;
> There's hell, there's darkness, there's the sulphorous pit,
> Burning, scalding, stench, consumption ...

From Shakespeare's *King Lear*

In March 1986 Clare Short MP stood up in the House of Commons during a debate concerning amendment of the Obscene Publications Act 1959 and declared that she was going to introduce a 10 Minute Rule Bill into the House of Commons in an attempt to get 'girlie' pictures in the tabloid newspapers banned. Impulsive as her declaration was, she followed it through. Soon after, a Bill to ban Page 3 type images was introduced: the Bill failed at its second reading.

But then the Bill itself was never the real point of the Page 3 campaign. I could not support it anyway, however sympathetic I felt to Clare Short's boldness and persistence, because it sought to deal with women's degradation through censorship — a mechanism which has a notorious capacity to rebound on its maker. What was more interesting and more important about the Page 3 campaign was the way in which it galvanised women up and down the country, who wrote in their thousands to Clare Short, to other MPs, to the women's magazines, to agony aunts, expressing something near to hatred of the Page 3 image. And how this, in turn affected Clare Short's politics, producing in her, for the first time, a belief and a delight in the collective power of women. The Page 3 campaign made her into a feminist, I would say.

This article is a fairly straightforward case study of Clare Short's Bill. It looks in some detail at the parliamentary and extra-parliamentary aspects of the campaign, and particularly at the arguments put forward by all the women who wrote in support of Clare Short. For while these women don't, on the whole, see themselves as feminists, the feelings they describe and the vocabulary they use are often the very arguments of feminism at its most articulate and unambivalent. And the single question that consistently nags at me is: how, *other* than legislation, can the anger of all these women be effectively mobilised?

Page 3: Its History and Meaning

In November 1969, Rupert Murdoch, the Australian newspaper proprietor who now owns News International, bought up a failing tabloid called the *Sun* — (once, the radical *Daily Herald*, it had been converted into the *Sun* in 1964). In one of the endless circulation battles that mark the official history of Fleet Street, Murdoch's aims was to beat the then 'upmarket' tabloid the *Daily Mirror* by turning the *Sun* into as popular, that is, 'downmarket' a paper as possible. He succeeded: within a year of launching the *Sun*, the paper's circulation had doubled, and soon after that it passed the two million mark.

The introduction of Page 3 girls was part of that circulation war, yet according to one of Murdoch's biographers, Michael Leapman:

> The feature by which the *Sun* became best known was the daily picture of a bare-breasted woman, usually on Page 3, but that did not begin until nearly a year after the launch. It was not Murdoch's idea, nor indeed a conscious strategem at all. Lamb (the *Sun*'s first editor) simply decided to do it one day and reaction was so positive, he thought he should carry on with it. The *Mirror* felt obliged to do the same for a while. (*Bare-Faced Cheek: The apotheosis of Rupert Murdoch*, Michael Leapman, 1983)

The Page 3 girl is important because she is one particular icon out of a variety of icons which illustrate how men — the culture in general — look at women. *Her* particularity lies in the way she combined the erotic and the denial-of-the-erotic within the one image. By this I mean: the display of naked, firm and usually big breasts are clearly erotic in intent, and yet this intent is immediately denied by the context in which the Page 3 girl is placed, i.e. the humorous caption, the sweet smile, the very use of the word 'girl'.

The explicit denial of the erotic is essential to those who produce — and participate — in Page 3 pictures. Both proprietors and Page 3 models are keen, however disingenous they are about it, to stress the asexuality of what they do. They talk about Page 3 in terms of 'health' and 'cheerfulness': the invocation of an assumed natural-ness about nakedness is central to their defence. Linda Lusardi, the glamour model (who with Samantha Fox has put up the most spirited defence of Page 3) described the pictures to *Woman* magazine in an article on May 24 1986, as:

> Quite harmless. Page 3 girls aren't doing anything in the papers they wouldn't do on the beach. They're clean, happy pictures ... It's always what you hide that people are after. It used to be ankles. In fact, maybe kids will think about nudity in a nice way because of them.

Linda Lusardi and Samantha Fox go out of their way to de-eroticise themselves by continually being in pictures with their mums and dads. 'To Linda Lusardi and her parents it's a laugh' ran the accompanying caption in *Woman* magazine.

News International spokesman, Arthur Brittenden, told *Woman*, also in their May 24th article:

> I don't see any harm in it. They are all nice girl-next-door types. There's nothing provocative in Page 3 any more than in the pictures of girls in art galleries. If the readers felt it was *unpleasant* then we would soon hear from them. (My emphasis)

Arthur Brittenden's use of the word 'unpleasant' is interesting. For in using it, he is fixing on a crucial aspect of the meaning of the Page 3 girl: he is describing her as much in terms of what she is *not* as what she is. Or, as Samantha Fox, put it in an interview with *New Musical Express*, on April 12 1986: 'Listen, there's all the difference between a pair of boobs and you know ... down there.' The Page 3 girl performs a delicate balancing act between the different meanings attached to the two halves of a woman's body, and therefore of woman's very self. It plays on the tension that exists in the perception of what you might call the male collective unconscious between the relative dangers and pleasures of each part, and their fear that one will have victory over the other: in other words, that woman's nice, good mothering side will be drowned by her bad, sexual side.

But the Page 3 girl does not simply play on this tension. She comes down clearly on the one side. The Page 3 girl is sexual enough to be a turn on for men, but she's not quite sexual enough to be independently sexual, for herself. That smile, the revelation of bosoms only, that willingness to service — all show that when the titillation is over, she'll still be there for men. In that sense, the Page 3 girl serves a reassuring function. She mitigates men's ever-present terror of women's sexuality, women's independence, and the consequences of that independence.

It is certainly more than a co-incidence that the first Page 3 picture appeared in the *Sun* in 1970, which was also the first proper year of women's liberation in this country.

The Bill Itself

Clare Short described the genesis of her Page 3 Bill to me as follows (all quotes from Clare Short are from an interview with me in early 1987).

> I was not at all involved in the issue before. For me, it was triggered by the Churchill Bill and the enormously irritating and hypocritical debate that accompanied it. It would have made certain kinds of television violence illegal. I stood up during this debate and said, 'It is true that people are worried about sexual crime, but such clauses as scenes that show "terrifying cruelty to children and animals" would apply also to documentary or political images, like showing what was going on in Vietnam. OK, it's true people are concerned about women, but then let's be simple and clear: let's get rid of Page 3. I thought of it on the spot. I decided to bring in a 10 Minute Rule Bill.
>
> It was only since coming into the House of Commons that I got to see more of the tabloids. They were getting on my nerves. I stumbled on to this whole thing, but the response of other people, well, of women kept me going. No-one took much notice at first. It was reported slightly, in the *UK Press Gazette* and then in regional papers ... but as a result of that reporting, I got 150 letters, from women.
>
> Once I'd decided to do this 10 Minute Rule Bill — its a stupid procedure really [a 10 Minute Rule Bill is one form of Private Member's Bill which at the very least allows an MP a ten minute speech in the House of Commons in support of the principle of their Bill: if the first reading is successful, it is published as a Bill and begins its parliamentary course]. I was determined to do the thing properly. I was quite careful about the phrasing of it so it would cover Page 3 only. I thought you can't do it all at once, can't get rid of porn. It would go underground anyway. So instead of hunting out the most vile porn, I thought: start in the middle and go for the thing that everyone's exposed to all the time.

Short's 10 Minute Rule Bill contained two main propositions. Firstly, 'to make illegal the display of pictures of naked or partially naked women in sexually provocative poses in newspapers' (for this purpose, newspapers were defined as 'any paper containing public news and published daily or on Sunday'). Secondly, to penalise any 'person' found guilty of such an offence by imposing a fine of one pence per copy of the newspaper published; two pence per copy if the offence is repeated.

Had the Bill become law, this would have inflicted — within only a day or so — quite heavy penalties on most of the major tabloids. If you take the average circulation in the first half of 1987 of the *Sun* and the *Daily Mirror* as 3.9 million and 3.1 million respectively, then their first day fines would have come to £39,000 and £31,000 each.

By the time the Bill was introduced into the House on March 6th Clare Short had got considerable publicity. The press gallery was more packed than most MPs could remember. Short describes the Tories as 'childishly excited, sniggering and giggling in a most crude school boy fashion'. Opening the debate, she set out her arguments. For her, the strength of the case against Page 3 pictures lay in the extent of women's reaction against them. She described Page 3 as 'offensive' to women, distorting both young boys' and girls' attitudes to their sexuality, and adult female capability in general. Women, she said, also believe 'that there is some connection between the rising tide of sexual crime and Page 3 ... these pictures portray women as objects of lust to be sniggered over and grabbed at, and do not portray sex as something tender and private'.

In reply, Robert Adley described Clare Short's speech as

a *titillating* mixture of politics, prejudice and prurience' (my emphasis). He described the measure to ban Page 3 as barely credible, and a sexist measure that did not plan to outlaw 'beefcake' pictures of men as well.

Who will decide whether a woman is or not partially naked, whether or not her pose is sexually provocative? ... Clare Short would have our newspapers resembling *Pravda*. There are few pleasures left to us today. One that I enjoy is sitting on an underground train, watching the faces of the people who are pretending not to be looking at Page 3 of the newspapers. This [Bill] is a ridiculous proposal. I suggest that of all the measures that have been proposed to this House during this session, this Bill deserves the *booby prize* (my emphasis).

However, the presence of a significant number of Labour MPs ensured that the Bill passed its first reading 97–56 votes.

To the Conservatives, the tabloid press, and the *Sun* in particular, Short and her Bill were easy meat for caricature. In the *Sun*'s case, their reaction had more than a touch of hysteria to it — in part due to the dispute then current between the print unions and Murdoch over News International's move to Wapping. The Wapping dispute probably also explained why Short concentrated her fire on the *Sun*, rather than, say the *Daily Mirror* or the *Star*, both of which also carry 'girlie' pictures. The *Daily Mirror* is a traditional, albeit right-wing Labour paper.

Short told me how

> The *Sun* ran a vitriolic campaign against me. One day my sister told me that they had printed '20 facts about Crazy Clare' and I thought 'Oh God, what's it going to say?' But, in fact, when I actually went and bought the paper, I saw that the facts were mainly harmless. They also had free car stickers saying 'Stop Crazy Clare' and a write-in Freepost thing to get readers to protest against what I was doing.

The paper invited well-known ring-wing MPs and sexual moralists like Peter Bruinvels, Geoffrey Dickens and Terry Dix to show their public support for Page 3 by picking out their personal favourite 'lovelies'. And they ran a readership survey to prove just how attached their readers were to Page 3, the result of which has yet to be published. When the *Star* ran a phone poll of its readers' opinions of their Starbirds during this period, a clear majority of those ringing in declared themselves against the publication of these kinds of pictures (*Everywoman*, Nov 87).

Responses to the Bill: feminists and other women

> Our readers' response was overwhelming... mums, housewives, teachers, office and factory workers, teenagers and graduates — the message came through loud and clear that you're overwhelmingly fed up with Page 3 girls and overwhelmingly back MP Clare Short and her campaign to have them banned.
>
> (*Woman* magazine: August 30 1986)

As I said earlier, the most interesting thing about the Page 3 Bill was the way it mobilised individual women, up and down the country, in their thousands in support of Clare Short. She received personally over five thousand letters: about seven thousand letters were written in all. Usually, an MP might expect 20 or 50 letters for something controversial going through Parliament. Churchill said in the House when his Bill was going through that he'd got 180 letters, which he considered to be a lot. Women also wrote to other MPs, prominent women like agony aunt Clare Rayner, and in particular, to the top women's weekly magazine, *Woman*. *Woman* undertook a campaign in support of Clare Short: their survey returns, published on August 30 1986, showed 90% of readers against Page 3 pictures, and in favour of having them banned.

Woman have kept some of the thousands of letters sent to them: they range from a few lines scribbled on the back of a post card or a Christmas card to long cogently argued typescripts. A few were from men, but the vast majority were from women. Certain themes recur, the most common being that the existence of Page 3 models distorts both men's and women's view of what a 'normal' woman's body looks like, and that this puts enormous pressure on women battling with an already frail sense of self and sexuality. The women repeatedly refer to how terrible — how hurt, how irritated, how jealous — the pictures make them feel, how it reduces them to something small and inadequate. One woman wrote 'I know when I see my fiancé gawping, I think: why bother? I'll never look like that.' Linked to this is an anger and tenderness on behalf of women who have had, or might have to have, masectomies, 'I feel, and others share my view, that the showing of Page 3 girls must be extremely upsetting for women who have had a breast removed and for those awaiting surgery.' There is irritation at the hypocrisy that allows women to show their bodies in one public context (Page 3 for men's entertainment) but not in another (breastfeeding in public spaces was the most mentioned).

Page 3 models undermine women's dignity, their sense of separateness and efficiency at work. So said a group of women working in a Midlands factory: 'We're sick of all the crude and disgusting things men say to us at breakfast time while they are looking at Page 3s.' A woman who called herself a 'female executive' described an interview she had to conduct with an 'ordinary' man. 'While I was on the phone he flicked through a *Sun*. He got to Page 3 and showed me the picture, "Oh look, there's a picture of you in here!" It made me angry and sad that he would treat me, a professional woman in authority, as nothing different from a Page 3 girl. Quite simply, we both had breasts.'

Four out of five respondents to the *Woman* survey believed there was a link between Page 3 pictures and violence against women. There is a gut certainty that the image the pictures presented of women — passive, available, just there for sex — increase men's view of women as 'game' — for sex or violence. Sublimimal encouragement to violence is given when sexy pictures are juxtaposed with stories about violence against women on the same page. *Woman* added their editorial weight to this argument by beginning their survey report with a raw quote from a woman who had been raped: '. . . and while it was happening the man told me I was getting it because I looked like a Page 3 girl called Jackie. You always looked like you wanted it so bad, so here you are, Jackie, you can have it . . .'

What was surprising about the letters was that so many of them used such explicit feminist arguments and vocabulary. Certain words and phrases appeared repeatedly — exploitation/denigration/commodity/stereotype/passivity/availability/object — and yet much of this language is more resonant of the public face of feminism in the early 1970s than it is of the cooler, more sophisticated, more technical vocabulary of self-referring feminists writing or politicking in the 1980s. It's as if it has taken a decade or more for feminist ideology to filter through to women once so completely outside feminism — and most of whom still don't consider themselves connected to feminism at all (or are even actively hostile to it) — and yet now those very women are arguing more passionately than a lot (but not all) of second or third generation feminists.

Whatever the truth of that, it is impossible not to conclude that the views expressed in the letters, and echoes so strongly by *Woman* magazine itself — and other mass circulation women's weeklies — represents a core opposition by millions of women in this country to Page 3, and that this in turn signifies a dramatic bifurcation of opinion between men and women on the issue.

All this was in marked contrast to the feminist response to Clare Short's Bill. Anti-censorship and libertarian feminists were, reluctantly, against any attempt to ban Page 3 by law; foreseeing the dangers, especially in this repressive political climate. Yet even among those who *supported* Clare Short, there wasn't much excitement about the Bill. It never became one of those campaigns that feminists claim as their own. It was treated as: a good thing, yes, but a good thing going on a long way away. This may have something to do with the long-established distance between feminist and parliamentary politics. It may be because feminists don't read the tabloids, and even if they do, they bring to that reading a feminism, capital F, that already explains, already armours them against what they are going to find there. So, there is none of the surprise, none of the sheer hurt or the fury — emotions that stem principally from a sense of powerlessness — which characterised *Woman* readers' response.

Some of this is to do with political fatigue. Feminism and feminists have been analysing and campaigning on women's representation in the media for so long (over a decade and a half) that certain kinds of knowledge have become a little wearily held over the years and there is a lack of a genuine feminist imagination about how to make certain changes. Also, the absolute nature of feminism's position on the issue has been clouded over by the increasing diversity and complexity, not only of the media and its use of imagery, but of our own politics in relation to these questions. For instance, questions around style, diverse sexualities and erotic imagery are now hotly debated among feminists, so that no-one is quite sure any more which images are degrading, which progressive, which subversive. Who dares say? Nothing is so simple, and a simplicity of perspective can fuel a more dynamic politics, while awareness of complexity can paralyse.

The Future

Amidst considerable publicity, Clare Short's original Bill failed to get a second reading in April 1987. At the time of writing (early 1988), Clare Short still plans to re-introduce it. What lessons can be learned from the 1986 campaign?

During the 1986 campaign, women seemed to adopt one of two basic positions on the bill. The first fused enthusiasm for the objects of the Bill with support for the Bill itself; the second reluctantly withheld support from the Bill because of the censorship implications, but from then on... got stuck. However, there is a third political position which combines the best of both of the above. This position recognises the complexity of issues of representation, i.e. that statute law does not deal in advance with the context of an image, and therefore censors *the thing itself* regardless of context. (Clare Short thought she had got over this problem by specifying that her Bill only applied to a daily or Sunday newspaper: but you only have to consider what would happen if a radical daily paper tried sometime in the future to use images of naked or partially naked women, for 'progressive' purposes, to see how the law could be used). The law is not a flexible instrument: worse, it is interpreted by ever more politically inflexible persons.

But the anti-censorship argument does not — and should not — negate Clare Short's basic aim, which is to find some means of giving expression to many women's anger, their feeling of being exploited by the Page 3 image.

The question, therefore, is: what expression?

The most imaginative idea that has been suggested so far is that women should boycott the *Sun*, the *Star*, the *Daily Mirror* and *Sunday Sport*, that they should refuse to buy these papers and that they should refuse to let them into their homes. And they should do this publicly and loudly: with locally arranged pickets, protests, and news coverage. If Clare Short is to introduce her Page 3 Bill, then this could provide a focus for nationwide campaigning — as long as it could be understood that there was a diversity of opinion regarding legislation within the campaign.

A last word on diversity and identity: it should be recognised within the campaign that Page 3 is a single issue; that it will mobilise some women and not others; that it will mobilise many women who may not be feminists, and it will alienate many women who *are* feminists and who just don't care that much about Page 3, or are involved in other things. But such conflicts in purpose and identity actually don't matter very much. For it has been one of the failures of feminism that it has not embraced some of the necessary limitations of politics: it has stopped seeing that politics is often about single public acts that have a beginning, a middle and an end, and do not always have to carry within them a completely correct programme, or a fully worked out identity. Such single public acts may trigger off further action. They may not. The main point is that, in some measure, they will change the world, and women's perceptions of the world, and that is what is important.

SEX AND CENSORSHIP: THE POLITICAL IMPLICATIONS

Catherine Itzin

The scene is a river bank, 'north of the River Thames'; the time an August morning in the year 54 BC. Three brothers — young male Celts — come out of the river naked from their swim. Earlier they have slit the throat of an Irish tramp and set the dogs after the one who got away. They 'horse' about, mock-fight and talk about the 'dogs tearing down the enemy somewhere in the woods'. One of them is training to be a priest: they talk about religion, magic, power. They are having fun. Suddenly three Roman soldiers walk out of the woods, and see the Celts. 'Three wogs,' says one. The Romans talk about killing them; the Celts talk about escaping. Neither understands the other's 'foreign' language: that this would be the case is obvious; that they are actually all speaking in English makes of it a deeply ironic point, especially as they are making derogatory and racist comments about each other. The Celts are caught unawares and unarmed, except for a knife. They are afraid. The soldiers immediately stab one Celt in the belly: 'he pulls himself along the ground, screams, rests — a progress that continues during the rest of the scene, gradually slowing'. Then they kill a second Celt. The one that is left, the apprentice priest, is held by one soldier while the other strips, slashes his buttocks with a knife, holds his thighs and begins to bugger him. The dialogue is about the Roman Empire: imperialism. The rape fails: he can't 'get it up anymore', so his knocks his victim unconscious and goes off for a swim, to clean off the shit. The remaining soldier treats the young Celt kindly, until he awakens speaking Latin, whereupon the soldier turns on him: 'Fucking Latin-talking nig-nog! Suck me off.'

(This is the third scene of the first act of *The Romans in Britain* by Howard Brenton, first performed at the National Theatre in October 1980.)

The photograph is captioned 'Beaver Hunters'. Two white men, dressed as hunters, sit in a black Jeep. The Jeep occupies almost the whole frame of the picture. The two men carry rifles. The rifles extend above the frame of the photograph into the white space surrounding it. The men and the Jeep face into the camera. Tied onto the hood of the black Jeep is a white woman. She is tied with thick rope. She is spread-eagle. Her pubic hair and crotch are the dead centre of the car hood and the photograph. Her head is turned to one side, tied down by rope that is pulled taut across her neck, extended to and wrapped several times around her wrists, tied around the rearview mirrors of the Jeep, brought back across her arms, crisscrossed under her breasts and over her thighs, drawn down and wrapped around the bumper of the Jeep, tied around her ankles. Between her feet on the car bumper, in orange with black print, is a sticker that reads: 'I brake for Billy Carter'. The text under the photograph reads: 'Western sportsmen report beaver hunting was particularly good throughout the Rocky Mountain region during the past season. These two hunters easily bagged their limit in the high country. They told HUSTLER that they stuffed and mounted their trophy as soon as they got her home.'

(This is a description of a cover of a magazine called *Hustler*, from Andrea Dworkin's *Pornography: Men Possessing Women*, The Women's Press, 1981.)

Hustler magazine displays a cartoon called 'Chester the Molester' (part of a series depicting child molestation as humour), in which a man wearing a swastika on his arm hides behind a corner, holds a bat, and dangles a dollar bill on a wire to entice a little girl away from her parents. The child and her parents all wear yellow stars of David: each member of the family is drawn with the stereotypical hooked nose of anti-semitic caricature.

(From Susan Griffin's *Pornography and Silence*, the Women's Press, 1981)

* * *

Within days of opening, Howard Brenton's *The Romans in Britain* had caused a front-page, leader-column furore in the media. It was the scene above which was the ostensible cause of the 'shock drama', 'nude storm', 'sex row', 'scandal'. Sir Horace Cutler, then leader of the GLC (offended by the male nudity as much as the simulated buggery), threatened to withdraw the GLC's substantial grant to the National Theatre. After a complaint from Mary Whitehouse (self-appointed guardian of public morals who 'hadn't seen the play and didn't intend to'), the Obscene Publications Squad at Scotland Yard went along to consider whether the play infringed the Theatres Act of 1968. Marxist playwright Edward Bond defended the play in a *Guardian* feature and such famous men as Harold Pinter, Christopher Hampton, James Saunders, and Steve Gooch replied in the letters column. In the meantime lawyers and police were reporting to the Director of Public Prosecutions, who would report to the Attorney General, who would decide whether a prosecution could be brought under the Theatres Act. The answer was no. That was the autumn of 1980.

In March 1981, the GLC decided (because of *The Romans*) not to increase its grant to the NT, which meant effectively a 15% cut in subsidy, what NT director, Sir Peter Hall, described as a 'case of censorship by subsidy'. And Mary Whitehouse, having failed to get the DPP to prosecute, issued a private summons against Michael Bogdanov, the play's director, accusing him under the 1956 Sexual Offences Act of 'having procured the commission by a man of an act of gross indecency with another man'. In June 1981 Bogdanov appeared at Horseferry Road Magistrates Court where he was committed for trial at the Old Bailey for procuring an act of gross indecency between two actors. The defence asked whether if in a production of *Hamlet*, the director could be charged with procuring the death of Polonius — but to no avail. Furthermore the magistrate concluded: 'I must interpret the law as it stands and not as it might be. It may be absurd, but had Mr Bogdanov been a woman he would have no case to answer.' And: 'If anyone took part in a rehearsal in which a woman in a play was raped, that would not be an offence.'

In March 1982, 'The Romans Trial Drama' reached the stage of the Old Bailey where Mrs Whitehouse's lawyer swore he had seen an erect penis penetrating a bare male backside and the prosecution suggested it was nothing but an erect thumb. On the third day, the judge pronounced that Mr Bogdanov did indeed have a case to answer. But before the farce could continue to its climax, the DPP — in an unprecedented move — stopped the trial 'in the public interest' (before, as it happens, Bogdanov was allowed to speak in his own defence). The law had been tested, and the door opened for further such prosecutions. Whitehouse & Co were well pleased. It all cost in excess of £60,000 — £40,000 paid for by public funds.

What are we to take as the meaning of all this? That (as Mrs Whitehouse claimed) a play at the National Theatre would make young men rush out and commit buggery in the streets? That the 1956 Sexual Offences Act (designed to oppress homosexual men in their private lives) was meant to apply to a serious playwright in a major subsidised theatre in 1982? That the judge really thought that a genuine procurement had taken place on the stage, such as might occur in the public conveniences at Piccadilly Circus? I would suggest some 'things' altogether more sinister. Through the smokescreen of this idiocy, two singular facts stand out:

1) The rape of a woman in a play would not be an offence.
2) Considerable time and money — the State's — was spent in an exercise whose ultimate goal would be to suppress a play about imperialism in general, and the British military presence in Northern Ireland in particular.

* * *

Pornography is big business. In the United States it is a four and a quarter billion dollar business, bigger than the record and film industries combined (though it should also be noted that parts of the record and film industries participate in and profit specifically from pornography).

Hustler magazine (see description of cover and cartoon strip above) is what is called 'soft porn': i.e., relatively inoffensive, reasonably socially acceptable — quite harmless really. Certainly it is freely available for sale through most newsagents (and supermarkets in the US), along with a wide variety of magazines showing women in various states of undress and kinds of 'provocative' poses. 'Soft porn' is in the middle range of the 'ordinary, legal girlie' magazine market. It includes such 'acceptable' images as page after page of lurid crotch shots of women's genitals. Or as on the cover of a June 1978 issue of *Hustler*, a woman stuffed head first (bottom 'provocatively' up) into a meat grinder, coming out the other end as mince, sporting a 'government stamp' reading 'Grade A Pink' (which is a euphemism for women's genitals). Or from the cover of another magazine, a woman on her back, legs in the air and wide open, while a man bores into her vagina with a pile driver. This is 'mild' pornography, sold alongside the comics, with the sweets and cigarettes.

The 'hard core' stuff includes scenes from films such as: 'castration, cannibalism, flaying, the crushing of breasts in vices, exploding vaginas packed with hand grenades, eyes gouged out, beatings, dismemberings, burnings, multiple rape, and any and every other horror that could ever befall the human body'. For 'human' read 'female'. This was Polly Toynbee's account in the *Guardian* in October 1981 of things she had, as a member of the Williams Committee, watched. She had also witnessed 'women engaged in sexual intercourse with pigs and dogs', and women killed on screen (in what are called snuff movies). Hard porn magazines use close-up photographs of women's bodies bound, gagged and hung, genitals exposed; children being seduced and raped (with titles like 'Good Sex with Retarded Girls'). There are laws which regulate the sale of hard-core pornography, but it is freely accessible to those (men) who want it.

In the mid-70s the Home Office set up the Williams Committee on Obscenity and Film Censorship. The Committee met thirty-five times over two and a half years, viewed the whole range of pornography just noted, and reported. (The Report was published in 1979 by HMSO and in 1981 by Cambridge University Press.) The Williams Committee concluded that the key problem was defining what is 'indecent', and that there was little evidence that pornography harms people (except in the few cases where participants in photos might have come to harm — i.e., as Polly Toynbee noted, 'the poor, unhealthy, unhappy, many Third World children' or the 'South American prostitutes who were actually sexually murdered in films').

The Williams Committee recommended 'the greatest possible freedom from censorship combined with rather stringent restrictions on the open display of material'. I will refrain here from comment, and let the contradiction between their evidence and their conclusions speak for itself. In any case, their report and recommendations were ignored by the Home Office, presumably for being 'excessively censorious'. And an Indecent Displays (Control) Act was passed in 1981 with a penalty of £1000 or two years in prison for anyone 'presenting an indecent display'. It is rarely enforced, perhaps because of difficulties in defining what is indecent?

Reading the description of *The Romans in Britain* and the *Hustler* magazine (forget the hard-core pornography for the moment) one must be struck by the similarities, if only in that they are concerned with sex and violence. Yet *The Romans* is condemned, and *The Hustler* is condoned. What is the meaning of this apparent contradiction?

* * *

Censorship in the theatre was officially ended by the Theatres Act of 1968, replacing an act which had been in force unchanged since 1843. Theatre censorship had officially originated in 1543, 425 years earlier, in an act of government which ordered any plays which challenged the authorised religion to be 'abolished, extinguished and forbidden'. During the 1540s and 1550s a number of royal proclamations and orders regarding prohibition and licensing were passed, including the institution of the Revels Office in 1545. From the opening of the first professional theatre in London in 1576, the Master of the Revels operated with ever wider and increasing powers as the official censor. As Richard Findlater points out in his book *Banned, A Review of Theatrical Censorship in Britain* (McGibbon & Kee, 1967), censorship was from the beginning associated with arbitrary, personal suppression of freedom, protected by the Crown.

From its beginning in the reign of Henry VIII, censorship was concerned with protecting both State and Church against religious and political attack, rather than with questions of good taste or bad language. It was imposed as part of the attempt to stamp out Catholic resistance to the Reformation and to affirm loyalty to Henry as head of Church and State. The stage was feared as a religious pulpit and as a political platform, and that remained the case for over four hundred years.

The purpose of censorship from beginning to end has been *political*: suppression. The ostensible concern with issues of morality (from the reign of Queen Anne in the eighteenth century only, at the turn of the century, and in the debate leading up to the 1968 Theatres Act) can be seen from Findlater's fascinating history to have been but the sheerest of hyprocisies, and a smokescreen for the suppression of social and political ideas antagonistic to the state and the social status quo. The suppression of the plays of Ibsen and Shaw are good examples of this hypocrisy in practice. Shaw's *Mrs Warren's Profession* was banned from the stage for over thirty years, ostensibly because of the sexual offensiveness of its subject, prostitution. Of course, the play was critical of sexual double standards and the institutionalisation of prostitution: that was the real reason for its suppression.

It is not surprising, then, that the liberal and left position with regard to censorship has always been consistently against it, and in favour of individual freedom of speech and movement. On that level, it is not surprising either, that the 'liberal' Williams Committee would conclude in favour of the freedom to produce, sell and consume pornography. Nor, in this context, is it surprising that a play critical of British imperialism in Ireland might face an attempt at suppression.

For myself, I have campaigned in this very same left/liberal tradition against censorship in the theatre in the pages of *Tribune*, and *Theatre Quarterly* in the seventies, and in my book *Stages in the Revolution: Political Theatre in Britain Since 1968* (1981, 1982). Now my views have changed. I will continue to campaign against the censorship of such plays as *The Romans in Britain*. But I will now actively campaign for the censorship of pornography. I see no contradiction whatsoever in these positions. For I have now had an insight into the *meaning* of pornography, and, significantly, into the *meaning* of Howard Brenton's play in relation to pornography. I can see now that the 'freedom' of pornography is posited on the 'censorship' of women: that the price of the 'freedom' given to those who publish and purchase pornography (men) is freedom denied to its objects (women).

Andrea Dworkin, in her excellent book, analyses every detail of the cover of *Hustler* to show how it is primarily a demonstration of male power of women, how 'the degradation of women exists in order to postulate, exercise and celebrate male power'. She points out how the men are self-possessed while the woman, bound to the hood of the Jeep, is possessed, without a 'self'. (It is common in pornography for women's faces to be covered, invisible to the camera: part of the function of pornography is the obliteration of the humanness of women.) She points out that the photo celebrates the physical power of men over women; how the power of terror is basic to the image; and how the power of 'naming' (language — and here Dale Spender's *Man-Made Language*, RKP, 1980, is relevant) transforms her into an animal. She points out how the photo is a demonstration of ownership: the woman is stripped to nothing and displayed as a prize, a commodity, while the men flaunt their wealth and possessions. (The parallel with similar common images in advertising — of women draped over cars — is strong and not at all incidental.) She points out that the woman is either dead, or will be. The photo, if it has anything to do with sex at all, shows sex as power and money. Its key message, however, is that pornography has nothing to do with sex, but rather with the silencing of women, the denial of the humanness of women, the 'death' of women. Pornography is violence. The violence is not just in the exploitation and degradation of real women (and children) in its making, but in the fear induced in all women by the knowledge that such images of themselves as violated objects exist, and in its validation *for* men, *of* men in their role as oppressors.

The images of pornography — whether they are on billboards

and television screens (women's bodies used to sell commodities) or come from under the counter (where women's bodies are the commodity) — instruct men in how to see women as dehumanised, as objects; instruct men in the value (lessness) of women, in the exploitation of women, in violence against women.

There still persists an 'illusion' that there is no provable connection between pornography and violence (as the Williams Committee concluded, for example). The truth — the irony — is that pornography *is* violence. Against women by men. The violence is institutionalised and it is internalised (by women, which accounts in part for their 'tolerance' and sometimes 'participation' in it).

What Susan Griffin's equally fascinating book does is show how this particular form of oppression of women is related to other forms of oppression and violence in society. Thus she picks the cartoon from *Hustler* as one of many examples of pornography and anti-semitism, which she studies at length, in depth, as she does the relationship between pornography and racism. Griffin: 'Finally one comes to recognise that the contents of the racist mind are fundamentally pornographic ... the pornographic mind and the racist mind are really identical ... Just as the racist is obsessed with a pornographic drama, the pornographer is obsessed with racism.' Thus there is a porn magazine entitled *Inter-Racial Spanking*, with a naked black woman tied up and beaten by a fully-dressed white man; and Nazi pornography is popular (a typical feature is 'Hitler Spanking', a man in Nazi uniform, made up to resemble Hitler, with a woman over his knee, naked except for black stockings and high heels). And so forth.

Susan Griffin takes us along the path from the thicket of advertisements which use women's bodies, or parts of women's bodies to sell consumer goods, through the jungle of soft and hard pornography to ... Belsen and the Bomb. She shows how the violence that is war is not separate from the violence that is pornography. They are both on the same continuum. They are both products of capitalism now. They have always been products of patriarchy.

What is 'offensive' to some people about *The Romans in Britain* is, I think, not that it contains a scene of 'pornography' and violence, but that it demonstrates (unequivocally and persuasively as it is artistically a 'good' play) that pornography *is* violence. And that (just as Susan Griffin argues) violence is integrally related to the violence of racism, the violence of fascism, the violence of imperialism,

the violence of war. It is, incidentally, a fairly impressive presentation of patriarchy as an oppression prior to and independent of
capitalism.

The play isolates three periods of imperialism in Britain: that of
the Romans against the Celts in 55 BC (though note the way the
'Irish' are treated by the Celts); that of the Saxon invasion in AD 535
and that of the British in Northern Ireland now (the latter two
periods are ingeniously presented simultaneously). Brenton shows
the side of history which ruling-class, male-created history books
ignore, showing how behind every great, celebrated war (exclude not
the Falklands war) and every glorious so-called golden age there has
been death, destruction, violence and corruption. The SAS officer
on the Irish border at the end of the play has a vision of his British
army machine gun as a Roman spear and a Saxon axe. Same story,
different actors.

The 'sensitive' scene of homosexual rape demonstrates the racism
implicit in imperialism (the Celts are wogs) and exposes some of the
hollow rhetoric of religion (my God's better than yours, so bang-
bang, you're dead). The scene functions as a metaphor of violence.
In this sense it could be genuinely threatening and tempting to
suppress, because it exposes what it is convenient to capitalism and
to patriarchy to keep obscured: i.e., the meaning of power.

'When will peace come?' asks the SAS officer before suiciding
himself at the end of an IRA pistol. Possibly with the end of
capitalism and its products: certainly with the end of patriarchy and
its products. But 'peace' would mean that 'the boys couldn't read
their comics (pornography)' and that 'the boys couldn't play with
their toys (knives and guns and nuclear weapons)' and that the 'boys
couldn't play their games (war)': in short that the boys would have to
give up their power. Surely that cannot seem such an awfully boring
thing to have to do if one recognises that the breasts crushed in vices
and the exploding vaginas and the Fiat car ads and the Falklands
War and the nuclear arms race and starvation in the Third World all
come in the same patriarchal package, wrapped up in the profits of
capitalism. What is at stake is life on earth.

So I see no contradiction in campaigning against political
censorship and for the censorship of pornography. The end is the
same: the liberty of, the liberation of all human beings. God forbid
that people are denied the freedom to say and think and read what
they like — though in the case of pornography, for 'people' read
'men'. But when will God forbid (and Christianity has made a

substantial contribution to the 'pornographic' mind) that this freedom is bought at the expense of women's humanity?

Susan Griffin effectively asks: what is freedom? And she distinguishes between the idea of *liberty* to do as one likes and a vision of human *liberation*. While the liberty of pornography exists uncensored, half of the population will remain in its chains.

There are certain 'freedoms' we elect to forego — like killing each other — and which we legislate against. Insofar as the meaning of pornography is the 'death' of women, then it must be another 'freedom' we elect to forego. For the sake of the survival of humanity.

Postscript

This essay was originally commissioned in 1982 for a special 'theatre' issue of *Red Letters*, a literary journal of the left. It was subsequently reprinted in *Gamut* in Canada in 1983 and in *Gulliver* in Germany in 1984. Since it was first published, there have been a number of developments in the pornography industry (which has got much bigger, now a 10 billion dollar a year industry in the USA, no figures available for UK) and in campaigns by women to eliminate pornography.

In the USA Andrea Dworkin and Catharine MacKinnon have created civil rights anti-pornography legislation described elsewhere in this book, and there are initiatives to legislate against pornography using this women's rights model in Canada and West Germany. In this country, the MP Clare Short introduced an Indecent Displays Act in 1986 (dubbed the 'Page 3 Bill') in an attempt to remove the daily portrayal of nude and semi-nude young women from the pages of the tabloid press. Predictably, the Bill failed.

Clare Short re-introduced her Page 3 Bill in 1988, at the same time as she launched the Campaign Against Pornography with Barbara Rogers, editor of *Everywoman* magazine who published 'Pornography and Sexual Violence: Evidence of the Links' (the unedited transcript of the Hearings held by Minneapolis City Council when it was considering whether to add the Dworkin/MacKinnon legislation against pornography to its existing civil rights legislation). CAP's policy is 'not against sex, sex education or frank discussion', but 'against pornography which shows women in a degrading or humiliating way, sometimes with violence being inflicted and often with the message that women enjoy this and want to be abused.'

There is also in this country a civil liberties and women's rights based Campaign Against Pornography and Censorship (CPC) which has been formed by a group of lawyers, journalists, writers, women's rights campaigners and trades unionists. CPC's aim is to provide information about every aspect of pornography, to publish research on evidence of harm to women, and on the pornography industry, to pursue legislation against pornography on the grounds of sex discrimination and incitement to sexual hatred and violence, and to promote actions, such as boycotts, against the pornography industry. CPC's policy statement is published as an appendix to this book.

As a member of the Women's Rights Committee (and now an elected member of the Executive Committee) of the National Council of Civil Liberties, I proposed a resolution at the 1987 AGM of the NCCL which affirmed the NCCL's policy of freedom of speech and expression, but noted that the NCCL's opposition to all forms of censorship had not been absolute: that they had quite correctly accepted restrictions directed at avoiding identifiable harm, as in the case of race hatred literature and the incitement to racial hatred. I therefore proposed that the Race Relations Act 1976 be used as a model for legislating against pornography: making it unlawful to publish or distribute material likely to stir up sexual as well as racial hatred. I proposed that pornography which was 'threatening, abusive and insulting' (using the terminology of the Race Relations legislation) or degrading and damaging to women be defined as that which 'depicts violence or involves violence or criminal offence in its manufacture'. I proposed that pornography, defined in these terms — representing a combination of sex and violence, and the degradation of women — be legislated against on the 'grounds that it can be an incitement to sexual hatred and contribute to acts of violence against women in the form of sexual abuse, sexual assault, sexual harassment, rape and murder', the evidence of which has been extensively published and accepted by Federal Courts in the USA. As a result of this initiative, the NCCL is currently reviewing its policy on pornography and child pornography.

In Toronto in 1983 when the City Council attempted to ban pornography from Pay TV, Councillor Anne Johnstone argued in favour of the ban on grounds that there already existed in Canadian law and the Canadian Broadcasting Act the accepted prohibition of 'hate literature' or 'material that defames, abuses, degrades or otherwise turns public opinion against any segment of society because of race.' 'This,' she said, 'is protection of human rights. The intent and application of this legislation is not to prevent the portrayal of victims. It is to prevent the portrayal of people to be victimised.' 'But why,' she asked, 'did the legislation overlook the largest single, identifiable group of our society, the female gender?' She argued that women deserved at least the same rights and protection from 'incitement to hatred' as was extended to black people. In speaking against pornography she quoted from my essay published here, in which, she said, she felt the 'question of censorship had been appropriately addressed.' Censorship is about the limitation of freedom: eliminating pornography is about promoting the freedom of women: the human rights of women.

Women campaigned for over 50 years to get the vote. It may take women 50 years or more to get rid of pornography, but the effort appears to be well and truly under way.

Catherine Itzin
June 1988

CENSORSHIP IN IRELAND: A WOMAN'S RIGHT TO INFORMATION?

Anne Conway

> The qualified right to privacy, the rights of association and freedom of expression and the right to disseminate information cannot be invoked to interfere with such a fundamental right as the right to life of the unborn child which is acknowledged by the Constitution of Ireland.

This extract from the Dublin High Court ruling of December 1986 against two Dublin women's clinics, forbidding them to provide a non-directive pregnancy counselling and abortion referral service, exemplifies the all-pervasive scope of censorship in Ireland. Ireland and Chile are the only countries which constitutionally deny women abortion. The High Court ruling interpreted the constitutional prohibition on abortion to cover the dissemination of information about it.

The background to this extensive censorship lies in the division of the country in 1922 into two confessional states. Restrictions on civil rights have characterised both states; the straitjacket of church state control in all areas of life in both the six and the twenty-six counties has given a particular character to censorship in Ireland. Church influence has dictated that not only is censorship related to political issues, but also to matters of private morality and sexuality and to views which do not coincide with Church thinking. This does not only affect practising Catholics, but also citizens of other religions and none, who are all subjected to the particular Irish Catholic view of acceptable moral behaviour.

From their inception, both states were felt to be illegitimate by a large section of the population; both have virtually permanent emergency legislation, draconian police powers and extensive censorship. For example, many of the great literary figures and artists who were part of Ireland's cultural renaissance at the turn of the century, such as Yeats, Beckett and Joyce, had their works banned in the past. The social repression which followed the partition of the country — virtually a counter-revolution — has been the source of the extensive censorship against women's rights practised throughout Ireland.

In the 1923 Censorship of Films Act, the censor was authorised to cut or refuse a license to films which were 'subversive of public morality'. The Censorship of Publications Board, established in 1930, was clerical-dominated and had the power to prevent the sale and distribution of any publication it considered obscene. The publication or distribution of literature advocating birth control was made an offence. It was only in the sixties, with the opening up of the Irish economy to multinational investment, that a relaxation of censorship temporarily occurred. Traditional social and moral values were challenged by the growth of the women's liberation movement, as the early campaigns of the movement centred around issues of sexuality. Yet it was not until 1977 that the movement succeeded in having the ban lifted on the publication of a Family Planning handbook censored under the Obscene Publications Act.

The slow and uneven move away from socially repressive legislation and censorship came to a halt as Ireland moved into the eighties. In the political climate of economic recession and a return to traditional Catholic values, a vicious campaign was launched against women. The right-wing Catholic group, the Pro-Life Amendment Campaign, succeeded after just one meeting with the leaders of the main political parties in securing a promise to hold a constitutional referendum giving equal rights to the foetus. The passage of the referendum in 1983 copper-fastened existing anti-abortion legislation and gave rise to the legal case brought by the Society for the Protection of the Unborn Child against the pregnancy counselling and abortion information service of the women's clinics. The High Court ruling of December 1986 was upheld by the Supreme Court in March 1988 and the clinic services remain closed. Women now seeking information on how to obtain a safe legal abortion in Britain must obtain the information themselves through a network of friends or relatives living in Britain, through popular British women's magazines, or through an informal network of helplines in a few of Ireland's main cities.

The censorship net has continued to expand. The Censorship Board in 1987 banned a book dealing with sexuality and sexual problems — *The Joy of Sex* — and the right-wing have recently launched a campaign against sex education in secondary schools. In October 1987 Radio Telefis Eireann brought in guidelines prohibiting discussion on abortion on live programmes. The guidelines warned that programme makers were 'vulnerable' to exploitation by opponents of the ruling and that they would 'possibly be liable to prosecution for conspiracy to corrupt public morals' if abortion advice is given over the air, perhaps by a telephone caller to a chat show.

As a result of the court rulings prohibiting the clinics giving abortion advice and information, women as a group suffer a far greater degree of censorship than any other sector of Irish society. Section 31 of the Broadcasting Act, which bans Sinn Fein, including their elected representatives, from the national airwaves, has helped create the climate for censorship on abortion information. If duly elected representatives are silenced from speaking for their constituency, it is an easier step to gag women and deny the individual the right to her sexual self-determination. Section 31 covers the airwaves, while censorship of abortion information extends to the whole of the mass media and beyond, forcing the issue of abortion underground and ultimately to the backstreets.

Since SPUC led the attack on the women's clinics there has been a sharp increase in the instances of censorship. Popular feminist writer, Nell McCafferty, was banned from appearing on radio and television for expressing Republican sympathies, under Section 18 of the Broadcasting Act, which covers incitement to violence and which had not been previously invoked. The ban was subsequently relaxed to cover live broadcasts only. Another woman journalist, Jenny McKeever, was dismissed from her job in Radio Telefis Eireain for a two-sentence, innocuous interview with a Sinn Fein leader. And in April 1988 a West Belfast community worker and writer was suspended from her job by Belfast City Council for writing an article in the *Irish Times* defending the people of West Belfast from some of the more lurid attacks on them by the British press. The suspension was lifted after a campaign by her trade union.

It is true that any relaxation of the censorship laws could bring with it an influx of pornography, and that such a consequence will have to be faced by feminists here. But for the present the reality is that in recent months, both broadcasters and politicians have openly called for political censorship to be extended. It is hard to separate all the different aspects of censorship from one another. Each aspect feeds off the other; they are complementary and create a climate in which views and opinions considered unacceptable are censored. The worst victims of this are women.

THE US ORDINANCES: CENSORSHIP OR RADICAL LAW REFORM?

Liz Kelly

When I wrote a piece for *Trouble and Strife* (Kelly 1985) on the pornography ordinance drafted by Andrea Dworkin and Catharine MacKinnon I was mainly concerned to make British feminists aware of what I felt was a critically important debate between US feminists. The context in which I am now writing (March 1987) is in some senses very different and in others precisely the same. I still feel that the actual intention behind, and content of, the ordinance is poorly understood by many feminists. However, the grounds on which the debate took place have been the basis for a number of conferences. The interesting discussions we could have had about the ordinance were undercut by an insistence by some feminists that what was at issue was free speech and censorship. Whilst it is necessary to go over and update the basic information in that earlier article, I want to argue a case in this chapter: that the ordinance itself was not about censorship but was an attempt at radical (feminist) law reform.

The Legislative History of the Ordinance

In 1983 Dworkin and MacKinnon were teaching a course on pornography in Minneapolis. At the same time the city council was discussing a new zoning law to limit the public availability of pornography to particular geographic areas. A number of community groups approached Dworkin and MacKinnon; their concerns being that zoning legislation disproportionately affected poorer neighbourhoods. Whilst agreeing with this, Dworkin and MacKinnon were also concerned that current obscenity legislation failed to address the harm pornography does to women. They came up with a new approach based on civil rights; the Minneapolis city council asked them to draft a bill (ordinance) based on this idea.

In the US, city councils can pass legislation relating to their area of jurisdiction; such laws are called ordinances. If any such law involves complex legal issues it may be referred to the District Court where a judge makes a ruling about whether it is constitutional. Further appeals are possible right up to the Supreme Court.

Dworkin and MacKinnon drafted an ordinance and hearings took place in which supporting evidence was given by individual women (many of whom had worked in the sex industry and/or gave testimony about how pornography was implicated in sexual violence they had experienced), feminist groups, social researchers and local community groups. Whilst the ordinance was passed by the Minneapolis city council, it was vetoed by the mayor. Indianapolis city council, with the guidance of MacKinnon, introduced a similar ordinance. Here it was passed by the city council and supported by the mayor, but ruled unconstitutional by the District Court. An appeal was lodged by the mayor of Indianapolis. (Further attempts to introduce versions of the ordinance took place in Los Angeles, Suffolk County, Long Island and Cambridge, Massachusetts.)

It was at this point that a group of feminists (Feminists Anti-Censorship Task Force — FACT) joined an anti-ordinance coalition which included Indianapolis Video Shack, The Association of American Publishers, The American Booksellers Association and the US Civil Liberties Union. FACT produced a brief opposing the ordinance for the appeal hearing, which was signed by 76 well-known writers and academics, ten of whom were men. The spectre of groups of feminists opposing one another in a court of law preoccupied US radicals for months. An acrimonious debate took place on public platforms, in the alternative press and no doubt within women's groups and friendship networks.

The Court of Appeal ruled that the ordinance was unconstitutional and a further appeal to the Supreme Court was lodged. In his ruling in the Court of Appeal, Frank Easterbrook supported the analysis of pornography underlying the ordinance, but ruled that this could not supersede the absolute principle of freedom of speech encoded in the US constitution. He said:

> Depictions of subordination tend to perpetuate subordination. The subordinate status of women in turn leads to affront and lower pay at work, insult and injury at home, battery and rape on the streets. But this simply demonstrates the power of pornography as speech. (Quoted in *off our backs* XVI:4, p. 6)

In February 1986 the Supreme Court upheld the Court of Appeal's ruling. Rather than hearing any of the evidence, the judges chose to 'summarily affirm' the ruling; an unusual procedure. If they had simply upheld the previous ruling other city councils could have introduced versions of the ordinance. By affirming the ruling the Supreme Court made a national ruling; this means that no similar legislation can be introduced in the US. The day after this decision, the Supreme Court upheld the use of zoning as a way of restricting pornography.

What the Ordinance Actually Says

Dworkin and MacKinnon begin from a belief that pornography directly harms women (in both its production and consumption) and that it is a central element in maintaining male dominance. They argue that pornography is a form of sexual discrimination because it is a specific harm which has an impact on all areas of women's lives. The ordinance lists the direct harms to women as: 'dehumanization, sexual exploitaion, forced sex, forced prostitution, physical injury, and social and sexual terrorism and inferiority presented as entertainment'. The ordinance also specifies that through the promotion of contempt for women, pornography is also implicated in women's economic inequality, the prevalence of sexual violence and in restricting women's freedom as citizens, i.e. women's equal exercise of rights as guaranteed under the US Constitution.

Pornography is defined in the 1985 draft of the ordinance as:

... the graphic sexually explicit subordination of women, through pictures and/or in words, that also includes one of the following:
1. women are presented dehumanized as sexual objects, things or commodities; or
2. women are presented as sexual objects who enjoy pain or humiliation; or
3. women are presented as sexual objects who experience sexual pleasure in being raped; or
4. women are presented as sexual objects tied up or cut up or mutilated or bruised or physically hurt; or
5. women are presented in postures or positions of sexual submission, servility or display; or
6. women's body parts — including but not limited to vaginas, breasts, or buttocks — are exhibited such that women are reduced to those parts; or
7. women are presented as whores by nature; or

8. women are presented being penetrated by objects or animals; or
9. women are presented in scenarios of degradation, injury, torture, shown as filthy or inferior, bleeding, bruised or hurt in a context which makes these conditions sexual.

Drafted as a civil rights law the ordinance empowers individual or groups of women (in very limited circumstances men) to take a case against the producers/distributors of pornography. To take a case the woman has to show that the magazine/book/film/video/ photograph is both subordinating and covered by the definition of pornography. She also has to make one of four charges to show that she was directly harmed: that she was coerced into participating in the production of pornography; that she was forced to view pornography; that she was assaulted as a direct result of pornography. In each of these cases the pornography in question has to be specified. The final charge is for trafficking; here the woman appears for women as a group and the case rests on demonstrating that the public availability of pornography constitutes a violation of women's civil rights.

To take account of the complexity of women's involvement in the sex industry, thirteen conditions are cited which *are not* acceptable as a defence in cases brought under the ordinance. They include: previously appearing in porn, signing a contract, that no physical force was used and/or that payment was received. Because cases would be heard in civil courts, there are no criminal penalties — the only sanctions available to the court are fines and stopping the production/sale of any pornography that is found to be subordinating within the definition, and directly implicated in harm. Where fines are imposed these are to be paid direct to the woman/ women taking the case.

The FACT Brief

The FACT brief rests on two fundamental disagreements with Dworkin and MacKinnon: that pornography is not central in maintaining women's oppression and that feminists should not be involved in campaigning for legal reform which restricts freedom of speech. Choosing 'anti-censorship' as part of their name reflects their assumption that the ordinance would result in censorship; a point I will return to later along with a comment on the issue of what is 'central' in women's oppression. There are six basic points in the FACT brief:

- Pornography is not central in maintaining gender inequality. The ordinance does not address the more important ways in which women are denied equality. Feminist energies should be directed at acts not images; thus we should focus on the acts of coercion in pornography, rape and battery, which are covered by already existing legislation.
- The terms 'subordinating' 'degrading' and 'sexual objectification' are not defined in the ordinance; thus judges will be able to define them. FACT suggest that this may result in feminist art, self-help health guides, and so on being prosecuted.
- The ordinance is sexist, as it represents men and women as fundamentally different. It suggests women are weak, in need of protection, unable to make their own decisions. Women appear as helpless victims who do not seek or enjoy sex and who cannot enter into legally binding agreements. It presumes all men are conditioned by pornography to commit acts of aggression and believe mysogynist myths.
- The ordinance asumes a simple link between words/images and behaviour. Men learn about gender roles in many places; the family is probably more important than pornography. Porn does not explain violence against women which existed before it was widely available.
- Women's experiences with pornography are mixed; some women get erotic pleasure from it. The meanings of pornography are varied, it can be an affirmation — particularly for sexual minorities.
- There are serious dangers in restricting sexually explicit speech. The inevitable alliance with the New Right on this issue is disturbing.

It has been suggested in *off our backs* that a number of the FACT signatories supported only some of the brief's arguments and were swayed by fears about state censorship. There is no doubt that this was the terrain on which the debate took place, foreclosing any real discussion of the ordinance itself. Feminists had to be on one side or the other; the sides being defined by FACT supporters as pro or anti censorship. Few discussions took place on whether an amended version of the ordinance might produce a broader consensus — one had to be either for or against it. Those of us who were interested and broadly sympathetic to this fundamentally different approach to pornography and the law, but who had questions we wanted to discuss, were silenced. If we voiced sympathy than that meant we accepted the ordinance, if we asked questions then we must be opposed to it. There was no space for discussion and open debate. Few opportunities were available for the majority of active feminists to work through the complex issues involved.

The Non-Debate

I find the grounds of the FACT brief unconvincing and at times contradictory. For example, whilst telling us we must focus on acts and not images, the brief proceeds to criticise the ordinance for not addressing the sexist imagery that abounds in the mass media.

However, within the brief there are some more specific points related to the drafting of the ordinance which feminists in other countries wanting to explore this approach may have to address (the ordinance itself has been re-drafted several times). For example, whilst the ordinance contains a tight and detailed definition of pornography the critical term 'subordinating' is not defined. There is also the question of whether the non-acceptable forms of defence to charges brought under the ordinance amount to defining women as legal minors and whether this would set a precedent for other legislation.

I am increasingly convinced that the suggestion that lesbian erotica or feminist health books could be prosecuted is a misreading of the ordinance; lesbian pornography may be another matter. The possibility that, if the ordinance had been passed and taken the place of obscenity laws, gay books and bookstores might be less targetted than they are now, was never discussed. The definition of pornography in the ordinances is considerably less vague than 'obscenity', 'prurient interests' and 'community standards' — the terms of current obscenity legislation in many countries. In totally opposing this new approach and refusing to offer any alternatives, FACT supporters end up implicitly suggesting that current obscenity legislation is in some way preferable to the ordinance.

The whole FACT brief smacks of a strange alliance of views between socialist feminists, liberal feminists and libertarians: freedom of speech is a supreme value; state intervention in any area should be minimal, and direct demonstrations of harm have to be proved. The fact that the ordinance is designed to precisely achieve what liberals have always demanded — prove harm — mysteriously disappears.

At no point, to my knowledge, did FACT engage in discussing the testimony of women that porn had indeed harmed them; that these were acts, some of which are not covered by existing legislation. The evidence is there for anyone who wants to see. In Linda Marchiano's moving testimony of her coercion in the making of the film *Deep Throat* she tells us that we can see the bruises on her body if we care to look (Lovelace and McGrady 1980). This one case demonstrates how unrealistic FACT's suggestion is that we separate out acts of violence from the production of pornography — they were inextricably linked. Linda Marchiano's experience also illustrates how one of the predominant themes in pornography — that women enjoy rape and violence, that rape is really sex — is played out in reality. There is a mutually reinforcing connection between pornography and the explanations/excuses men offer for their abusive behaviour. Just focusing on the act, for example, of rape under rape law, will never undermine the ease with which rapists are able to plead the consent defence. The credibility of this form of defence is reinforced daily in the content of pornography.

Unlike the FACT signatories, I do not see pornography as just words and images — it is produced by actions and like advertising it is intended to have an effect (Kappeler 1986) — even if this is limited to wanting to look at some more of it. One of the basic points underlying the ordinance and present in MacKinnon's recent writings is that women's subordination is increasingly sexualised, made erotic (MacKinnon 1987). It is this analysis that informs Dworkin and MacKinnon's proposition that pornography is central to women's continued oppression. Whilst this analysis may be most applicable to Western capitalist societies, merely stating, as the FACT brief does, that pornography hasn't always been so prevalent does not undermine the argument. The analysis is, in fact, an explanation of why pornography, and the sex industry more generally, has grown so rapidly over the last 20 years. Simplistic analyses of capitalist commodity production do not amount to an adequate alternative explanation. Women who oppose both the ordinance and feminist anti-pornography campaigns more generally cannot just assert that pornography is not central. They have to engage much more directly with this analysis of how women's oppression has been transformed and maintained.

Feminism is based on the fundamental belief that women have been and are systematically oppressed and on a political commitment to end that oppression. The suggestion in the FACT brief that the ordinance is sexist, in that it makes women's systematic oppression visible in law, comes close to denying the fundamental reality on which feminism is based. The suggestion that the ordinance is flawed because it fails to address every aspect of women's oppression in one law is just plain silly.

What I still find extraordinary is that the feminist opposition totally failed to address what is most interesting about the ordinance. First, that it attempts to embody feminist and women-centred definitions in a legislative format and second, that it seeks to empower women rather than the police or the state. It almost seems a deliberate misreading to stir up fear of state censorship. There is quite simply no case unless a woman takes one and feels she can demonstrate each of the three stages of proof required by the ordinance. The only consequences if she wins her case are financial penalties to those making vast profits. There seems to me no direct benefit to the state from this process. The end result if, and only if, a large number of women both achieve successful prosecution and are awarded substantial damages, may be that some pornographers wind up their business, or shops stop selling it, as it is no longer profitable. This is a long-term prospect and it would be the result of individual choice, not state coercion.

As I understand it, censorship means preventing someone from speaking or publishing/distributing their views. The chief focus in discussions has tended to be state censorship, and amongst radicals there has been a tendency to see all forms of state censorship as attacks on fundamental human rights. It is impossible within this simplistic definition of the issues to engage in dialogue. It has, however, become increasingly accepted within radical thought that some restrictions on speech/the written word/visual representation are permissable and even desirable. We all restrict the views we publish in our publications; we do not give space to overtly fascist, racist or sexist views. Precisely what the difference between this sort of restriction and that condemned because it is done in the name of the state must be specified. Where the restrictions are based on the suppression of oppositional political viewpoints we surely need to distinguish between those which are progressive and those which are oppressive. Would we regard it as a fundamental challenge to human rights that a Black majority government in South Africa placed restrictions on racist discourse? Do we regard it as a fundamental challenge to basic human rights that the Sandinistas made pornography illegal in Nicaragua?

Maybe the argument turns on who it is that is doing the restricting and whether their intentions are 'honourable', i.e. the nature of the state in Western capitalist nations. If we believe that states in these countries are irredeemably patriarchal, racist and classist, then all radicals must cease campaigning for any legal reforms, be it for access to abortion, protecting or extending trade union rights or anti-discrimination legislation, and concentrate on total transformation. But most Marxists today agree that the state is a site of struggle with relative autonomy, within which it is possible to win reforms, however limited they might be and that these struggles are a vital part of radical political action. The recent shift to the right in the West should be a spur to more determined struggle, rather than a fatalistic suggestion that fighting for radical change in such a climate is too dangerous. This latter position lurks between the lines of the FACT brief and was explicit in Adrienne Rich's defence of her signing of it: 'I am less sure than Dworkin and MacKinnon that this is a time when further powers of suppression should be turned over to the State.' (Letter in *off our backs* XV:6). Twentieth century history is replete with examples of the dire consequences of radicals retreating into defensive and reactive politics.

The ordinance non-debate was yet another re-run of the arguments for and against feminists taking on the issue of pornography. Quite why, for some feminists, campaigning against sexist images in the media is acceptable but campaigning against pornography is not still escapes me — particularly when campaigns against sexist advertising are directed towards the removal of offensive imagery. Indeed a number of feminists who oppose state intervention want to have it both ways. Lynne Segal, for example, accepts that pornography is offensive to women and supports direct action against it, but also wants to defend the analysis of some of the signatories of the FACT brief that use of pornography is an acceptable sexual practice (Segal, 1987, Chapter 3).

In reading and listening to a number of arguments against the ordinance and/or any campaigning for legal restrictions on speech and representation, I was reminded of the 'wait until after the revolution' injunctions we encountered from the male Left so consistently in the early 1970s. The history of socialist transformations unfortunately tell another story. Where women subordinated their feminist politics to the 'greater cause', the subsequent society continued to subordinate women. It is only where women have continued to organise as women, to raise their demands during the revolutionary struggle, that progressive change continues. We cannot afford to drop any issues or demands. For pornography not to be a target of feminist activism, the onus is on those who disagree to show that it has *no role* in perpetuating women's oppression. This case has not yet even been argued.

What I would like to see is some critical but constructive discussion of the actual content and intent of the ordinance, along with a serious debate of precisely what forms of restrictions, on speech are acceptable. We know that certain forms of speech represent a threat to someone's or some group's basic human rights — rights to survival, safety, equality, democracy and dignity. It is not a basic human right to make a profit, exploit others or speak/act with total disregard of the consequences.

Bibliography

FACT Brief
Susanne Kappeler, 1986, *The Pornography of Representation*, Polity Press.
Liz Kelly, 1985, 'Feminists v Feminists — legislating against porn in the USA', *Trouble and Strife* 7, 4–10.
Linda Lovelace and Mike McGrady, 1980, *Ordeal*, Citadel Press.
Catharine MacKinnon, 1987, *Discourses on Women and Law*, Harvard University Press.
off our backs, XV:5, 6, 7; XVI:4.
Lynne Segal, 1987, *Is the Future Female? Troubled Thoughts on Contemporary Feminism*, Virago.

FALSE PROMISES: FEMINIST ANTI-PORNOGRAPHY LEGISLATION IN THE US

Lisa Duggan, Nan Hunter and Carole S. Vance

(Excerpted, with permission, from an article in Varda Burstyn (ed.), *Feminists Against Censorship*, Douglas & McIntyre, Toronto, 1985.)

In the United States, after two decades of increasing community tolerance for dissenting or disturbing sexual or political materials, there is now growing momentum for retrenchment. In an atmosphere of increased conservatism, evidenced by a wave of book banning and anti-gay harassment, support for new repressive legislation of various kinds — from an Oklahoma law forbidding schoolteachers from advocating homosexuality to new antipornography laws passed in Minneapolis and Indianapolis — is growing.

The antipornography laws have mixed roots of support, however. Though they are popular with the conservative constituencies that traditionally favour legal restrictions on sexual expression of all kinds, they were drafted and are endorsed by antipornography feminists who oppose traditional obscenity and censorship laws. The model law of this type, which is now being widely copied, was drawn up in the politically progressive city of Minneapolis by two radical feminists, author Andrea Dworkin and attorney Catharine MacKinnon. It was passed by the city council there, but vetoed by the mayor. A similar law was also passed in Indianapolis, but later declared unconstitutional in federal court, a ruling that the city will appeal. Other versions of the legislation are being considered in numerous cities, and Pennsylvania senator Arlen Specter has introduced legislation modeled on parts of the Dworkin–MacKinnon bill in the U.S. Congress.

Dworkin, MacKinnon and their feminist supporters believe that the new antipornography laws are not censorship laws. They also claim that the legislative effort behind them is based on feminist support. Both of these claims are dubious at best. Though the new laws are civil laws that allow individuals to sue the makers, sellers, distributors or exhibitors of pornography, and not criminal laws leading to arrest and imprisonment, their censoring impact would be substantially as severe as criminal obscenity laws. Materials could be removed from public availability by court injunction, and publishers and booksellers could be subject to potentially endless legal harassment. Passage of the laws was therefore achieved with the support of right-wing elements who expect the new laws to accomplish what censorship efforts are meant to accomplish. Ironically, many antifeminist conservatives backed these laws, while many feminists opposed them. In Indianapolis, the law was supported by extreme right-wing religious fundamentalists, including members of the Moral Majority, while there was *no* local feminist support. In other cities, traditional procensorship forces have expressed interest in the new approach to banning sexually explicit materials. Meanwhile, anticensorship feminists have become alarmed at these new developments and are seeking to galvanize feminist opposition to the new antipornography legislative strategy pioneered in Minneapolis.

One is tempted to ask in astonishment, how can this be happening? How can feminists be entrusting the patriarchal state with the task of legally distinguishing between permissible and impermissible sexual images? But in fact this new development is not as surprising as it at first seems. Pornography has come to be seen as a central cause of women's oppression by a significant number of feminists. Some even argue that pornography is the root of virtually all forms of exploitation and discrimination against women. It is a short step from such a belief to the conviction that laws against pornography can end the inequality of the sexes. But this analysis takes feminists very close — indeed far too close — to measures that will ultimately support conservative, anti-sex, procensorship forces in American society, for it is with these forces that women have forged alliances in passing such legislation.

This is therefore a critical moment in the feminist debate over sexual politics. As anticensorship feminists work to develop alternatives to antipornography campaigns, we also need to examine carefully the new laws and expose their underlying assumptions. We need to know why these laws, for all their apparent feminist rhetoric, actually appeal to conservative antifeminist forces and why feminists should be preparing to move in a different direction.

The antipornography ordinances passed in Minneapolis and Indianapolis were framed as amendments to municipal civil rights laws. They provide for complaints to be filed against pornography in the same manner that complaints are filed against employment discrimination. If enforced, the laws would make illegal public or private availability (except in libraries) of any materials deemed pornographic.

Such material could be the object of a lawsuit on several grounds. The ordinance would penalize four kinds of behavior associated with pornography: its production, sale, exhibition or distribution ('trafficking'); coercion into pornographic performance; forcing pornography on a person; and assault or physical attack due to pornography.

Under this law, a woman 'acting as a woman against the subordination of women' could file a complaint; men could also file complaints if they could 'prove injury in the same way that a woman is injured'. The procedural steps in the two ordinances differ, but they generally allow the complainant either to file an administrative complaint with the city's equal opportunity commission (Minneapolis or Indianapolis), or to file a lawsuit directly in court (Minneapolis). If the local commission found the law had been violated, it would file a lawsuit. By either procedure, the court — not 'women' — would have the final say on whether the materials fit the definition of pornography and issue an injunction (or court order) preventing further distribution of the material in question.

The Minneapolis ordinance defines pornography as 'the sexually explicit subordination of women, graphically depicted, whether in pictures or words'. To be actionable, materials would also have to fall within one of a number of categories: nine in the Minneapolis ordinance, six in the Indianapolis version. (See Appendix II for text of the original Minneapolis ordinance, from which the excerpts of the legislation quoted in this chapter are taken.)

Although proponents claim that the Minneapolis and Indianapolis ordinances represent a new way to regulate pornography, the strategy is still laden with our culture's old, repressive approach to sexuality. The implementation of such laws hinges on the definition of pornography as interpreted by the court. The definition provided in the Minneapolis legislation is vague, leaving critical phrases such as 'the sexually explicit subordination of women', 'postures of sexual submission' and 'whores by nature' to the interpretation of the citizen who files a complaint and to the civil court judge who hears the case. The legislation does not prohibit just the images of gross sexual violence that most supporters claim to be its target, but instead drifts toward covering an increasingly wide range of sexually explicit material.

The most problematic feature of this approach, then, is a conceptual flaw embedded in the law itself. Supporters of this type of legislation say that the target of their efforts is misogynist, sexually explicit and violent representation, whether in pictures or words. Indeed, the feminist antipornography movement is fuelled by women's anger at the most repugnant examples of pornography. But a close examination of the wording of the model legislative text, and examples of purportedly actionnable material offered by proponents of the legislation in court briefs suggests that the law is actually aimed at a range of material considerably broader than what proponents claim is their target. The discrepancies between the law's explicit and implicit aims have been almost invisible to us, because these distortions are very similar to distortions about sexuality in the culture as a whole. The legislation and supporting texts deserve close reading. Hidden beneath illogical transformations, nonsequiturs, and highly permeable definitions are familiar sexual scripts drawn from mainstream, sexist culture that potentially could have very negative consequences for women.

The Venn diagram illustrates the three areas targeted by the law, and represents a scheme that classifies words or images that have any of three characteristics: violence, sexual explicitness or sexism.

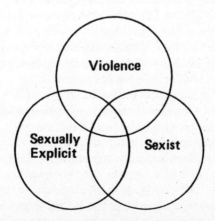

Clearly, a text or an image might have only one characteristic. Material can be violent but not sexually explicit or sexist: for example, a war movie in which both men and women suffer injury or death without regard to or because of their gender. Material can be sexist but not sexually explicit and violent. A vast number of materials from mainstream media — television, popular novels, magazines, newspapers — come to mind, all of which depict either distraught housewives or the 'happy sexism' of the idealized family, with mom self-sacrificing, other-directed and content. Finally, material can be sexually explicit but not violent or sexist: for example, the freely chosen sexual behavior depicted in sex education films or women's own explicit writing about sexuality.

As the diagram illustrates, areas can also intersect, reflecting a range of combinations of the three characteristics. Images can be violent and sexually explicit without being sexist — for example, a narrative about a rape in a men's prison, or a documentary about the effect of a rape on a woman. The latter example illustrates the importance of context in evaluating whether material that is sexually explicit and violent is also sexist. The intent of the maker, the context of the film and the perception of the viewer together render a depiction of a rape sympathetic, harrowing, even educational, rather than sensational, victim-blaming and laudatory.

Another possible overlap is between material that is violent and sexist but not sexually explicit. Films or books that describe violence directed against women by men in a way that clearly shows gender antagonism and inequality, and sometimes strong sexual tension, but no sexual explicitness fall into this category — for example, the popular genre of slasher films in which women are stalked, terrified and killed by men, or accounts of mass murder of women, fuelled by male rage. Finally, a third point of overlap arises when material is sexually explicit and sexist without being violent — that is, when sex is consensual but still reflects themes of male superiority and female abjectness. Some sex education materials could be included in this category, as well as a great deal of regular pornography.

The remaining domain, the inner core, is one in which the material is simultaneously violent, sexually explicit and sexist — for example, an image of a naked woman being slashed by a knife-wielding rapist. The Minneapolis law, however, does not by any means confine itself to this material.

To be actionnable under the law as pornography, material must be judged by the courts to be 'the sexually explicit subordination of women, graphically depicted whether in pictures or in words that also includes at least one or more' of nine criteria. Of these, only four involve the intersection of violence, sexual explicitness and sexism, and then only arguably (see Appendix I). Even in these cases, many questions remain about whether images with all three character-istics do in fact cause violence against women. And the task of evaluating material that is ostensibly the target of these criteria becomes complicated — indeed, hopeless — because most of the clauses that contain these criteria mix actions or qualities of violence with those that are not particularly associated with violence.

The section that comes closest to the stated purpose of the legislaton is clause (iii): 'women are presented as sexual objects who experience sexual pleasure in being raped.' This clause is intended to cover depictions of rape that are sexually explicit and sexist; the act of rape itself signifies the violence. But other clauses are not so clearcut, because the list of characteristics often mixes signs or by-products of violence with phenomena that are unrelated or irrelevant to judging violence. We might be willing to agree that clause (ii) — 'women are presented as sexual objects who enjoy pain' — signifies the conjunction of all three characteristics, with violence the presumed cause of pain, but the presence of the words 'and humiliation' at the end of the clause is problematic. Humiliation may be offensive or disagreeable, but it does not necessarily imply violence.

A similar problem occurs with clause (iv): 'women are presented as sexual objects tied up or cut up or mutilated or bruised or physically hurt.' All these except the first, 'tied up', generally occur as a result of violence. 'Tied up', if part of consensual sex, is not violent and, for some practitioners, not particularly sexist. Women who are tied up may be participants in nonviolent sex play involving bondage, a theme in both heterosexual and lesbian pornography. (See, for example, *The Joy of Sex* and *Coming to Power*.) Clause (ix) contains another mixed list, in which 'injury', 'torture', 'bleeding', 'bruised' and 'hurt' are combined with words such as 'degradation' and 'shown as filthy and inferior', neither of which is violent. Depending on the presentation, 'filthy' and 'inferior' may constitute sexually explicit sexism, although not violence. 'Degradation' is a sufficiently inclusive term to cover most acts of which a viewer disapproves.

Several other clauses have little to do with violence at all; they refer to material that is sexually explicit and sexist, thus falling outside the triad of characteristics at which the legislation is supposedly aimed. For example, movies in which 'women are presented as dehumanized sexual objects, things, or commodities' may be infuriating and offensive to feminists, but they are not violent.

Finally, some clauses describe material that is neither violent nor necessarily sexist. Clause (v), 'women . . . in postures of sexual submission or sexual servility, including by inviting penetration', and clause (viii), 'women . . . being penetrated by objects or animals', are sexually explicit, but not violent and not obviously sexist unless one believes that penetration — whether heterosexual, lesbian, or autoerotic masturbation — is indicative of gender inequality and female oppression. Similarly problematic are clauses that invoke representations of 'women . . . as whores by nature' and 'women's body parts . . . such that women are reduced to those parts'.

Texts filed in support of the Indianapolis law show how broadly it could be applied. In the amicus brief filed on behalf of Linda Marchiano ('Linda Lovelace,' the female lead in *Deep Throat*) in Indianapolis, Catharine MacKinnon offered *Deep Throat* as an example of the kind of pornography covered by the law. *Deep Throat* served a complicated function in this brief, because the movie, supporters of the ordinance argue, would be actionnable on two counts: coercion into pornographic performance, because Marchiano alleges that she was coerced into making the movie; and trafficking in pornography, because the content of the film falls within one of the categories in the Indianapolis ordinance's definition — that which prohibits presenting women as sexual objects 'through postures or positions of servility or submission or display'. Proponents of the law have counted on women's repugnance at allegations of coerced sexual acts to spill over and discredit the sexual acts themselves in this movie.

The aspects of *Deep Throat* that MacKinnon considered to be indicative of 'sexual subordination' are of particular interest, since any movie that depicted similar acts could be banned under the law. MacKinnon explained in her brief that the film 'subordinates women by using women . . . sexually, specifically as eager servicing receptacles for male genitalia and ejaculate. The majority of the film represents "Linda Lovelace" in, minimally, postures of sexual submission and/or servility.' In its brief, the City of Indianapolis concurred: 'In the film *Deep Throat* a woman is being shown as being ever eager to oral penetration by a series of men's penises, often on her hands and knees. There are repeated scenes in which her genitalia are graphically displayed and she is shown as enjoying men ejaculating on her face.'

These descriptions are very revealing, since they suggest that multiple partners, group sex and oral sex subordinate women and hence are sexist. The notion that the female character is 'used' by men suggests that it is improbable that a woman would engage in fellatio of her own accord. *Deep Throat* does draw on several sexist conventions common in advertising and the entire visual culture — the woman as object of the male gaze, and the assumption of heterosexuality, for example. But it is hardly an unending paean to male dominance, since the movie contains many contrary themes. In it, the main female character is shown as both actively seeking her own pleasure and as trying to please men; a secondary female character is shown as actually directing encounters with multiple male partners. Both briefs described a movie quite different from the one viewers see.

At its heart, this analysis implies that heterosexual sex itself it sexist; that women do not engage in it of their own volition; and that behaviour pleasurable to men is repugnant to women. In some contexts, for example, the representation of fellatio and multiple partners can be sexist, but are we willing to concede that they always are? If not, then what is proposed as actionnable under the Indianapolis law includes merely sexually explicit representation (the traditional target of obscenity laws), which proponents of the legislation vociferously insist they are not interested in attacking.

Some other examples offered through exhibits submitted with the City of Indianapolis brief and also introduced in the public hearing further illustrate this point. Many of the exhibits are depictions of sadomasochism. The court briefs treat SM material as depicting violence and aggression, not consensual sex, in spite of avowals to the contrary by many SM practitioners. With this legislation, then, a major question for feminists that has only begun to develop would be closed for discussion. Instead, a simplistic reduction has been advanced as the definitive feminist position. The description of the material in the briefs focused on submissive women and implied male domination, highlighting the similarity proponents would like to find between all SM narratives and male/female inequality. The actual exhibits, however, illustrated plots and power relations far more diverse than the descriptions provided by MacKinnon and the City of Indianapolis would suggest, including SM between women and female dominant/male submissive SM. For example, the Indianapolis brief stated that in the magazine *The Bitch Goddesses*, 'women are shown in torture chambers with their nude body parts being tortured by their "master" for "even the slightest offense" . . . The magazine shows a woman in a scenario of torture.' But the brief failed to mention that the dominants in this magazine are all female, with one exception. This kind of discrepancy characterized many examples offered in the briefs.

This is not to say that such representations do not raise questions for feminists. The current lively discussion about lesbian SM clearly demonstrates that this issue is still unresolved. But in the Indianapolis briefs all SM material was assumed to be male dominant/female submissive, thereby squeezing a nonconforming reality into prepackaged, inadequate — and therefore dangerous — categories. This legislation would virtually eliminate all SM pornography by recasting it as violent, thereby attacking a sexual minority while masquerading as an attempt to end violence against women.

Analysis of clauses in the Minneapolis ordinance and several examples offered in court briefs filed in connection with the Indianapolis ordinance show that the law targets material that is sexually explicit and sexist, but ignores material that is violent and sexist, violent and sexually explicit, only violent or only sexist.

Certain troubling questions arise here, for if one claims, as some antipornography activists do, that there is a direct relationship between images and behavior, why should images of violence against women or scenarios of sexism in general not be similarly proscribed? Why is sexual explicitness singled out as the cause of women's oppression? For proponents to exempt violent and sexist images, or even sexist images, from regulation is inconsistent, especially since they are so pervasive.

Even more difficulties arise from the vagueness of certain terms crucial in interpreting the ordinances. The term 'subordination' is especially important, since pornography is defined as the 'sexually explicit subordination of women.' The authors of this legislation intend it to modify each of the clauses, and they appear to believe that it provides a definition of sexism that each example must meet. The term is never defined in the legislation, yet the Indianapolis brief, for example, suggests that the average viewer, on the basis of 'his or her common understanding of what it means for one person to subordinate another' should be able to decide what is pornographic. But what kind of sexually explicit acts place a woman in an inferior status? To some, *any* graphic sexual act violates women's dignity and therefore subordinates them. To others, consensual heterosexual lovemaking within the boundaries of procreation and marriage is acceptable, but heterosexual acts that do not have reproduction as their aim lower women's status and hence subordinate them. Still others accept a wide range of nonprocreative, perhaps even nonmarital, heterosexuality but draw the line at lesbian sex, which they view as degrading.

The term 'sex object' is also problematic. The City of Indianapolis's brief maintains that 'the term sexual object, often shortened to sex object, has enjoyed a wide popularity in mainstream American culture in the past fifteen years, and is used to denote the objectification of a person on the basis of their sex or sex appeal ... People know what it means to disregard all aspects of personhood but sex, to reduce a person to a thing used for sex.' But, indeed, people do not agree on this point. The definition of 'sex object' is far from clear or uniform. For example, some feminist and liberal cultural critics have used the term to mean sex that occurs without strong emotional ties and experience. More conservative critics maintain that any detachment of women's sexuality from procreation, marriage and family objectifies it, removing it from its 'natural' web of associations and context. Unredeemed and unprotected by domesticity and family, women — and their sexuality — become things used by men. In both these views, women are never sexually autonomous agents who direct and enjoy their sexuality for their own purposes, but rather are victims. In the same vein, other problematic terms include 'inviting penetration', whores by nature' and 'positions of display.'

Through close analysis of the proposed legislation one sees how vague the boundaries of the definitions that contain the inner core of the Venn diagram really are. Their dissolution does not happen equally at all points, but only at some: the inner core begins to include sexually explicit and sexist material; and finally expands to include purely sexually explicit material. Thus 'sexually explicit' becomes identified and equated with 'violent' with no further definition or explanation.

It is also striking that so many feminists have failed to notice that the laws (as well as examples of actionable material) cover so much diverse work, not just that small and symbolic epicentre where many forms of opposition to women converge. It suggests that for us, as well as for others, sexuality remains a difficult area. We have no clearly developed framework in which to think about sex, equivalent to the frameworks that are available for thinking about race, gender and class issues. Consequently, in sex, as in few other areas of human behaviour, unexamined and unjustifiable prejudice passes itself off as considered opinion about what is desirable and normal. And finally, sex arouses considerable anxiety, stemming from both the meeting with individual difference and from the prospect — suggested by feminists themselves — that sexual behaviour is constructed socially and is not simply natural.

The law takes advantage of everyone's relative ignorance and anxious ambivalence about sex, distorting and oversimplying what confronts us in building a sexual politic. For example, anti-pornography feminists draw on several feminist theories about the role of violent, aggressive or sexist representations. The first is relatively straightforward: that these images trigger men into action. The second suggests that violent images act more subtly, to socialize men to act in sexist or violent ways by making this behaviour seem commonplace and more acceptable, if not expected. The third assumption is that violent, sexually explicit or even sexist images are offensive to women, assaulting their sensibilities and sense of self. Although we have all used metaphor to exhort women to action or illustrate a point, antipornography proponents have frequently used these conventions of speech as if they were literal statements of fact. But these metaphors have gotten out of hand, as Julie Abraham has noted, for they fail to recognize that the assault committed by a wife beater is quite different from the visual 'assault' of a sexist ad on TV. The nature of that difference is still being clarified in a complex debate within feminism that must continue; this law cuts off speculation, settling on a causal relationship between image and action that is starkly simple, if unpersuasive.

This metaphor also paves the way for reclassifying images that are merely sexist as also violent and aggressive. Thus, it is no acc-ident that the briefs supporting the legislation first invoke violent images and rapidly move to include sexist and sexually explicit images without noting that they are different. The equation is made more easy by the constant shifts back to examples of depictions of real violence, almost to draw attention away from the sexually explicit or sexist material that in fact would be affected by the laws.

Most important, what underlies this legislation and the access of its analysis in blurring and exceeding boundaries is an appeal to a very traditional view of sex: sex is degrading to women. By this logic, any illustrations or descriptions of explicit sexual acts that involve women are in themselves affronts to women's dignity. In its brief, the City of Indianapolis was quite specific about this point: 'The harms caused by pornography are by no means limited to acts of physical aggression. The mere existence of pornography in society degrades and demeans all women.' Embedded in this view are several other familiar themes: that sex is degrading to women, but not to men; that men are raving beasts; that sex is dangerous for women; that sexuality is male, not female; that women are victims, not sexual actors; that men inflict 'it' on women; that penetration is submission; that heterosexual sexuality, rather than the institution of heterosexuality, is sexist.

These assumptions, in part intended, in part unintended, lead us back to the traditional target of obscenity law: sexually explicit material. What initially appeared novel, then, is really the re-appearance of a traditional theme. It's ironic that a feminist position on pornography incorporates most of the myths about sexuality that feminism has struggled to displace.

The Minneapolis and Indianapolis ordinances embody a political view that holds pornography to be a central force in 'creating and maintaining' the oppression of women. This view appears in summary form in the legislative findings section at the beginning of the Minneapolis bill, which describes a chain reaction of misogynistic acts generated by pornography. The legislation is based on the interweaving of several themes: that pornography constructs the meaning of sexuality for women and, as well, leads to discrete acts of violence against women; that sexuality is the primary cause of women's oppression; that explicitly sexual images, even if not violent or coerced, have the power to subordinate women; and that women's own accounts of force have been silenced because, as a universal and timeless rule, society credits pornographic constructions rather than women's experiences. Taking the silencing contention a step further, advocates of the ordinance effectively assume that women have been so conditioned by the pornographic world view that if their own experiences of the sexual acts identified in the definition are not subordinating, then they must simply be victims of false consciousness.

Not only does pornography not cause the kind and degree of harm that can justify the restraint of speech, however, but its

existence serves some social functions, which benefit women.
Pornographic speech has many, often anomalous, characteristics.
One is certainly that it magnifies the misogyny present in the culture
and exaggerates the fantasy of male power. Another, however, is that
the existence of pornography has served to flout conventional
sexual mores, to ridicule sexual hypocrisy and to underscore the
importance of sexual needs. Pornography carries many messages
other than woman-hating: it advocates sexual adventure, sex
outside of marriage, sex for no reason other than pleasure, casual
sex, anonymous sex, group sex, voyeuristic sex, illegal sex, public
sex. Some of these ideas appeal to women reading or seeing
pornography, who may interpret some images as legitimating their
own sense of sexual urgency or desire to be sexually aggressive.
Women's experience of pornography is not as universally victim-
izing as the ordinance would have it.

The consequences of enforcing such a law, moreover, are much
more likely to obstruct than advance feminist political goals. On the
level of ideas, further narrowing of the public realm of sexual speech
coincides all too well with the privatization of sexual, reproductive
and family issues sought by the far right — an agenda described very
well, for example, by Rosalind Petchesky in 'The Rise of the New
Right' in *Abortion and Women's Choice*. Practically speaking, the
ordinances could result in attempts to eliminate the images
associated with homosexuality. Doubtless there are heterosexual
women who believe that lesbianism is a 'degrading' form of
'subordination'. Since the ordinances allow for suits against
materials in which men appear 'in place of women', far-right
antipornography crusaders could use these laws to suppress gay
male pornography. Imagine a Jerry Falwell-style conservative filing
a complaint against a gay bookstore for selling explicit materials
showing men with other men in 'degrading' or 'submissive' or
'objectified' postures — all in the name of protecting women.

And most ironically, while the ordinances could do nothing to
improve the material conditions of most women's lives, their high
visibility might well divert energy from the drive to enact other, less
popular laws that would genuinely empower women — comparable-
worth legislation to equalize male and female pay scales, for
example, or affirmative action requirements for hiring and
promoting women workers, or fairer property and support principles
in divorce laws.

Far-right elements recognize the possibility of using the full potential of the ordinances to enforce their sexually conservative world view, and have supported them for that reason. Feminists should therefore look carefully at the text of these 'model' laws in order to understand why many believe them to be a useful tool in *anti*feminist moral crusades.

The proposed ordinances are also dangerous because they seek to embody in law an analysis of the role of sexuality and sexual images in the oppression of women with which even all feminists do not agree. Underlying virtually every section of the proposed laws there is an assumption that sexuality is a realm of unremitting, unequalled victimization for women. Pornography appears as the monster that made this so. The ordinances' authors seek to impose their analysis by putting state power behind it. But this analysis is not the only feminist perspective on sexuality. Feminist theorists have also argued that the sexual terrain, however power-laden, is actively contested. Women are agents, and not merely victims, who make decisions and act on them, and who desire, seek out and enjoy sexuality.

Editors' footnote: The United States Supreme Court subsequently ruled that the Indianapolis ordinance violated free speech right by its censorship of ideas, and was thus unconstitutional.

CENSORSHIP IN THE NAME OF FEMINISM

Lisa Duggan

(Reprinted and abridged, with permission, from *The Village Voice* October 1984. Note that the ordinance was invalidated in 1986.)

Indianapolis is an unlikely place for an anti-pornography crusade. Its busy, immaculate downtown is free of porn shops; even convenience stores and newsstands carry only an occasional copy of *Playboy* or *Penthouse*. Hardcore pornography is hard to find. During a recent visit to the city, it took me three days to locate the local porn district — a pathetic collection of "adult businesses" at 38th Street and Shadeland Avenue, in a depressed commercial area of empty parking lots, boarded-up storefronts, and small shops about 20 minutes east of the city's center. Adult Toy and Gift, a heterosexual porn shop with live peep shows, sits alongside the Annex, a gay men's porn shop, and the Doll House, a go-go bar. There are other porn shops scattered in outlying areas of the city and surrounding Marion County. There are also adult movie theaters and an occasional massage parlor. But these are few and far between. For a city of a million and a half, Indianapolis is remarkably porn-free.

Yet in the last year Indianapolis has become the site of an extraordinary anti-pornography effort. It is the first American city to sign into law an amendment to its civil rights ordinance defining "pornography" as a form of sex discrimination. The legislation would allow individuals to sue in civil court to ban specified sexually explicit materials and to collect damages for the harm done by the pornographers. It was written by radical feminists Catharine MacKinnon and Andrea Dworkin. The Indianapolis action was extraordinary because an ostensibly feminist initiative was supported not by local feminist groups but by neighborhood associations, conservative Republican politicians, right-wing fundamentalists, and members of the Moral Majority — a coalition unique in American politics.

The new law is not yet in effect. Less than 90 minutes after it was signed by the mayor, a collection of publishers, booksellers, broadcasters, and librarians, joined by the ACLU [American Civil Liberties Union — US equivalent to the British NCCL], challenged the measure in federal district court on Constitutional grounds, as a violation of First Amendment protection of free speech. Judge Sarah Evans Barker's decision is pending, and it is likely to have a wide impact. Scores of other U.S. cities are awaiting her decision before enacting their own versions of the law.

Regardless of the judicial outcome, the passage of this law in Indianapolis is a landmark event. It constitutes the first success of a new legislative strategy on the part of anti-pornography feminists. For the first time, organizations such as Women Against Pornography (WAP) are advocating state censorship of films, books, and magazines deemed degrading to women. In doing so, they've provided traditional procensorship forces with a new way to attack the First Amendment. They've also allied themselves with the most antifeminist forces in the culture, those who are opposed to ERA [the Equal Rights Amendment], abortion, gay rights, and affirmative action (the list could go on). That this has been done is appalling — that it has been done in the name of feminism is frightening.

Since the election of Ronald Reagan and the growth of the New Right as a force in national politics, the fundamentalist right wing in Indianapolis has been strengthened. Consequently, public morality campaigns of various sorts have appeared with a confident vigor. Two years ago, Reverend Greg Dixon, pastor of the Indianapolis Baptist Temple and a former Moral Majority official, led the Coalition for a Clean Community on a march against immorality in the city's downtown. About 2500 marchers cheered when Republican mayor William Hudnut III declared Clean Community Day. In Indianapolis, reactionary extremists enjoy a degree of political legitimacy almost unimaginable to most northeasterners.

The religious right in Indianapolis opposes pornography on scriptural and moral grounds as propaganda for promiscuity. But they aren't the only anti-pornography campaigners in the city. Neighborhood groups have organized against porn for a mixed bag of reasons. Some are angry that commercial interests have the power to determine what goes into their neighborhoods. Some are motivated by fear and bigotry and express concern that pornography promotes interracial sex and homosexuality. Some would like to close only the porn shops in their own neighborhoods; others would eliminate all sexually explicit materials from the face of the earth.

Ron Hackler of the citizens for Decency of Marion County, for example, explains that his group was founded to oppose the little complex at 38th & Shadeland on behalf of the residents of the adjacent neighborhood. But the Citizens have branched out since then. They plan to ally themselves with the national organization, Citizens for Decency Through Law, a group that advocates the elimination of porn through vigorous enforcement of obscenity laws. According to the group's brochure, pornography causes crime, venereal disease, and "dangerous societal change" through its depiction of "everything from beastiality [sic], sodomy, rape, fornication, masturbation, piquerism, orgies, homosexuality, and sadomasochism." It's quite a leap from a desire by residents to gain some control over their neighborhoods to a vision of sex leading to Armaggedon.

Pressure this past year from the motley collection of anti-porn groups in Indianapolis led Mayor Hudnut, a Presbyterian minister, to look for new ways to battle pornography. Obscenity laws hadn't proved effective. Although the city's zealous antivice prosecutor and police department had been willing to make the arrests, their cases repeatedly failed to persuade juries or were thrown out on technicalities. The zoning law used to restrict "adult businesses" had been tied up in court challenges as well (there is now a new zoning law, however). Mayor Hudnut finally received inspiration from an unlikely source — the progressive city of Minneapolis and radical feminists Dworkin and MacKinnon.

Dworkin and MacKinnon didn't plan to write a new municipal law against pornography. In the fall of 1983, they were teaching a class at the University of Minnesota, presenting and developing their analysis of the role of pornography in the oppression of women. Each woman is known for her advocacy of one of the more extreme forms of anti-pornography feminism — the belief that sexually explicit images that subordinate or degrade women are singularly dangerous, more dangerous than nonsexual images of gross violence against women, more dangerous than advertising images of housewives as dingbats obsessed with getting men's shirt collars clean. In fact, Dworkin and MacKinnon argue that pornography is at the root of virtually every form of exploitation and discrimination known to woman. Given these views, it's not surprising that they would turn eventually to censorship — not censorship of violent and misogynistic images generally, but only of the sexually explicit images that cultural reactionaries have tried to outlaw for more than a century.

Dworkin and MacKinnon were invited to testify at a public hearing on a new zoning law (Minneapolis's "adult business" zoning law had been stricken in the courts also). When they appeared, they testified *against* the zoning strategy and offered a surprising new idea instead. Dworkin railed at the City Council, calling its members "cats and dogs" for tolerating pornography; MacKinnon suggested a civil rights approach to eliminate, rather than merely regulate, pornography. City officials must have enjoyed the verbal abuse — they hired the women to write a new law and to conduct public hearings on its merits.

In Minneapolis, Dworkin/MacKinnon were an effective duo. Dworkin, a remarkably effective public speaker, whipped up emotion with sensational rhetoric. At one rally, she encouraged her followers to "swallow the vomit you feel at the thought of dealing with the city council and get this law in place. See that the silence of women is over, that we are not down on our backs with our legs spread anymore." In contrast, MacKinnon, a professor of law, offered legalistic, seemingly rational solutions to the sense of panic and doom evoked by Dworkin. In such a charged atmosphere, amid public demonstrations by anti-porn feminists — one young woman later set herself on fire to protest pornography — the law passed. It was vetoed by the mayor on constitutional grounds.

Indianapolis, though, is not Minneapolis. When Mayor Hudnut heard of the Dworkin/MacKinnon bill at a Republican conference, he didn't think of it as a measure to promote feminism, but as a weapon in the war on smut. He recruited City-County Council member Beulah Coughenour — an activist in the Stop ERA movement — to introduce the law locally. A Republican conservative, she is a member of the lobbying group Pro-America; she sent her children to Reverend Dixon's Baptist Temple schools. A city council member for nine years, Coughenour had been considered a minor figure in Indianapolis politics, but she displayed unexpected skill in overseeing the passage of the anti-porn bill.

Coughenour's first smart move was to hire MacKinnon but not Dworkin as a consultant to the city in developing the legislation. MacKinnon was the legal brains behind the law, after all (and is probably still the only person to fully understand the legal theory behind it). MacKinnon is also "respectable". She wears tailored suits and gold jewelry; her hair is neatly pulled back in a bun. She looks like a well-heeled professional and sounds like an academic. Of the law's coauthors, she was most likely to be accepted by Indianapolis's conservative city officials. Dworkin's style would not have gone over in Indianapolis — there are no crowds of anti-porn feminists to galvanize into action, while there are innumerable tight-laced conservatives to be alarmed by the feverish pitch of Dworkin's revival-style speeches, not to mention her overalls and unruly appearance.

MacKinnon worked closely with Coughenour from the start. She advised city officials in the drafting of the law, but by her own admission she made no contacts with local feminists. In addition, she accepted Coughenour's claim that right-wing fundamentalists were not involved with the law and its progress through the council. In talking to MacKinnon, one gets the impression of someone so immersed in the theory of the law that she never noticed the local politics behind it. When she gave her testimony at the public hearing on the anti-porn bill, she went so far as to describe Indianapolis as "a place that takes seriously the rights of women and the rights of all people . . ." Apparently, she didn't know that her supporters in the police department were involved in the videotaping and beating of gay men in the city's downtown only weeks before.

Many local feminists were surprised to discover that Indianapolis was a place that took "seriously the rights of women", and they responded angrily to MacKinnon's distortion of their situation. An outsider had been brought in to represent "the" feminist position, and this had been done by their political adversaries. Sheila Suess Kennedy, a Republican feminist attorney, submitted written testimony to the council in which she said, "As a woman who has been publicly supportive of equal rights for women, I frankly find it offensive when an attempt to regulate expression is cloaked in the rhetoric of feminism. Many supporters of this proposal have been conspicuously indifferent to previous attempts to gain equal rights for women." (In 1980 Coughenour had attacked Kennedy in a local political race because of her feminism.) Kathy Sarris, president of Justice, Inc., an Indiana statewide lesbian and gay rights organization, and another feminist opponent of the measure, commented, "It has not occurred to Mayor Hudnut to put women in leadership positions in city-county government; why is he now so concerned with the subordination of women in pornography?" During his tenure, Hudnut has refused to meet with lesbian and gay rights advocates.

In organizing the public hearing on the law, Coughenour was careful to make sure it wouldn't turn into a circus but rather be a forum for rational exchange and sympathetic testimony. This was in direct contrast to how she would stage manage the final vote. At the public hearing, MacKinnon explained the legal theory of the bill for more than an hour in academic terms that seemed to pass right by the council members. The remaining proponents didn't speak about the law at all but about the pain of rape and abuse, or about the terrors of "unnatural acts" and "sodomy". A woman from the prosecutor's office introduced the psychological studies that anti-pornography activists claim prove that porn causes sexual violence. Social psychologist Edward Donnerstein, one of the experts cited, appeared before the full council two weeks later to stress that his studies showed the effects of violent images on attitudes, not the effects of sexually explicit materials on behavior. Donnerstein has since complained that his studies are being misused in anti-pornography campaigns.

Opposition to the law was organized by Michael Gradison, in the Indiana Civil Liberties Union office. Predictably, civil liberties attorneys were appalled by the bill's breadth and vagueness. In addition, many members of the city's black community were upset that complaints about porn, under the law's provision, would be screened by the city's Equal Opportunity Board, a body already overloaded with complaints about racial and sex discrimination. A representative of the Urban League asked that council members consider what would happen to antidiscrimination efforts in the city once the Office of Equal Opportunity was swamped with examples of pornography to rule upon. Two members of the gay community suggested to the council that it consider strengthening antiviolence, antiabuse laws or provide additional services for victims, rather than support censorship.

Oddly, there were no right-wing fundamentalists present at the public hearing. This, no doubt, contributed to MacKinnon's belief that they were not directly involved. It was only after the hearing that Coughenour called Reverend Dixon and asked for his help. The law was in trouble. Although it had been passed out of committee, many council members had serious doubts about its constitutionality, its practicality, the cost of litigating it in federal court. Dixon called a meeting of the Coalition for a Clean Community and got to work, phoning council members to assure them that this law was not a "back door" attempt to legitimate feminism: a vote for this law would be a vote against smut. Dixon turned out nearly 300 of his supporters for the final vote on the measure — a vote at which MacKinnon was not present.

Reverend Dixon's political activism played a decisive role in passing the anti-porn law in Indianapolis. During the final discussion before the vote many council members were equivocating. But every time a doubt was voiced, Dixon's supporters, crowded into council chambers, grumbled; every time praise was uttered, they broke out in applause. In the end, it was the most conservative councillors who felt the pressure and passed the law — overwhelmingly. All the Republicans on the council voted yes. All the Democrats, including those black councillors concerned with strengthening civil rights enforcement in the city, voted no. The total was 24 to 5.

Now that the passage of the law is a fait accompli and cities around the country await Judge Barker's decision on its constitutionality, it's worth asking the obvious question: what the hell happened in Indianapolis? Radical feminists allied with the Moral Majority? A censorship law as a means to gain equality between the sexes? It's confusing, and of course the principals involved have different interpretations of what occurred.

Reverend Dixon believes that he helped galvanize the war on smut by supporting a new weapon in the public arsenal. Ron Hackler of the Citizens for Decency has more modest hopes. He has tried to raise public awareness of the problem posed by pornography, so that obscenity laws (which he actually prefers to anti-porn legislation) can be more vigorously enforced. Obscenity laws, he thinks, could eliminate a wide variety of sexual materials, including: "The explicit depiction of sexual acts ... felatio and cunnilingus close up in living color, the erect penis in sex acts, and things that are of no particular value. They're offensive to most people, they lead to an unrealistic expectation of people as they view sex ..." He also added, "we saw movies of men taking artificial penises and shoving them up the rear end of other men, tying up a man and one man banging his penis against another man's penis. Maybe that's not obscene, I don't know — it's kind of stupid."

MacKinnon sees events in Indianapolis quite differently than Dixon and Hackler. She told me the coalition that supported and passed the law represented "women who understand what pornography does and means for women in this culture, and therefore think that we should be able to do something about it, and men who do not want to live in a society in which the subordination of women is enjoyed, profited from, and is a standard for masculinity." This is undoubtedly the coalition MacKinnon would like to have seen, but as a description of events in Indianapolis, her statement is profoundly out of touch with political reality. She acknowledges that supporters came from "diverse points on the political spectrum", but she believes that the Indianapolis coalition reconstituted alignment "on a feminist basis" — an assessment that ignores the explicitly *anti*-feminist politics of the law's right-wing supporters.

MacKinnon is also convinced that, if some supporters of the law are really after "obscene" materials rather than "subordinating" ones, they're "doing something stupid". The civil rights approach, she says, will not meet their demands. But supporters of the law such as Reverend Dixon and Ron Hackler understand the limitations of the civil rights ordinance. Dixon, in fact, hopes that the law will be combined with obscenity and prostitution busts and the recriminalization of homosexuality. MacKinnon to the contrary, these anti-pornography campaigners are not doing something stupid. They are working to organize a public morality crusade, and they believe that the attention focused on this law has helped them.

Still the question persists — how have feminists managed to ally themselves with right-wing moralists on this issue? What is it about pornography that attracts such energy from such disparate places? If one looks closely at the Indianapolis "coalition" one sees first the great advantage to the politicians who managed to hold it together. The names of Mayor William Hudnut and Beulah Coughenour have appeared in the national press for the first time in their political careers. There is nothing like the combination of sex and violence to generate public interest and media attention. But another look reveals the outlines of a symbolic campaign on the part of various anti-pornography "true believers".

Right-wing moralists see pornography as representative of social disorder. Its depictions of nonmarital, nonreproductive sex invoke the threatening social changes associated, for them, with divorce, birth control, abortion, miscegenation, and homosexuality. Pornography is understood as a threat to the sanctity and authority of the patriarchal family, and it is made to stand for gender confusion and sexual chaos. In this context, right-wing moralists can agree with feminists that "pornography degrades women", because women's sexuality outside the family is itself seen as cheapened and degraded. Reverend Dixon and Phyllis Schlafly agree that it is women, as upholders of morality and the home, who should lead the fight against pornography.

Neighborhood groups do not necessarily share the cosmology of right-wingers when they set out to fight pornography. In part they are responding to the real-world association of porn shops with organized crime in cities throughout America. But neighborhood groups in Indianapolis also see porn shops and pornography as symbolic substitutes for social change in the community. Economic decline and increased crime are blamed on the porn shop — as are the fears of some white residents about racial integration. It is imagined that if the porn shop were closed, all would be well again; the happy secure neighborhoods of the nostalgia-laden past could be restored.

The radical feminist anti-pornography campaign, represented in Indianapolis by MacKinnon (and only MacKinnon), is also engaged in symbolic politics. Pornography is made to stand in for all misogyny, all discrimination, all exploitation of women — in their view, it not only causes but constitutes the subordination of women. The commodification and objectification of women's bodies is believed to reside more centrally in pornography than in mainstream media; this society's culture of violence against women is said to radiate from, rather than be reflected in, pornography. The campaign against porn is thus a symbolic substitute for a more diffuse, but more necessary, campaign against the myriad forms of male domination in economic life, in political life, in sexual life. Pornography serves as a condensed metaphor for female degradation. It is also far easier to fight, politically, in the conservative climate of the Reagan years — far easier now to gain support for an anti-porn campaign than for affirmative action, abortion, lesbian rights.

What all these anti-porn zealots have in common is a conviction of the special power of sexual representation to endanger. For some it endangers the family, for some community, for others the well-being of women. All are agreed that sexually explicit images must be controlled — though each group would differ as to *which* images are most in need of control — in order to control the perceived social danger, in order to prevent ruin, decay, obliteration. The groups allied against porn in Indianapolis also share a vision of sexuality as a terrain of female victimization and degradation; none of them offers a vision of female sexual subjectivity, of female power and joy in the sexual arena.

Feminists have engaged in such symbolic campaigns before. In the 19th and early 20th centuries, for instance, some British and American feminists waged campaigns against prostitution and for "social purity", and they achieved legislative success with the help of conservative allies. However, the strengthening of laws against prostitution had the effect of worsening the condition of prostitutes, making them yet more vulnerable to victimization at the hands of law enforcement officials, as well as pimps and johns. The raising of the age of consent in the early 20th century, also accomplished with feminist support in the United States, had the result of empowering institutions of juvenile justice to persecute and incarcerate adolescent girls for the "offense" of sexual activity. In all these cases, conservatives ultimately exercised more power in determining how laws, once enacted, would finally affect women's lives — more power than feminists then imagined.

One of the insights gained by feminist historians, who have examined such social legislation, is that a "feminist issue" or "feminist law" does not exist in the abstract: it is the alignment of political and cultural forces that gives meaning to issues and laws. In Indianapolis, local feminists were invisible except for the handful who opposed the anti-porn law. *No* effort was made to distinguish clearly the feminist from the conservative position. As a result the visibility of reactionary, antifeminist forces was enhanced — exactly the opposite of what MacKinnon intended.

And it's not only in Indianapolis that the reactionary, antifeminist position has been enhanced. The MacKinnon/Dworkin bill has contributed to a moral crusade that is threatening to expand to other places on a wider scale. In Suffolk County, Republican legislator Michael D'Andre has recently introduced a version of the anti-porn law that emphasizes the repressive potential of the MacKinnon/ Dworkin approach by asserting that pornography causes "sodomy" and "destruction of the family unit", as well as crimes and immorality "inimical to the public good". In Washington, Pennsylvania senator Arlen Spector is broadening his congressional hearings on child pornography to investigate the effects of adult porn on women. President Reagan has also announced his intention to establish a federal commission to study pornography and offer legislative action. Imagine the administration that brought you the Family Protection Act introducing measures to control pornography. Imagine anti-pornography feminists helping to legitimate such a nightmare.

If the discussion of sexuality surrounding the anti-porn law in Indianapolis had resulted in increased awareness of feminist issues, in the increased visibility and social/political power of feminists, in the enhanced ability of feminists on both sides of the issue to define and control the terms of debate, perhaps it could have been useful. But it didn't. Instead, Catharine MacKinnon joined with the right wing in invoking the power of the state against sexual representation. In so doing, she and her supporters have helped spur a moral crusade that is already beyond the control of feminists — anti-porn or otherwise. And that moral crusade can only be dangerous to the interests of feminists everywhere, and to the future of women's rights to free expression.

THE MEESE COMMISSION ON THE ROAD

Carole S. Vance

(Abridged, with permission, from a longer article in *The Nation, Aug 2-9*, NY 1986)

In 1985 Edwin Meese, Reagan-appointed Attorney General of the USA, appointed a Federal Commission to find 'new ways to control the problem of pornography'. On July 9 1986 the Commission's report was released, recommending a repressive agenda for controlling sexual images and texts: vigorous enforcement of existing obscenity laws and the passage of draconian new measures.

The Commission was chaired by Henry Hudson, a vigorous anti-vice prosecutor from Arlington, Virginia. Six of the remaining ten commissioners had previously taken public stands opposing pornography and supporting obscenity law as an means to control it, and included fundamentalists and conservatives. The remaining four constituted the commission's moderate bloc; the three women in this bloc signed a statement that, while abhorring 'the exploitation of vulnerable people' in pornography, rejected 'judgemental and condescending efforts to speak on women's behalf as though they were helpless, mindless children'.

The Show Trial

Any pretense of objectivity that the commission might have wished to claim was dispelled by its glaring and persistent biases in gathering and evaluating evidence. The list of witnesses invited to testify was no more open than the commissioners' minds: 77 percent supported greater control, if not elimination, of sexually explicit material. Heavily represented were law-enforcement officers and members of vice squads (68 of 208 witnesses), politicians and spokespersons for conservative antipornography groups like Citizens for Decency through Law and the National Federation for Decency.

Of the 'victims' of pornography, many told tales of divorce, promiscuity, masturbation and child abuse — all, in their view, caused by sexually explicit material. For these born-again victims, the remedy for complex social problems was found in renouncing pornography and sexual sin. The vice cops on the staff energetically recruited the alleged victims to testify, assisted by antipornography groups and prosecutors. The same zeal was not applied to the search for people who had positive experiences.

Witnesses appearing before the commission were treated in a highly uneven manner. Commissioners accepted virtually any claim made by antipornography witnesses as true, asking few probing questions and making only the most cursory requests for evidence or attempts to determine witness credibility. Those who did not support more restriction of sexually explicit speech were often met with rudeness and hostility, and their motives for testifying were impugned. The panelists asked social scientist Edward Donnerstein if pornographers had tried to influence his research findings or threatened his life. They asked actress Colleen Dewhurst, testifying for Actors' Equity about the dangers of censorship in the theater, if persons convicted of obscenity belonged to the union, and if the union was influenced by organized crime. They questioned her at length about the group's position on child pornography.

There were many instances when the commission flagrantly isolated ordinary rules of fair procedure. These defects, and the serious constitutional questions raised by the panel's recommendations, are reviewed in 'Polluting the Censorship Debate' by American Civil Liberties Union legislative counsel Barry Lynn.

The Meese commission conducted a show trial in which pornography was found guilty. But producing an updated discourse about pornography and sex proved difficult despite the staff's tight control over witnesses, topics and rules of evidence. The chief supporters and beneficiaries of the commission were conservatives and fundamentalists whose main objection to pornography is its depiction — and they believe, advocacy — of sex outside of marriage and procreation. The Justice Department knew that this position would no longer sell outside the right wing. The attack on sexually explicit material had to be modernized by couching it in more contemporary and persuasive arguments, drawn chiefly from social science and feminism. So the pre-eminent harm that pornography was said to cause was not sin and immorality but violence.

Conservatives have been gunning for the 1970 report on the

President's Commission on Obscenity and Pornography, a major obstacle to the social agenda on sex, because that exhaustive review found no evidence that sexually explicit material caused antisocial behavior. The report recommended that restrictive laws governing adults' access to sexual materials be repealed and that the government undertake massive sex-education programs for adults and young people. The goal of the Meese commission was to overturn the 1970 panel's findings, and so it has. A mirror image, the Meese report finds that pornography causes harm — individual, social, moral and ethical. It recommends restrictive legal measures, but it declines to support sex-education programs. The conservative tenor and goals of the report can hardly be disguised. A drive against pornography may be the Administration's sop to conservative groups frustrated by their lack of total victory on abortion and school prayer — the social issue on which Reagan delivers.

Updating the Harms of Pornography

Conservatives found it harder than they expected to enlist social science in their cause. With $500,000, in contrast to the 1970 commission's $2 million (in 1967 dollars), the Meese commission was unable to fund any research and had but one part-time social scientist as a consultant. So it reviewed research conducted by other investigators. However, the staff either did not understand or else wilfully ignored the nuances of social science research. Star witnesses Edward Donnerstein and Neil Malamuth, who have conducted many of the interesting new experiments on sexually explicit images, testified with care. Aggressive imagery and mainstream media are more worrisome than sexual imagery and X-rated channels, they said. Caution is required in interpreting the necessarily artificial laboratory findings to naturalistic settings and to populations other than college boys. Causal inference to actual behavior like rape is unwarranted. Not all the social science testimony was so disappointing. Dolf Zillmann, a communications researcher from Indiana University, testified that nonviolent images of consensual sex have negative effects, including greater acceptance of extramarital sex, and his collaborator, Jennings Bryant, thundered that when porn comes into your life, 'forget trust, forget family, forget commitment, forget love, forget marriage!'

When it became clear that social science would not provide the indictment of pornography that he wanted, Hudson announced that harm should be evaluated according to two additional tiers of evidence: 'the totality of the evidence', which included victim testimony, anecdotal evidence, expert opinion, personal experience and common sense; and 'moral, ethical and cultural values'. This signals an abrupt departure from standard practice in social science and public health research.

The report's section on harms — written by Frederick Schauer — overstates the evidence, leaps to unsupported conclusions about what might be 'reasonably assumed' in social science, cites no research to support statements and appears to misunderstand what causality means in social science. The panel's conclusion that violent pornography causes sexual violence, reached 'unanimously and confidently' required 'assumptions not found exclusively in the experimental evidence', Schauer wrote. 'We see no reason, however, not to make these assumptions.' The rules of evidence spelled out here are casual, not causal.

The commission fared much better in its attempt to co-opt the language of antipornography feminists. One would think it was a difficult undertaking, since Hudson, Sears and the conservative cohorts were no feminists. Hudson usually addressed female commissioners as 'ladies'. He transmuted the term used by women's antipornography groups, 'the degradation of women', into 'the degradation of femininity', which conjured up visions of Victorian womanhood dragged from the pedestal. Beyond language, conservatives consistently opposed proposals that feminists universally support — for sex education, for example.

However, witnesses provided by women's antipornography groups proved more useful than social scientists. They were eager to cast their personal experiences of incest, childhood sexual abuse, rape and sexual coercion in terms of the 'harm' and 'degradation' caused by pornography. Some were willing to understate, and most to omit mentioning, their support for those cranky feminist demands so offensive to conservative ears: abortion, birth control, lesbian and gay rights. Other feminist groups, including COYOTE, the US Prostitutes Collective, the ACLU Women's Rights Project and the Feminist Anti Censorship Task Force (FACT, of which I am a member), criticized the panel's simple-minded attempt to link violence against women with sexual images and noted the irony of the Attorney General's concern for women at a time when the Administration has seriously cut back on women's programs. Protests were organized in conjunction with hearings in Los Angeles and New York.

The notion that pornography degrades women proved to be a particularly helpful unifying term, floating in and out of fundamentalist as well as antipornography feminist testimony. Speakers didn't notice, or chose not to, that the term 'degradation' has very different meanings in each community. For antipornography feminists, pornography degrades women when it depicts or glorifies sexist sex: images that put men's pleasure first or indicate that women's lot in life is to serve men. For fundamentalists, degrading sexual images show sex outside marriage, including many behaviors considered acceptable, even desirable, by feminist thinkers, such as masturbation and egalitarian lesbian sex.

Although the commission happily assimilated the rhetoric of antipornography feminists, it decisively rejected their remedies. Conservative men pronounced the testimony of Andrea Dworkin 'eloquent' and 'moving' and insisted on including her remarks in the final report. But antipornography feminists had argued against obscenity laws and in favor of ordinances, such as those developed for Minneapolis and Indianapolis by Dworkin and Catharine MacKinnon, which outlaw pornography as a violation of women's civil rights. The commission never seriously entertained the idea that obscenity laws should be repealed; given its conservative constituency and agenda, it couldn't have.

The report summarily dismisses Minneapolis-style ordinances, 'properly held unconstitutional,' because they infringe on speech protected under the first Amendment. But the panel cleverly, if disingenuously, argues that obscenity prosecutions against violent and degarding material are 'largely consistent with what this ordinance attempts to do,' ignoring the proponents' rejection of obscenity laws. They recommend that legislatures consider civil remedies against material that would be found obscene under current standards. This constitutes a major defeat for antipornography feminists. But unlike the loudly protesting social scientists — Donnerstein called the commission's conclusions bizarre — the antipornography feminists have not acknowledged the panel's distortion. They commend the panel for recognizing the harm of pornography and continue to denounce obscenity laws as 'anti-woman, anti-gay, beside the point and ineffectual,' without coming to grips with the panel's commitment to that approach.

Even more startling were MacKinnon and Dworkin's statements to the press that the commission 'has recommended to Congress the civil rights legislation women have sought', and this comment by

Dorchen Leidholdt, founder of Women Against Pornography: 'I'm not embarrassed at being in agreement with Ed Meese.' (She also supported the panel's efforts to publish Donald Wildmon's list of 'businesses that traffic in pornography'.) The only plausible explanation is that each group is strategizing how best to use the other. The Meese commission used feminist language to justify its conservative agenda, while antipornography feminist groups used the Meese commission to gain public recognition and legitimacy. It doesn't take more than a moment's reflection to see who came out on top.

The Definition

If orchestrating the new discourse was taxing, defining pornography was even harder, and in the end proved impossible for them. They did divide sexually explicit images into four categories: 1. violent; 2. not violent but degrading; 3. not violent and not degrading; 4. not sexually explicit but portraying nudity. However they were unable to agree as to what should be included in each category. In the non-violent but degrading category, some wished to include oral sex, anal sex, group sex, masturbation and any explicitly homosexual act. Although the moderates cited research which showed that the images in the non-violent, non-degrading category were not harmful, anecdotal evidence and common sense suggested to the conservatives that they indeed were.

Two important points emerge from this definitional swamp. First is the finding that all sexual images cause harm. On that one the conservatives won. The second is the invention of the category of violent pornography. This category is problematic, but moderates have accepted it as blindly as have conservatives. The reasons for this uncritical response are complex: a genuine concern about violence, particularly against women; a willingness to believe that depictions of violence or coercion in sexual images cause literal imitation; an ignorance and fear of sexually stigmatized behavior, particularly sadomasochism.

Underlying all this is our culture's confusion between sex and violence, attested to by the fact that it took the stop-rape movement ten years to educate the public that rape was an act of violence, not sex. But the confusion cuts both ways: if violence is misunderstood to be sex, sometimes sex is misunderstood to be violence.

What falls into the category of violent pornography? Some

material is suggested by recent social psychology laboratory experiments on "aggressive" and "nonaggressive" sexually explicit materials. ("Violent pornography" is not a social science term.) The studies commonly use specially made short cuts depicting a woman's rape: in one version she resist to the end; in the other she gives in and "enjoys" it. The negative attitudinal effects found with the second scenario — quite apart from questions of the duration of effects and generalizability — have been atttributed to a much broader range of material. To indict pornography this broadening is necessary, because the rape scenario appears in only a small fraction of commercial pornography. The commission's own content analysis of April 1986 top-selling pornographic magazines found an extraordinarily low rate of pictures showing "force, violence, or weapons": 0.6 percent, or 3 out of 512. This analysis and supporting data, which were included in early drafts, mysteriously disappeared from the final report.

But the commission used the term "violent pornography", defined as "actual or unmistakably stimulated or unmistakably threatened violence presented in a sexually explicit fashion", to cover a wide range of other materials. Leading the pack was the snuff film, a movie in which a real woman is purportedly killed. The snuff film was the hearings' unicorn; much talked about, long searched for but never found. Legions of vice cops testified that an actual snuff film had never been identified, despite diligent investigations. Some R-rated Hollywood movies were also candidates for Class I. "Slice and dice" films such as *The Texas Chain Saw Massacre* offer scenes of eroticized violence, but they are not pornography because they are not sexually explicit.

The remaining candidate for inclusion in this category, then, was sadomasochistic imagery, of which the commission saw a great deal and found deeply upsetting. During the course of their discussions, S&M migrated from the "degrading" to the "violent" class, more by a process of osmosis than decision. The commission called no witnesses to discuss the nature of S&M, either professional experts or typical participants. They ignored a small but increasing body of literature that documents important features of S&M sexual behaviour, namely consent and safety. Typically, the conventions we use to decipher ordinary images are suspended when it comes to S&M images. When we see war movies, for example, we do not leave the theatre believing that the carnage we saw was real or that the performers were injured making the films. But the commissioners assumed that images of domination and submission were both real and coerced.

The exceptional status of S&M images was heightened by testimony about coerced performances in any and all pornography, such as Linda Marchiano's account of how her husband abused her in the making of *Deep Throat*. Although coercion could exist in the making of any image — sexual or nonsexual, S&M or non-S&M — popular prejudice transformed concern about coercion into another indictment of S&M images. A critique of coercion should have focussed on working conditions, not images. It helped that the images shown to the panelists were carefully selected so that the preponderance portrayed female submission and male dominance, thus framing sadomasochism in the context of gender inequality. Reverse images of male submission, common in the genre, or homosexual images, were rarely shown.

The Results

The most tangible results of the Meese commission will be increased prosecutions under existing obscenity laws and the passage of new ones. There will be a rash of state investigatory commissions and local hearings. The commission endorsed citizen action groups, recommending lawful extra-legislative actions to reduce the availability of sexually explicit material, a 'network of sex spies' (Barry Lynn). Most dangerously, the rhetoric about the harms of pornography may incline judges and juries to make subjective judgements, and contradict the assumptions of our legal system, which regulates bad actions rather than the books, speech or political theories that might arguably cause them. The genius of the Meese commission lies in its ability to make plausible in regard to sexual words and images a standard that is totally implausible in any other sphere.

The commission's chances of success — despite internal dissent, criticism by social scientists and widely publicized lawsuits by *Playboy* and *Penthouse* — remain high. The commission has with uncanny intuition gone to the heart of our culture's symbolic infrastructure about sex: sex degrades women; sex and violence are intimately linked, perhaps identical. To the extent that the commission has tapped fears usually expressed in conservative terms and has repackaged them in contemporary language, its findings will have appeal.

A total return to the sexual landscape of the 1950s is improbable. Too many changes have occurred in sex roles, families and sexual expression to permit the rollback conservatives have in mind. Yet sexual liberalization is enormously fragile, in part because it is so dependent on other social changes now under heavy assault from the right, in part because even progressives perceive sexuality as still too shameful and private an issue for which to mobilize a vigorous public defense. Some of us who have benefited from it believe that sexual modernization is not political, just personal. The right knows better.

DOES VIEWING PORNOGRAPHY LEAD MEN TO RAPE?

Alice Henry

off our backs, a monthly feminist news magazine based in Washington, DC, has actively covered the controversy surrounding anti-pornography ordinances in the United States. They ran a long news story by one of the supporters of the Minneapolis ordinance when it was first proposed, followed by stories on the ordinances proposed in Indianapolis, and in a suburb of New York City.

The debate within feminism broke wide open when the Feminist Anti-Censorship Task Force (FACT) circulated a brief against the ordinance which many feminists signed. At a National Women and the Law Conference in 1985, Catharine MacKinnon (pro-ordinance) and Nan Hunter (a signer of the FACT brief) were paired off in a debate which *off our backs* reported in some detail (June 1985). The debate was quite bitter, particularly because Catharine MacKinnon implied that her opponent was not really a feminist, for example saying that Nan Hunter was there 'to speak for the pornographers, although that will not be what she says she is doing.'

One issue in the controversy was whether current research proved that viewing pornography increases aggression against women. MacKinnon claimed, 'Our hearings in Minneapolis produced overwhelming evidence of the damage done by pornography. Researchers and clinicians documented what women know from our lives: that pornography increases attitudes and behaviors of aggression and other discrimination, principally by men against women. This relation is causal. It is better than the smoking–cancer correlation, and at least as good as the data on drinking and driving . . . Why is it that women — lawyers — feminists, want to require that we reach the acts, not the speech, when the acts are being done in large part because of the speech . . . Why can there be a law for every other abuse, but when harmed women want to move against pornographers, women — feminists — calling themselves feminists — say that *this* is something that there should not be any law about?'

I thought it would be a good idea to take a hard look at the testimony backing up the Minneapolis ordinance. Unfortunately, no statistical correlations between viewing pornography and becoming aggressive were reported; for the purposes of presenting the evidence to a lay audience, the methodological apparatus was stripped away. You can assess the material that was presented for yourself — the testimony is now available in Britain, published by *Everywoman*. But because not everyone is going to go back and look at the 'real' research reported in professional journals, complete with statistical apparatus and details of the methodology, I wrote a short review of the most cited literature for *off our backs*. This article is based on that review.

*   *   *   *

When they tried to get the anti-pornography ordinance passed by the Minneapolis city council, advocates of the ordinance called on social psychologists to give evidence on whether acts of aggression like rape and battery are inflicted when or after pornography has been viewed. Recent research by several liberal men with a good publication record, respected in their field and about to publish a book on the subject, looked at these questions from a point of view quite sympathetic to feminists. It seemed that if pornography led men to rape, they would find the evidence.

It is not unusual for legislators to listen to the testimony of social scientists, even if it is notoriously difficult to demonstrate in the usual social psychological experiment that some stimulus (like pornography) presented in a set-up situation (like a lab) would produce the same response in real life. First off, there's the question of whether college boys behave like most other men. Even if you believe they respond to pornography like other men, what about the differences between the lab context and 'real life'? When a person knows they are in an experiment, he or she can't help but try and figure out what the experimenter is up to, or what he or she is supposed to do. The so-called 'subject' often treats the experiment like a game. Being shown a porn movie in a classroom situation is hardly like the way a man goes about viewing porn in the outside world. In the classroom, the viewer hasn't actively chosen to see a porn movie. In real life, one scenario might be that a bunch of lads get together, decide to see a 'sex film', get some cans of lager to go with it, have a good laff together watching the flick, then go out looking for a fuck. This is sexism in action, and they might rape.

But how do you separate out how much of a cause the porn flick was? There are so many other things involved. They actively chose to see the porn movie. They were ready to laugh at women and to look for a woman to rape. They may have raped if they hadn't seen the film; lots of men have raped without seeing porn. And clearly, just because a man has seen some porn, or even monumental amounts of porn, he is not necessarily going to go out and rape.

While real life is a tangled mess of reasons to rape, hopefully a clever piece of research could show the 'pure' effect of viewing porn just by showing porn to some, and other material to the others.

Is this reasonable? It depends on whether you think people are ever passive receptors. If you think cutting down on other stimuli, or interfering factors, helps you isolate the effect of a message, you might try to do experiments like the ones used as evidence at the Minneapolis hearings. But even on a basic perceptual level, psychologists have shown that people respond to change and constancies, not to single stimuli. At the level of a complex stimulus like a porn movie, the whole social context is of utmost importance. People, men included, aren't simple machines where you push a button 'why don't you do this' and they go along and do it.

So it is no surprise that the research asking whether porn leads to rape doesn't come close to showing whether men are more likely to rape if they are exposed to pornography. Still, the researchers were happy enough to testify at the Minneapolis hearings.

Edward Donnerstein presented some of his findings, claiming that men become de-sensitised after seeing violent porn films, and then go on to be less sympathetic to women who have been raped. Without the technical apparatus, it was difficult to evaluate his conclusions. The city councillors could make of it what they wanted. As a feminist, and one who wants to look at evidence, I went to the library and read through the most cited articles. This summary is presented to give readers an idea of what the experiments are like. Malamuth and Donnerstein have published a book containing a great deal of the research on these lines.

Some Examples of Research on Porn

What is the background of this research? In a 1982 article, Neil

Malamuth and Edward Donnerstein wrote:

> There are theoretical reasons for being particularly concerned about
> the fusion of sexuality and aggression in the media. First, the
> coupling of sex and aggression in these portrayals may result in
> conditioning processes whereby aggressive acts become associated
> with sexual arousal, a powerful unconditioned stimulus and
> reinforcer.

The first question might be, 'Is aggressive pornography sexually
arousing?' According to Malamuth's and Donnerstein's review of
what research there was, for most men, aggressive pornography is
less sexually arousing than non-aggressive pornography. The
exception was convicted rapists, who said viewing rape was just as
exciting as viewing consenting sex. However, they did not find
violent pornography more exciting.

At that point, Malamuth and Donnerstein say there is 'little
evidence at this time to indicate that exposure to aggressive
pornography increases a person's sexual responsiveness to such
stimuli'. Their conclusion casts doubt on their initial idea that the
'coupling of sex and aggression in these portrayals may result in
conditioning processes whereby aggressive acts become associated
with sexual arousal'.

Nevertheless, viewing aggressive porn could have other effects. It
could make men more likely to believe that women who have been
raped really enjoy or want rape. In a 1979 study, Malamuth found
that whether or not a man looked at rape and sadomasochistic
material from *Playboy* and *Penthouse* made no difference in how he
later evaluated whether a woman was raped. Malamuth and
Donnerstein say that might be because the stuff in *Playboy* and
Penthouse did not show women enjoying rape. So they showed some
college boys two films, *Swept Away* and *The Getaway*, and looked at
whether they were more likely to accept rape myths than students
who saw two neutral films.

There did not seem to be much difference. Those who saw the
films showing women enjoying forced sex scored 50 and and the
controls scored 47 on the 'rape myth acceptance' scale. Malamuth
and Check write that the differences between those who viewed the
movies with scenes of forced sex and those who did not 'did not
reach acceptable levels of significance'.

However, in the review article summarising their research,
Malamuth and Donnerstein say this particular piece of research is
'the strongest evidence to date to indicate that depictions of sexual

aggression with positive consequences can adversely affect socially important perceptions and attitudes'. It's not good evidence, but the review article suggests it is.

Nevertheless, even if viewing aggressive porn does not increase sexual arousal, and does not lead to accepting rape myths, it might promote aggression against women. Donnerstein conducted several studies in which male or female lab assistants posing as fellow students gave poor evaluations of essays the 'subjects' wrote by giving the 'subjects' nine small shocks. Next, the 'subjects' were shown one of several types of short (4–5 minutes) films, which either included:

- aggressive porn scenes in which the woman is shown enjoying violent sex
- aggressive porn scenes in which the woman does not enjoy the violent sex
- porn scenes with no violence
- scenes with no sex but with violence against women
- neutral films — no sex, no violence

After viewing the film shorts, the student subjects were put in a situation where they could negatively evaluate (by giving a shock, they assumed) the person who had evaluated them.

If the female lab assistant posing as a subject had not given them a negative evaluation by giving a shock, the students gave a low level of shock no matter what sort of film they saw. The conclusion might be that seeing a violent porn movie did not in and of itself make students aggress (give an electric shock to) a female lab assistant.

If the female lab assistant negatively evaluated them, and the students were then shown the 'violent' films (with or without sexual content) the students were slightly more likely to give a shock to the lab assistant.

In the same type of situation (negative evaluation by a woman lab assistant, and later given the chance to shock her) and shown one of four short films, male students gave the least shock after viewing a neutral film and after a non-aggressive porn film. They gave more shock after seeing an aggressive, but not sexually (woman beaten by a man) film, and most shock after viewing an aggressive porn film.

Interestingly enough, after viewing both short porn films and after the one showing a man beating a woman, the student subjects also gave a higher shock to *male* lab assistants. Why should this be? Perhaps porn shorts showing men behaving badly gives the students the idea it is okay to shock the male lab assistant who gave them a hard time.

This experiment is not set up to show that 'seeing porn leads to commiting violence'. It is closer to a situation of 'wanting to commit violence' (having been aggressed upon by the lab assistant, which could be taken as a stand-in for other reasons for misogyny, or the usual incentives men have to aggress against women) and then receiving a message that it is okay to aggress ('disinhibition') leading to aggression against women.

In conclusion, Malamuth's review of their research on the effects of viewing aggressive pornography indicate that when a man is already motivated to aggress against a woman or man, viewing aggressive pornography may make him slightly more likely to convert his anger into aggressive behavior. But there does not seem to be anything 'special' about aggressive porn. Like any attempt to encourage behavior, it only works on some people some of the time. Certainly Malamuth and Donnerstein found no evidence of 'conditioning processes whereby aggressive acts become associated with sexual arousal'. The lack of evidence may be because of imperfections in the experiments. Still, not finding what you were looking for *is* a finding. It is all too easy to continue thinking, 'I didn't find it this time, I'll keep on looking.'

The Evidence Presented at the Minneapolis Hearing

The evidence presented by Donnerstein at the Minneapolis anti-pornography law hearings was based on male college students' attitudes towards various pornography films, and the effect of viewing these films on their evaluation of a rape trial. One group saw 'R-rated' films showing scenes of sexual violence or violence against women in a sexual context. The films were *Texas Chainsaw Massacre*, *Maniac*, *I Spit On Your Grave*, *Toolbox Murders* and *Vice Squad*. Another group saw 'X-Violent' films which were sexually explicit and included rape scenes or other forms of violence against women, but were not as explicit or graphic as the R-rated movies. Donnerstein says that in the X-rated violent movies, the 'women are shown reacting in a favorable way, e.g. sexually aroused, to aggression'. The third group was shown X-rated films — explicit sexual content, but no violence against women.

The students were asked to rate (usually on a scale from one to seven) how graphic and explicit the violence was; how bloody and gory the violence was; overall, how violent was the film; and how many violent scenes there were in the film.

The mean ratings consistently dropped from very high after seeing the first film to slightly less high after seeing the fifth film. For instance, students seeing *Chainsaw* or *Maniac* first rated them 6.8 on a scale of 7 on 'overall violence'. If they saw those films of day 5, after seeing four other R-rated films, they rated *Chainsaw* and *Maniac* around 6.2. Overall, most men rated these films at the very top of the scale, and the rest almost at the top of the scale both before and after viewing other 'R' films. The biggest drop was in the rating of 'how gory', from 6.5 or so on day 1, to 5 on day 5.

What do the drops in ratings mean? Are they 'de-sensitisation', in the sense of inability to see goriness, or 'sensitisation', in the sense of an increasing ability to make fine distinctions between really gory and badly acted goriness? Might some have switched to evaluating performance rather than the intended message, rotten as it might be? Presumably most of these students had never seen the likes of *Chainsaw* before, and might have developed a more sophisticated notion of just how gory a flick can be after seeing four miserably gory flicks.

Whether or not viewing porn leads a man to boredom, never wanting to see one again, or a search for more and more violent films surely depends on things like whether he wants to see violent porn in the first (and last) place, whether his friends approve of porn, and the whole bundle of values about being sexual.

What to do?

So far, the research has not come up with evidence that on its own, viewing porn leads men to rape. But, some feminists have argued, even if one man goes out and rapes on account of seeing some porn, we as feminists must seek to prevent this by taking away the porn. Besides, what if porn is like other fictional portrayals of violence, of evil, of hatred, in that it can influence what you think and do? If we think that porn contributes to rape, do we want to make it illegal and subject to criminal action?

I'm not sure that focusing on eliminating pornography from the newstands and video shops will cut it out of men's minds. Porn is easily invented in a sexist society — anyone can think up porn. I worry about focusing on sexual words and pictures as the words that we can make taboo, or unthinkable. That has been the conservative religious line for a long time. If the basic problem is sexism, why not outlaw all sexist thought — not just the ones keyed in on sex?

I know rape is violent sex, quite unlike consensual sex; why not focus on the violence, on the behavior? And isn't discussion — more words, not less — the best way to change someone's thoughts on the subject?

Bitter Debates

Feminists may all agree that porn is awful, but the disagreement on whether laws against it are the way forward have become acrimonious. Responding to the article I wrote in *off our backs* laying out this criticism of the social research testimony, MacKinnon wrote,

> Now, she (Alice) wrote, and you published, an entire article on the connection between pornography and how women are seen and treated that not only botches even the account of some very good research on the subject, but never mentions a single woman's actual experience. Not even *research* on women's actual experiences.
>
> Women have known for a long time that pornography is at the center of much discrimination against us, whether through attitudes or behavior, violent or less overt. Research is only beginning to uncover and substantiate some of these connections we experience every day. What do you call not caring to hear women when we say these things *do* happen to us, in favor of male researchers studying men predicting that such things *would* happen to us? Whatever you call it, I suspect it isn't feminism.
>
> All the woman-haters will be quoting you now.

I am bothered by the insinuation that whatever I'm doing, 'it isn't feminism'. It's not just me she throws out of feminism; MacKinnon has been making speeches saying that women who are sceptical about her civil rights ordinances against pornography are 'so-called feminists'.

There are many of us who think public protest against pornography is an essential strategy. I support pickets against porn and slide shows educating people about porn. I think direct action, like smashing sex shops, can be a useful tactic, especially if women do it as civil disobedience, expecting to be arrested. My reservations are about laws that make writing or selling pornography sueable or otherwise illegal, mostly because I don't think repression of ideas is an effective way to stop people from thinking them. It is more effective to openly criticise ideas as they come up.

Porn may indeed be part of the context, the message that it is okay to rape. The question is how to build a context that does not permit rape. Why not enforce laws against rape, insist that rapists be prosecuted effectively, get sex education into the schools — as well as providing an all-round feminist education? Merely not having pornography on the news stand isn't an effective deterrent to rape.

CENSORSHIP — AN ANALYSIS

Annie Blue

Censorship and freedom (of expression/action/movement/speech) are relative to power, and the nature of both depends on the power predominant at any given moment.

Censorship and Power — The Inseparable Couple, or, 'You can't have one without the other'.

The concept of censorship cannot be examined outside the context of power relations because censorship is essential to the maintenance of power. Women are controlled by acts of censorship which effectively limit and dictate the conditions of our existence and assign us to the status of an oppressed class. Only those who possess power — men — have the means of controlling/censoring/limiting those who do not. In our society men have economic, physical and social power; when women challenge this and name the means by which we are oppressed, we are identifying the acts of censorship which control us, maintain our position as a sex class, and at the same time uphold male supremacy.

Censorship — A Radical Feminist's Definition

Censorship is what men do/have done to women in order to control us and what they tell us we are doing when we try to stop them. Applications of the term under male supremacy are predictably flexible, contradictory, convenient and effective in silencing women. For example, action can (rightly) be taken via legislation against racist material, language, behaviour and so on, without thought of censorship, on the grounds that it incites racial hatred. When women demand action against pornography because it incites sexual hatred, this is called censorship. Again, the laws of libel and slander protect the individual from lies, but though women are falsely labelled as passive, available, subservient, willing objects, though what we are or want is lied about on a massive scale in pornography, when we demand an end to the lies this is called censorship.

Censorship and Freedom — The Mathematics of Freedom:
0 (no power) $\times$ 1,000r (rights) = 0 (no freedom)

Freedom is professed to be a basic 'human right'; theoretically everyone is entitled to 'it', but in reality there exists no such thing because 'freedom' is relative to power. Those who have power — men — dictate the nature of 'freedom', they decide and construct the nature of our 'freedoms' for us by allowing us certain 'rights'. These rights, e.g. women's rights, equal opportunities, which are supposedly basic and intrinsic, can be removed at any time without redress, can be used against us and are impossible to enforce without the co-operation and approval of the power holders. They are in fact merely privileges, accorded or withdrawn depending on the inclination of those in power, or on the climate of the time.

(To function as intended, equality of opportunity assumes a state of equality of persons that does not exist in a patriarchal society. Individual women's 'successes' are negated by the massive inequalities necessary for the continued subordination of all women. A woman may succeed in entering a field once reserved for men, but though she may be 'equal' she will have to work harder, to compromise, and may still be the target of verbal and physical abuse, sexual harrassment, discrimination, and rape, and is still defined by her sex in pornography. 'Equality of opportunity' lulls us into a false sense of security by offering an apparently attractive alternative to exploitation and oppression. It can also be dangerous because those in power can use it to justify their position and regain ground lost to women, for example in requiring that women's studies courses are open to men, and in other ways invading and policing women's space.)

In 'our' male-centred culture, women are relentlessly censored into unfreedom by custom, tradition, language, religion, the law, education, the whole male system. Our unfreedom is rigorously enforced, by definitions of 'normal' behaviour and femininity, by heterosexism, by pornography and all forms of male violence, by our objectification, by our economic status — whilst simultaneously we are assured that we are 'free' and told that everyone else has a 'right' to their 'freedom' also. This doublespeak (the male Authorised

Version of Reality) is intended to conceal the actuality of the woman-hating/censoring nature of male-centred culture which manufactures our options, restricts our actions, prescribes our reactions, divides us, packages us, bargains for us, ghettoises us, trades us, objectifies us, kills us, rapes us, beats us and tells us we are free.

The Censorship of Women's Existence — or, All the World's a Sportsfield but only Men are Really Players

Male dominance and control have engineered a culture which has evolved around male ideas, attitudes and experiences, attaching significance and importance to male existence and marginalising women's existence. In 'our' male-centred culture (MCC!) women have been assigned to the status of supporters, standing on the sidelines of a global sportsfield where men are the designers of the game, the rule-makers, tacticians, managers, players, referees, profit-makers, decision-makers; it is without exception a man's game. Women are allowed on the field of play only in prescribed roles, as cheerleaders perhaps or programme sellers, or maybe the team mascot. Occasionally we are permitted to participate as substitutes, but only when we have gone through rigorous training and proved beyond doubt that we are 'fit' to play, that we understand the tactics, promise to play to the rules and follow the game to the letter (Margaret Thatcher is a gem of a substitute right-back!). The substitutes pose no threat because they are immediately dropped if they don't play the game or perform well as players. The power behind the game is in the boardroom with the backers, the directors and the managers — the men who control the global sportsfield. The strength of the team is cemented in the locker room, another no-go area for women, with a language and a culture of its own, that bond players, managers, referees and moneymen alike and effectively keep women in our place — off the field.

In order to sustain and uphold our secondary role and in an effort to disguise it, women are given the 'freedom' to move along the sidelines and watch the game. We have all been well-grounded in crowd behaviour, we know how to be good sports and are well-rehearsed in when to cheer. In this way a feeling of participating/belonging is cultivated and we can come to believe in our importance as supporters — the team needs us and our energy is put into the game rather than one another. Some women have more privileged positions and more comfort, depending on colour, class, marital status, depending on whether we produce more players or service the team — but let any of us enter the field without permission, challenge the rules or protest from the sidelines that we have had enough, that the game renders us worthless and invisible, that we are enraged by our image — let any of us demand an existence separate from the game — and the wrath of the gamekeepers is swift and terrible. The penalties for attempting to change the tactics or challenge the rules include ridicule, legal action or verbal or physical abuse. The penalty for trying to transform or stop the game may result in detention in prison or a psychiatric institution, torture or death. But only this will do, for as the game goes on, women live and die on the sidelines.

To Legislate or Not to Legislate ... Heads You Win, Tails We Lose

Present legislation against pornography could be compared to a large plaster applied (late) to a main artery injury. Better than nothing but somewhat lacking in effectiveness.

The law and the legal system has long been recognised by the majority of feminists as patriarchy fossilised. Movement, when perceptible, is ecliptical. There is documented evidence of how it works systematically against women. We witness it in the pronouncement of judges, the habitually light sentences given to men for crimes against women, the treatment of women in rape cases, the failure to recognise rape in marriage as a crime, the trivialisation of wife battering and torture, the high percentage of women in prison for crimes from which men walk free, the comparatively high number of women in prison for indeterminate periods, legislation around prostitution and abortion, and so on and so on.

Feminists also agree that the whole system must be radically changed if male attitudes, values and assumptions are to be challenged rather than perpetuated.

Proposed new legislation (via a 'sex discrimination through pornography' bill which provides civil remedies) will be part of this same system; it will continue to be administered by white, middle-class men, and will entail individual women being put on trial (as in rape cases) in order to prove they are 'damaged'. So what is the immediate alternative? The Obscene Publications Act? The escalation of sadistic pornography, with even computer games rating 'X' certificates because they contain mutilated women's bodies? The sexualisation of girl children, reflected in the increase in child pornography at one end of the scale and the sale of make-up to five-year-old girls in popular stores at the other? What is the foreseeable end when explicit sexual violence against women is packaged to sell products and women are killed as a turn-on for men, in 'snuff' films that can be hired from some video shops from around £1.50 (as the researchers for Sara Daniels play 'Masterpieces' discovered)?

Tight legislation (incorporating ground covered by the Dworkin–MacKinnon ordinance) which re-defines pornography from a radical feminist perspective, moving away from patriarchal ideas of 'obscenity' and 'depravity', and towards naming it as male violence towards women, would go some way towards challenging the attitudes and values of the system. It would affirm that women will no longer be silenced. It would get the issues into the public arena. It would clarify the porn/erotica, porn/art blur. It may check the rapid slide of increasingly violent pornographic images into advertising, the media, etc, and thus into our everyday lives. In a system created by men for men, legislation against pornography will have its limitations, it can and probably will be used against us, but until the revolution ... what else do we have?

CENSORSHIP AND HYPOCRISY: SOME ISSUES SURROUNDING PORNOGRAPHY THAT FEMINISM HAS IGNORED

Sue George

Pornography has been seen by some feminists as the single most oppressive factor in society, rather than poverty, racism or other forms of institutionalised male power. Why? Do sexual depictions of women (leaving aside for the moment the question of violent pornography) necessarily oppress us? Should we try and get rid of all of them because some are pernicious? I believe that if pornography oppresses women (and I am not entirely convinced that it does), it is because it is the reflection of one end of the spectrum which allows few choices for women. A film of continuous sexual activity, real or faked, may be boring, insulting to women, or a turn-on, but it does not *cause* women's oppression. Its continual reflection *may* reinforce it, but it cannot cause it on its own. All depictions of women, even those coming from a consciously feminist viewpoint, reflect women's oppression. We cannot remove patriarchy from our heads just like that.

I will be looking here at some of the issues around pornography and censorship which have not yet been addressed satisfactorily, both in general and as they relate specifically to women in video, film and television (audiovisual media). I am not advocating an uncritical acceptance of pornography, but rather a deeper and more thorough appraisal of the issues involved. There are no easy answers to many of the questions raised here, and some of them are contradictory. These contradictions have to be resolved, not ignored in the hope they will go away.

One of the reasons I decided to write this paper was the degree of hypocrisy exhibited by a number of feminists — myself included, I began to realise — who publicly decry pornography whilst privately giggling about it and even using it themselves. When other feminists talk about porn and the harm they feel it has done we say nothing, or appear to agree, only afterwards raising our eyebrows to each other as we ask each other excitedly about the lesbian porn article in *Square Peg* or persuade our boyfriends to hire us videos (wanting to watch them, but not be seen to be wanting to). One of the reasons pornography has such a hold over us is because there is so little honesty about it. If this difference between public and private opinion is so great, there is obviously a great deal more for us to discuss.

Meanwhile, many other feminists remain fundamentally indifferent to pornography, despite being told frequently how pernicious it is.

We must also recognise that pornography is not just about power, but about sexuality, and sexuality is about emotion. Pornography is an extremely emotive issue, which many women do not dare discuss. We do not like to upset each other, which leads to stalemate.

There is no doubt that many women are turned on by things which are not unequivocally pro-woman (very little is). Simply turning away from those things without *fully* examining them solves nothing. Whatever it is we are repressing remains repressed and, feeding on guilt, grows ever more powerful. For a feminist, therefore, to enjoy pornography is to feel doubly guilty. Firstly, we are subject to the usual societal taboos; secondly, it is wrong because it is degrading to women, and other feminists would disapprove.

As women are able to watch war films, football matches, and indeed the vast majority of films or TV programmes where women are absent or in subservient positions to men, so women can do this in pornography as well. Just because women appear submissive in much porn does not mean that a woman watching it has to become submissive in her fantasies. Women can manipulate porn to fit their existing fantasies, as men do. Many anti-pornography campaigners cannot accept that women may choose to use porn. In their view, women are forced to use it by their men, who then inflict what they learn from porn on the women. This view only allows women to be victims, which we are not.

Representation

Initially linked to fertility, sexually explicit images of women go back to pre-history, and the use of such images for sexual titillation pre-dates photography by at least hundreds of years. The explicitness of readily available images in Europe and America has certainly increased dramatically over the past fifty or a hundred years, while the division of women into 'good' and 'bad' has become less absolute. Over this period many taboos have been broken and it is possible that, as sexuality has become a less forbidden topic, women have been allowed more humanity in this respect.

Some distinction definitely has to be made between different images available in porn. Surely there is a great deal of difference between images of women being horrifically abused and women doing things which, in the right circumstances, could be very pleasurable! The pornography I have seen (except that depicted in anti-pornography slide shows) has been of non-violent heterosexual and lesbian sex. It includes both 'soft core' porn, which can be bought in the newsagents, and 'hard core', where the sex is definitely not simulated, which cannot. (None of this has been violent, and the images are banned because they depict actual sex, not because they are violent.)

Much feminist objection to non-violent pornography is based around the issue of objectification. Both men and women are objectified in porn in that they are only seen as sexual objects. What can be seen as oppressive to women is that only a very small spectrum of women feature in pornography. In reality, almost everyone is fancied by someone, sometime, regardless of physical appearance. But if objectification of potential sexual partners is fundamentally degrading, then any depiction of people which does not reflect their entirety as human beings is degrading. Surely being sexually attracted to people you don't know is neither wrong nor avoidable. Few people escape 'fancying' or 'being fancied'; nor would they want to escape it.

It is in the area of sado-masochistic pornography where the most difficult questions about the links between image, fantasy and reality must be addressed. Although, as I have already stated, I have varying positive and negative responses to non-violent pornography, like so many other women I have strong feelings of revulsion against violent porn. For me, the strongest contradictions lie here: I do not want to see these images, but my anti-censorship commitment remains. The 'whatever turns you on' school of feminist porn may argue that these images have no, or only a tenuous, connection with reality. Some women have masochistic fantasies, they argue, and should they not be allowed to indulge them? But images which suggest that women like pain are not only going to be seen by women who like pain within *very* confined boundaries, they can be seen by anyone. But even when this happens, why should we assume that the majority of men seeing these images will be encouraged to become violent themselves?

Violence against women has always been around, and its actual connection with pornography per se has not been satisfactorily proved. Rapists sometimes cite pornography as an influence, but I would be reluctant to believe anything they said. How exactly is it an influence rather than an excuse, anyway? Perhaps it's because porn offers more than it can possibly deliver that it has been connected with incitement to rape. Inevitably, it offers everything and delivers nothing.

Racism and Representation

One of the issues from which everyone seems to have shied away is that of racism and sexuality. British society is repressed and puritanical in many ways, and the (white) women's movement and the left in general reflect this. This repression is demonstrated in a time-honoured phenomenon: the projection of sexuality onto other groups. Images of Black women in the media, mainstream or alternative, are few because Black women — or men — have not been allowed access to power within it. Where Black women do appear, they are almost invariably shown as sexual objects. There are few (if any) images of white female sexuality which are positive for feminists while remaining 'acceptable' to mainstream society. Yet it still seems acceptable to white feminists that Black women be overtly (hetero)sexual. How this operates can be seen most baldly in the music business. Tina Turner, for instance, is seen by many as sexuality incarnate. And it is interesting to note the reaction of white feminists to some of the African bands which have been playing in London over the past year. Many of these bands, Les Quatres Etoiles and Fela Kuti, for example, have female dancers/backing vocalists. Their primary function seems to be to provide a sexual element in the group, yet nowhere, ever, have I seen any comment about this. If white bands or singers had similar dancers they would be picketed. Yet at Les Quatres Etoiles' concert white (apparently) feminists and lefties were queuing up to dance on stage. I am not necessarily saying they shouldn't, but they should recognise their *own* desire to be publicly sexual and their own racism, which sees Black people as 'other' and exotic.

In traditional British culture (and many others too) sexuality is an extremely private matter, which is barely discussed. This allows pornography to flourish and accounts partly for its attraction. It also allows for the kind of racism detailed above. Before it will disappear, white people have to take responsibility for their own desires — something which doesn't appear to be imminent.

The Anti-Sex-and-Violence Lobby

The moral right in this country (and the USA) are subject to these fears and repressions, just like those who scorn their political opinions. Nevertheless, parts of the feminist movement have found connections with the anti-sex-and-violence lobby because of their anti-pornography stance. This amazes me. It has always been true that the moral right was anti-woman. They are operating from a 'family' standpoint, where the interests of the nuclear family, with unquestioned father at the head, are paramount. They believe that 'sex and violence' — they seem to see no difference — on television have partly caused the breakdown of the family. Authority must be vested in the parents (father) and sex education is dangerous because it takes away parents' rights. Never mind that the family is the site for so many sorts of oppression. But they have cunningly couched some of their arguments in terms with which feminists can agree. One of Victoria Gillick's more famous quotations involved her saying that women were being tied to the bedpost from an increasingly young age. But the reason the moral right want women to concentrate on their self-development rather than go early into sexual relationships is for the sake of their future husbands and families, not for themselves.

An axiom of the anti-pornography movement is that pornography leads to violence against women. But the moral right is not against violence against women. It is only against violence against women who are unimpeachably pure and *never* step out of line — surely something feminists would never support.

Now that lifetime monogamous heterosexuality is being seen by a growing sector of society — not just the moral right — as the only way to avoid the spread of AIDS, it is vital that debates about sexuality be brought onto our terms. Many forms and aspects of sexuality should be addressed in the space for discussion which AIDS has forced. But as the moral right often seems to blame women who have been raped (unless they are virgins, violently raped by strangers), so they blame people who contract HIV (unless it is through blood transfusion, deception by a bisexual husband, etc.). At present, propaganda about AIDS is based either on no sex before marriage, or on using condoms, if you *must* take a risk. No mention of the minimal risk run by lesbians, of course. Individuals' (society's) fear and guilt about sexuality is both exploited by the moral right, and most blatantly evident within it. No wonder that some of what they say has attracted people of such otherwise different opinions.

The moral right want legislation over what we are allowed to see to be ever-tightened. The most recent attempt to bring television under the remit of the Obscene Publications Act fizzled out before the June '87 election. However, further attempts seem inevitable. The most recent bill was designed to test whether material was 'grossly offensive to a reasonable person'. This is the moral right's criterion. But by their standards, a reasonable person would be a white, middle-class, church-going Tory (male), married with two children. The general public, in all its diversity, would not be considered fit to judge. And any legislation, whether over 'obscenity' on television, or pornography per se, would be introduced by those who already have the power in this country. They have no interest in real change, whether they are MPs, judges, owners of porn emporia, or the media in general. The power base is inimical to feminists and to women's interests in general. They know exactly what they want — the status quo or worse — and will use their legislation against what we want.

They are not interested in getting rid of pornography, simply in limiting its availability. 'Banning' pornography would be nothing more than a cosmetic exercise, designed to prevent children and 'respectable citizens' from being faced with 'sex for sale'. Such legislation has absolutely nothing to do with fighting women's oppression. For instance, laws already exist to limit the display of nakedness on the street. There used to be a mural of two semi-naked women opposite my office. Jeans were painted on them! As if there is any fundamental difference between pink legs and navy ones! They were still obviously advertising a 'sex' club. And while there is still a demand for it, pornography will continue to exist. Legislation might make it harder to obtain, more expensive, therefore more profitable to the producers and more deeply involved in criminality, but it would not destroy it.

Control of Women and the Audiovisual Media

The anti-sex-and-violence lobby focuses most closely on television because of its undoubted power over everyone's lives. Those who own and control the media like to think it reflects reality. Of course, that's nonsense: it depicts reality as they think it ought to be. Rather like the DHSS who believe women ought to be supported by men, whether they are not not, the majority of audio-visual professionals believe that their own view of reality (white, heterosexual, middle-class, male) *is* reality, and if it's not, it should be. People other than the above see reality somewhat differently, of course.

Aspects of the media which might be regarded as sexist — almost all of them — have such an enormous influence because they are everywhere. I believe that the more subtle the degrading image, the more influence it has, because the less questioned it will be. For instance, television images of women living through their husbands are legion, and in programme makers' terms, realistic. Such images are so influential because they are the stuff of television. The *absence* of positive images of women, particularly of *Black* women, is also enormously influential, both on those who are absent, and on 'society'. On the other hand, watching blatant pornography — which cannot be seen on TV — is a surreptitious and shameful act, even when consumed publicly. Its influence, therefore, is comparatively small.

Also frequently shown, both on TV and in the cinema, are 'women in peril' films. It can be convincingly argued that these films are a form of social control, persuading women that they should stay at home because the world is full of killers and rapists. Women in 'real life' both are, and are expected to be, frightened of men, rapists, etc. Yet women watch these films and are frightened silly. Why? Perhaps it is because although the films represent some sort of reality, they are not 'real life'. By being very frightened, in a situation which is not at all threatening, it is possible to work through and resolve real fears which have already been experienced.

Fighting Against Their Censorship — Building Our Own Images

How can we create the sort of images we want to create, and what are the problems involved? Despite the protests of the moral right, mainstream film and television operates within very narrow parameters. Trying to move outside those parameters brings women face to face with censorship. Women film and video makers struggling to create their own positive images are on the receiving end of this censorship. If, for instance, you are producing something for television (which few women have the chance to do) then you will be careful to make it 'acceptable' or it will not be shown. And independent film and video makers have to attract money from grant-aiding bodies, so they have to fall in with those bodies' funding criteria. Whatever happens, women generally receive less money than men, with the result that what they produce is less 'professional'. This can be used as an excuse not to exhibit it. For instance, Caroline Sheldon's film *17 Rooms (what lesbians do in bed)* — which is *not* about sex — was due to be screened in the gay series on Channel 4. It was held up for 'technical' reasons, and eventually not shown because it was too late to clear the music rights. These examples are 'indirect' censorship, but they are certainly effective!

A wide variety of strong images of women are being produced. In my opinion, erotic images by and for women should be made too. Many women feel that pro-women erotic images are not possible when sexuality is so patriarchally defined. But perhaps producing our own sexual images is one way in which we may begin to define it. If we don't produce these images ourselves, then someone one else will try to do it for us. Others say that whatever we produce, it will be consumed by men. Some women may feel that this is a risk worth taking. It is also possible that sexual images produced by women may simply not interest men particularly. But there is no denying the practical and political difficulties surrounding feminist erotica. There is, as yet, very little of it about. Lesbian erotica, produced in America, has just become available here. It is, of course, highly controversial. Feminist heterosexual erotic images do not seem to exist, and I am curious to know what they would be. At present, men are very anxious that their naked bodies should be invisible and erections are officially banned, probably because men fear their fragility. Where men are sexualised, it's usually for other men. Although women's production of these images would not in itself be an answer, it could play a part in the formation of a feminist-centred sexuality.

Strong, positive images are being created by women, Black people, and other under-represented groups to counteract the prevailing forms of representation. Of course, there are many practical problems from 'how can I get the money to make my film?' to 'is this really a positive image?' I believe that creating a feminist audio-visual culture is part of the solution to the misrepresentation of women in the media, and is part of the process of long-term change. At the same time as creating our own images, we also have to address current forms of representation. The majority of feminists appear to support, with reservations, the use of some kind of legislation to control pornography. But however attractive this might appear superficially, legislation will be used against us and offers no real solution. A real solution, which will include radically different representations of women in all our diversity, will not come through legislation. It will come from us. And it will only come when we begin to discuss, honestly, deeply and non-judgmentally, what we believe to be the truth.

Note: Although I work for the Women's Film, Televison and Video Network, these are my personal opinions, not those of WFTVN.

RAGE AND DESIRE: CONFRONTING PORNOGRAPHY

Pratibha Parmar

Since the publication in 1981 of *Pornography* — *Men Possessing Women* by Andrea Dworkin, feminists, most notably in Canada and North America, have been waging passionate battles and forging new political alliances around the question of pornography and censorship.[1]

Feminists in Britain have been slower to take on the issues in this area but there is no doubt that the zealous fervour so predominant in this most recent wave of feminist activity and debate has wafted across the Atlantic to Britain. This is not to say that discussions around such issues are a new phenomenon here. For instance, public debates around issues of sexuality, pornography, prostitution and birth control have a political history in 19th Century Britain. The work of feminist historians, such as Judith Walkowitz, has shown that there has been a history of tension between feminists who were involved in the Campaign to repeal the Contagious Diseases Acts passed in 1866 and 1869 and the social purists who were also engaged in the same campaign, but for reasons of morality rather than because such acts aimed to control women's sexuality.[2] The alliances that some feminists made with such moralists finally led to a further erosion of women's rights and as Varda Burstyn cautions:

> With the clarity of hindsight we can now see that many of the early feminists made a number of major errors in their campaigns on sexual issues, errors that hurt the women's movement as a whole and undermined its ability to fight for women on other fronts.[3]

One of the characteristics of debates on pornography has been a tendency to make universal generalisations about male power and sexual subjugation. Judging from the books and articles in various magazines that have been published in Britain in the last few years, it is clear that it is not only the rhetoric, language and theories of the anti-pornography lobby led by Dworkin which are being adopted almost wholesale, but also that their strategies calling for censorship are being aped. Political critiques of pornography have so far been dominated by feminists who see all men as the perpetrators/ collaborators in pornography and all women as their victims.

Debates around pornography and censorship raise complex issues which have significant implications for our daily lives and it is important that we attempt a sophistication in the language and concepts we use in our attempts to understand these issues. It is precisely the particular use of language and the rhetoric of the anti-pornography lobby which is disturbing and which I think reveals their contradictions. It is a language which allows a slide into confusing the multiple causes and forms of women's oppression with a single focus on one manifestation of their oppression.

For example, in the conclusion of *Pornography: Men Possessing Women*, Dworkin argues: 'We will know that we are free when the pornography no longer exists. As long as it does exist, we must understand that we are the women in it: used by the same power, subject to the same valuation, as the vile whores who beg for more.'[4]

Fear, rage and frustration are raw emotions which many of the anti-pornography theorists use to incite women to act out of a politics of outrage and anger. This, in itself, is not necessarily a bad thing. After all, the initial energy of the contemporary women's liberation movements in the west came precisely from such passionate feelings of righteous anger at women's oppression. But the political landscape of the mid-1980s is a bleak one, where repression is a fundamental part of many people's daily lives and anger alone will not bring about the fundamental economic and political changes that are so necessary. Thatcherite Britain is one divided dramatically between races, classes and communities. Severe economic pressure and cuts in the health services have greatly reduced many people's access to basic social services. The gap between those housed, fed and in employment and those without any of these basic survival tools has dramatically increased. The rise in racist murders and killings go unabated. Racist discourses around the origins of AIDS in Africa have been used as a way of justifying stricter immigration controls and increased harassment of Black visitors to Britain.

Women, too, have been a target of the current backlash. For example, the Alton Bill has attempted to erode women's existing limited rights of access to legal abortions. All the gains that women have made in the last few decades are slowly being chiselled away, not only through legislation, but also by the virulent ideology of the moral right. Poverty, racism, and violence against women and children have become very much a part of Britain in the 1980s, while increased police powers mean an increase in state control over people's movements and basic rights.

The last few years have also seen a dramatic moral and political backlash against the lesbian and gay communities as a direct result of the fear and panic created around AIDS. The media, the government and right-wing forces have not wasted any time. Existing anti-gay prejudices have been mobilised to orchestrate a systematic attack on the lesbian and gay communities. An example of this is the furore caused by a library book titled *Jenny lives with Eric and Martin* — an educational tool to show that gay men, too, can be parents and live as a family — available under parental control in libraries in Haringey in London. There, local and national right-wing forces joined together and organised public book burnings, while carrying placards which said AIDS=Gays=Death.

The Education Minister ordered the Inner Education Authority to ban the book because he claimed to 'speak up for parents who want school libraries to contain the best of our children's literature and to emphasise that a normal moral framework is the bedrock of the family'. The Parent's Rights Group led the main opposition against Haringey Council's progressive policies on lesbians and gays. Leaflets opposing the policy were published by 'Concerned Parents and Citizens of Haringey' in association with the 'The New Patriotic Movement'. The latter has been revealed as a far-right group with links to the Moonie World Unification Church. In June 1987, during the General election, Betty Sheridan, a founder member of the Parents Rights Group, appeared in national newspaper advertisements that said: 'My name is Betty Sheridan. I live in Haringey. I'm married with two children. *And I'm scared.* If you vote Labour, they'll go on teaching my kids about Gays & Lesbians, instead of giving them proper lessons.' The ads were financed by The Committee for a Free Britain who share an address with the Moonie Unification Church.[5]

The role that the media played in abetting this climate of moral backlash was paramount. The *Sunday Mirror* interviewed the head of Scotland Yard's Obscene Publications Squad (26/10/86), who proclaimed that such books were 'a source for sexual perverts to further their interests'. The *Daily Telegraph*, an equally right-wing paper, defended the censorship of *Jenny Lives with Eric and Martin* and used this as a springboard for a warning of 'the dangers of active, aggressive homosexual proselytising, in which a number of evil people have declared war on marriage and the family'.

The political tensions such a situation created was capitalised on by Mr. Wilshire, the Tory MP who proposed an amendment clause to the 1987 Local Government Act. Section 28, which has been passed into law, was to make it illegal for local councils to finance anyone or anything (including publications) which would 'promote homosexuality' or promote the teaching in schools of the acceptability of homosexuality as a 'pretended family relationship'. The implications of this clause are worse than horrific. In the area of cultural activity there could be a total ban on any images of lesbians and gay men, any films, videos or photographs that may have been funded directly or indirectly by progressive local councils.

It is only in the last five years that there has been a visible growth in lesbian and gay groups, centres, literature and visual materials — all of which have helped enormously to put homosexuality on the political agenda of local government. This has been despite the retrenchment of Thatcherism and largely due to the pressure lesbian and gay activists have put on local Labour councils who have adopted an equal opportunities policy towards issues of homosexuality. So much so that Thatcher's last election campaign focused much energy on discrediting Labour councils for their support of lesbian and gay issues. They issued posters, including one with the words: 'Young, gay and proud', 'Policing Classrooms' and 'Sex education taught in schools'. Another billboard showed the title of an American book, *Black Lesbian in White America* — plus the caption: 'DO YOU WANT YOUR CHILD TO RECEIVE AN EDUCATION LIKE THIS? (VOTE CONSERVATIVE)'. We were left in no doubt of the Tory Party's not-so-hidden agenda of eroding any of the progressive policies fought for so hard by the lesbian and gay communities.

In outlining the political landscape of Britain in recent years, my intention is to show that unless we are mindful of the moral backlash around the area of sexual politics, and the climate of fear and prejudice, there is every danger that calls for censorship of pornography will coalesce with similar demands coming from the new moral right.

The language of pornography

The majority of pornography is about the public depiction of sexual imagery of women, which is created, controlled and consumed by men and is one manifestation of women's oppression. But it is not the only one, nor is it the *central* cause of our oppression, as Dworkin and other anti-pornography supporters argue. I want to pose several challenges to the contention that pornography itself plays a major role in the general oppression of women. The prior agenda of such political conclusions is one which is familiar, and maybe even obvious, but nevertheless it needs to be restated. It is an agenda which sees women as a class oppressed first and foremost by a universal patriarchy, unmediated by race, class or history. It constructs women as victims, forever silenced and objectified, by a monolithic category of men who become 'them' — an undefined, entity, devoid of differences of class, race or access to power. As Ann Snitow argues, 'All are collapsed into a false unity, the brotherhood of the oppressors, the sisterhood of the victims.'[6]

But again this sisterhood of all women assumes that there are no significant differences between women, compared with the similarities of our experiences of pornography. I find such analysis both Eurocentric and nationalist. It is also insulting in its simplicity. Feminism has a long history of divisions created out of an inability of the movement to deal with differences of race, class and sexuality. It is precisely this refusal to recognise the differences amongst us and addressing all theories and campaigns from a supposedly unified female experience that prompted many Black women to organise autonomously in the early 1980s. Central to our experience in Britain has been the racism of the State, and this was reflected in the campaigns, for example, against immigration controls, against sub-standard education of Black children, against police brutality, against forced vaginal examinations of Asian women and forced sterilisation. Black women have been at the forefront of initiating analysis and action around the racism within the women's movement and have challenged much of the 'imperialist' theories and practices of white feminism.[7] Most of the writings that I have read on pornography do not in any way show an awareness of this history, or acknowledge and/or incorporate an understanding of how racial, class and cultural differences between women shape our subjective experiences of the world. They also make no attempt to explore how women may be affected differently by pornography because of their different subjectivities.

The historical processes of European thought and practice which regard images of Black women and men as the Other — i.e. more primitive and more sexual — are deeply rooted and ideologically inscribed within European culture.[8] Images, icons and stereotypes of Black female sexuality, in particular, are reproduced in contemporary pornography and subsequently received/read by white men and women. The process by which this happens should be important, if not necessary, consideration for *all* feminists engaged in unravelling the complex matrix of pornography and representation.

One of the central concerns of the Euro-American women's movement has been to understand the ideological construction of sexuality and to develop feminist critiques of sexuality and sexual practices within an overall analysis of the sexual subordination of women. Of course, within this overall scenario, radical feminist theories of women's subordination have differed from socialist feminist analysis. While it is no longer tenable to argue that these two perspectives are clearly demarcated, because of the many overlaps and permutations between them, nevertheless the dominant thread in much socialist feminist analysis has been an attempt to locate its arguments within a historically specific framework. Its strength has also been its uncovering of economic and material conditions which give rise to particular forms of women's subjugation. All this is completely absent from the anti-pornography lobby, which retreats into presumptuous generalisations about men and male power and about female sexuality.[9] There is an implicit assumption that somewhere and somehow there exists an unchanging and predefined female sexuality which is:

> romantic, egalitarian, natural, gentle, free of power dynamics, monogamous, emotional, nurturing and spontaneous. This feminist prescription reflects and reproduces the dominant cultural assumptions about women (and is premised) on the notion that women are victims of sex and that sex is degrading to women, but not to men.[10]

Such a position sees women's sexuality purely in relation to men and ignores the work many feminists have done to create their own sexual agenda, whether that is in relationship to men or not. Such a position is in fact anti-feminist in its refusal to acknowledge many women's successful attempts to conceptualise and define our sexuality independently of men. Furthermore, it calls on an essentialist notion of women's and men's nature and disregards the social construction of sexuality and fantasies. Women who admit to their contradictory sexual fantasies are accused of being victims of 'politically incorrect early conditioning'... contradictory because their responses to pornography evoke at one and the same time feelings of anger, rage, fear and humiliation, as well as pleasure, arousal and desire.

Within such a framework, women who engage in discussions or sexual practices which utilise concepts of power, desire and fantasy are made to feel guilty and dismissed as having 'internalised oppressive self-images'. The tragedy is that the spaces which many women have bravely created to continuously question and redefine their sexuality, either in relation to men or to other women, is being eroded by the guilt-inducing moralism of the anti-pornography lobby.[11] It is as if such women are being asked to purge themselves of the 'evil' that has been ingrained into their psyches and which they need to cleanse themselves of, in order to emerge as 'good' and 'pure'. Given the virulent moral overtones of the current right-wing backlash against women and the pressure to reprivatise sexual identity, such formulations around 'evil' and 'pure' are alarming.

Our psyches around sexual desire, pleasure and fantasies are contradictory and problematic. But there is not an inevitable slide from acknowledging or even accepting any one of these fantasies for ourselves, to what we directly do in our everyday life and relationships. Instead we should welcome our fantasies as signals or clues to exploring and discovering our sexual desires and pleasure.

Censorship

While it is crucial to challenge the very basis on which the anti-pornography lobby propogates its arguments by criticising their political formulations of pornography, it is equally important to confront their call for legal sanctions against it. Censorship of any kind has always had disastrous and repressive effects for communities without access to power. Censorship exists in many different areas and is not only confined to sexuality.

The unofficial exclusion of Black women from writing and publishing and from many public spaces is a form of censorship which has existed both within and outside of the women's movement, Black people in South Africa speaking out against the apartheid regime have and are experiencing vicious state censorship. Irish women involved in the struggle for self-determination in

Northern Ireland have been imprisoned and harassed by the occupying forces of the British. In effect, they have been censored. There are countless other such examples where people have had to bear the brunt of repression arising out of attempts to censor their radicalism, which challenges their subjugation and domination. There is no doubt that Clause 28 was brought in as a way of censoring and silencing many of the positive and combative efforts by lesbians and gay men to become visible and have a voice in the social, cultural and political life of society.

Dworkin/MacKinnon Ordinance

The Dworkin/MacKinnon ordinance, which seeks to enable anyone to bring a civil suit against anything deemed to be 'offensive' and hence 'pornographic', poses several problems. What puzzles me is how women who have defined all men as the enemy can ask the 'patriarchal state' to intervene on their behalf and pass laws in the interests of women. Expecting the state to behave in a benevolent manner is naive. Black women and Irish women who have experienced the brutality of the British state first hand have no such callow notions. The very state that condoned forced vaginal examinations of Asian women at Heathrow airport, a practice which amounted to both sexual and racial harassment, is the same one to which some Dworkin/MacKinnon followers in Britain are appealing.

It is also not very clear who or what they are asking to be censored. Is it the consumers or the porn kings who control the means of production, or is it the imagery itself? There are differences in the strategies adopted by groups such as Women Against Violence Against Women (WAVAW) in their campaigns against pornography and the strategies of women such as Catherine Itzin, who has initiated a legal campaign against pornography in Britain, although they all share the same language.

Revolutionary/radical feminists have a history of unthought-out and simplistic practices in their attempts to combat violence against women on the streets. It is this history which informs and shapes to this day their responses to pornography. In the late 1970s many women, mainly white, organised Reclaim the Night demos demanding that the streets be made safe for women — these marches usually went through Black areas, thus reinforcing racist ideas about Black men as perpetrators of sexual crimes against white women. It was also in the late 1970s that the Yorkshire Ripper was brutalising and murdering many women. As a reaction against police calls for women not to venture out at night on their own, some revolutionary feminists, part of WAVAW, called for a curfew on all men. Such a demand in towns and areas where there were substantial Black populations was deeply offensive and racist. It reflected a complete ignorance on the relationship of Black communities to policing, when time and time again Black men had been picked up on the streets for no good reason and harassed by the police.

In a recent interview, Annie Blue from WAVAW said:

> We see all pornography as violence against women. We'd like a law that uses this radical feminist definition of its function in society. It's a double-edged sword, because it would give more power to the police and state, but in the present climate, it's the best of two evils. What else have we got?[12]

To pose the police and the state as 'the better of two evils' in such a crass, naive and unpoliticised manner is highly dubious. This throws into question the basis/definition of feminism that such women are working with. A position which does not acknowledge, understand or even incorporate an analysis of the state and policing in relation to *all* women should be challenged in its claim to feminism.

The legal lobby is led by Catherine Itzin, who has argued that 'pornography was a cause of sex discrimination' and that the women who partake in pornography 'are victims, usually poor and exploited'. She then went on to argue that just as 'negroes were kept in slavery rather than have their full citizenship rights recognised', so it is with the struggle that Dworkin/MacKinnon have had in passing their ordinance in the U.S. In arguing for similar anti-pornographic legislation in Britain, she uses the example of the Race Relations Act 1976 as a model to work from and suggests that such legislation would incorporate the Dworkin/MacKinnon definition of pornography.[13]

What makes me angry about such formulations is the easy manner in which women such as Itzin use the race analogy to give credence and strength to their arguments. To collapse the denial of basic human rights of slaves with the objectification of women in sexual imagery is not only racist but extremely opportunistic. To attempt to equate the mass genocide of whole nations and communities of African people with sexual subjugation of women betrays an indecent ignorance of the economic, cultural and political machinations of slavery. It diminishes both African history and women's struggle for control over our sexuality. What I am criticising here is the equation of two historically specific processes of exploitation and oppression. Women are, have been, and continue to be brutalised in and through pornography, but this has to be challenged, changed and criticised in its own terms and not through emotive recourse to other historical parallels. The fundamental problem lies with the basic presumption of anti-pornographers that pornography is the root of all evil, and it is this which allows them to make this erroneous and racist equation. The tendency to create such parallels between different struggles comes from a need to give added weight, historical legacies, to modernist concerns. But why should this be necessary?

Nor is the Race Relations Act a piece of legislation which has had much effect in safeguarding the interests of Black people in Britain. In fact it has often worked against our interests, as Sona Osman shows elsewhere in this collection. Nor has such legislation stopped the police from contributing to the rise in the murders and street attacks on Black people. Catherine Itzin argues that unlike pornography, at least 'you can't buy racist material in newsagents' and this in itself constitutes a powerful statement'.[14] But why and how does she then explain the rise in racist murders, assaults and attacks both on the streets and in Black people's homes?

The state is not neutral, and this has been demonstrated time and again, not only by Black people's experiences, but also through the miners' strike in 1983/4 and by women at Greenham Common. It is suicidal to consider possibilities of strategic alliances with the state. Of course, this is different from making progressive demands of the state. Many social and political movements around the world have made demands of the state as a legitimate and sometimes successful strategy for change. But Catherine Itzin, who is attempting to make 'incitement to sexual hatred' a civil offence, does not reveal any sophisticated understanding of such distinctions or strategies.

A second problem is that Dworkin's definition of what is pornographic can be interpreted in a variety of ways, depending on who is doing the interpreting. So, what a High Court judge, usually a white heterosexual man, believes to be pornographic may and will inevitably be quite different to what anyone of us may interpret or define as pornographic. Indeed, when there are so many differences between feminists on this, how can you ask a judge or a judicial system which has itself proved to be anti-women to arbitrate? Having such definitions will also inevitably lead to a policing of everyone's desires, fantasies and sexuality. Who decides what images are permissible and which ones are not?

Anti-pornography theory collapses a variety of sexual images into a generalised statement that all pornography is violence against women. But as Ann Snitow has argued convincingly:

> A definition of pornography that takes the problem of analysis seriously has to include not only violence, hatred and fear of women, but also a long list of other elements, which may help explain why we women ourselves have such a mixture of reactions to the genre ... we need to be able to reject the sexism in porn without having to reject the realm of pornographic sexual fantasy as if that entire kingdom were without meaning or resonance for women ... Without history, without an analysis of complexity and difference, without a critical eye toward gender and its constant redefinitions, some recognition of the gap — in ideas and feelings — between the porn magazine and the man who reads it, we will only be purveying a false hope to those women whom we want to join us: that without porn, there will be far less male violence, that with less male violence there will be far less male power ... [15]

Power of Imagery

We live in a highly visual culture that is controlled by the institutions of the mass media, whose primary aim is to increase consumerism through advertising and to present the world through the eyes of a dominant elite. Every day we are presented with images which appear 'natural' and yet bear hardly any resemblance to the reality of most people's lives. The power of images is unquestionable and what is needed is an unmasking of the hidden agenda of the media and the role representation plays within cultural and political life.

A dominant premise of the pro-censorship lobby is their understanding and/or analysis of the powerful influence which sexual imagery of women has over men. They posit a direct correlation between pornography and violence against women. I do not want to argue this point on the grounds of whether such a correlation has a scientific and/or statistical basis; instead I would argue that complex issues around visual representation cannot be reduced to a simple formula of pornography = violence against women.

Much work has been done and is continuing to be done in the

women's movement around issues of women's representation in mainstream media, through advertising, films and television. The power of images to inform, misinform, manipulate and feed into notions of female and male roles has long been recognised by feminist cultural activists. Some women have consistently challenged the notion that we are just passive recipients or mere victims of the media, even though we are influenced by it. More recently, such work has been stated by many Black women and men concerned to challenge the racist and sexist representations of Black people, both within mainstream media and in independent bodies of work. The struggle over imagery and for self-representation and self-definition has been established as a legitimate political struggle by many Black cultural activists.[16] Black photographers, artists, writers and film makers are not only working to control the content of their representation, but are also building infrastructures which give us control over the means of production of our work. We are using our respective creative mediums to discover and explore issues relating to racial, sexual and cultural identities.

This area of work, too, has suffered from interference and censorship. Take, for example, the film, *A People's Account* about the uprisings in Broadwater Farm and Handsworth, and the suffering as a result of police action of two Black women, Cherry Groce, who was left paralysed after being shot, and Cynthia Jarret, who died of a heart attack. The film was made in 1986 by Ceddo, a Black film and video workshop. Channel 4 and the IBA have pulled it off the screen three times, arguing that it is too one-sided. This film provides a rare forum for the voices of Black people who live on these estates and who experienced police violence. For once, we are spared the overwhelming presence of the white dominant voices, painting pictures of 'barbaric, and 'savage' Black rioters. The film has still not been seen on Channel 4, who originally funded it, and it has been censored by them jointly with the IBA, purely on the grounds of political bias. Censorship of this kind is clearly about control. When it comes to the visual representation of and by Black people, women, gay men and lesbians, the problem, without doubt, is that when anyone of us from these groups begin to challenge the dominant imagery (which is often exploitative, racist, sexist and homophobic) the shackles of censorship are snapped on before any resistance can be mustered up.

To conclude, I want to restate my argument that most women from their different subjectivities do and will continue to find what they define as pornography both enraging and problematic. What we don't need is a regression to victimisation theories of women's oppression which see women only as sexual victims and passive recipients of authoritarian patriarchal institutions. What we *do* need is a greater sophistication in the language and analysis of pornography than has been witnessed so far[17] — an analysis which takes into account the complexity of different subjectivities and their respective relationship to institutions of power and of the state. Inevitably, how we fight politically against pornography, violence against women and censorship will ultimately depend not only on how we define and name the problems, but also on how we wage struggles around other aspects of our political agendas and visions.

Notes and References

1. Andrea Dworkin, *Pornography: Men Possessing Women*, The Women's Press, 1981.
2. Judith Walkowitz, *Prostitution and Victorian Society: Women, Class and the State*, Cambridge University Press, 1980.
3. Varda Burstyn, 'Political Precedents and Moral Crusades: Women, Sex and the State', in *Women Against Censorship*, edited by Varda Burstyn, Douglas and McIntyre, Vancouver and Toronto, 1985.
4. Andrea Dworkin, op cit p. 224.
5. Jan Parker and Chris Baker, Association of London Authorities Briefing Paper on Section 28, January, 1988. (Internal document.) My thanks to Jan Parker for useful discussion in this area.
6. Ann Snitow, 'Retrenchment Versus Transformation: The Politics of the Anti-Pornography Movement' in *Women Against Censorship*, op cit p. 113.
7. See, for example, Hazel Carby, 'White Women Listen! Black Feminism and the boundaries of Sisterhood' in *The Empire Strikes Back: Race and Racism in 70s Britain*, edited by the Race and Politics Group, Centre for Contemporary Cultural Studies, Hutchinson, 1982. Also see 'Many Voices One Chant: Black Feminist Perspectives': *Feminist Review*, Autumn 1984.
8. See Sandra L. Gilman, *Difference and Pathology: Stereotypes of Sexuality, Race and Madness*, Cornell University Press, 1985.
9. See Dworkin, op cit, in particular pages 13 to 24, where she expounds on the seven tenets of male power and supremacy.
10. Donna Turley, 'The Feminist Debate on Pornography', *Socialist Review*, no 87–88, May–August, 1986.
11. Susan Ardill and Sue O'Sullivan, 'Difference, Desire and Lesbian Sadomasochism' in *Feminist Review* 23, Summer 1986.
12. Sarah Baxter, 'Women Against Porn', in which she quotes Annie Blue, *Time Out*, March 23–30, 1988.
13. Catherine Itzin, April 20th 1987, in *London Daily News*.

14. Catherine Itzin, quoted by Sarah Baxter, op cit.
15. Ann Snitow, p. 117, op cit.
16. See, for instance, 'Black Image, Staying On', a special issue of *Ten:8 (photographic magazine)*, no. 16, 1984.
17. Except for the excellent anthology *Women Against Censorship*, op cit, and a collection of articles entitled, *Caught Looking: Feminism, Pornography and Censorship*, edited by Kate Ellis et al, published in USA, 1987. Unfortunately, bookshops in Britain refuse to stock this enjoyable and well-argued collection because of images/illustrations which they deem 'pornographic'.

Acknowledgements:

I would like to thank Vron Ware, Paul Gilroy, Shaheen Haque and Sue O'Sullivan for their constant support, encouragement and useful comments on my earlier drafts and to Gail Chester for her patience.

THE CENSORING OF REVOLUTIONARY FEMINISM

Sheila Jeffreys

For some years now, those feminists who see pornography as the propaganda of womanhatred have been accused by the sexual liberals here and in the USA of being censors. Fear and loathing have erupted from the sexual liberals towards the feminists they see as so threatening. I would like to ask who is censoring whom? I do know that the policies of the anti-pornography campaigners are being censored by virtually the whole of the left, liberal, academic, cultural, media establishment. I shall give a few examples here of how this censorship works from my experience and then offer a couple of suggestions as to why this savage censorship by the defenders of 'free speech', the anti-censorship lobby, is taking place.

For five years I have taught on the Open University Summer School 'The Changing Experience of Women'. This year I have not been appointed and received a standard letter informing me that there were few vacancies and many interested tutors. The tutors who taught with me on the sexuality module have been reappointed. What did I do wrong? Last summer, for the first time, I showed the New York Women Against Pornography slide show in an optional evening session. I was in trouble immediately.

I asked other tutors if they would take small discussion groups after the slide show, because a very large number of students had chosen to attend and needed small groups in which to air their reactions. Students from one group subsequently complained that the tutor who was with them tried to calm down their rage and horror by telling them that the slides needed to be seen in their context, that they were just representations, (those familiar with cultural studies argot will recognise this common ploy to deflect women's fury at images of womanhating), and that women could not know what men would make of these images. The tutor said that one of the most shocking, a woman being passed head first through a meat grinder with only her legs showing, was really a joke and should not be taken seriously. Some of the students were well aware of what men would make of such slides, since they had had pornography used on them as children by male relatives. What men make of pornography is not obscure to women.

I objected in support of these students, at the way their rightful outrage at the slides had been invalidated by a tutor. Yet I understood that I was likely not to be reappointed. The sexual liberal tutor was complaining about the slides being shown because they 'upset' women. It is usual for the anti-censors to campaign for freedom of expression. One might naively have expected that the anti-censors would support the right of women to see what is actually in porn magazines. But the usual concerns of the freedom lobby go out of the window when it comes to feminist anti-porn campaigners. The rights of the pornographers to produce and market porn are to be protected along with the right of men to see porn and to take women to see porn in contexts of their choosing, i.e. porn cinemas, or their living rooms, but the right of feminists to show women pornography in a political context is not to be defended.

In response to expressions of concern by tutors and students at the failure to reappoint me, I received a letter from the chair of the course team. She said that she had received complaints that the showing of the slide show had caused stress to tutors and students. She explained that she did not see the decision she had made as a political or discriminatory one.

In the USA, a campaign named FACT (Feminist Anti-Censorship Task Force) was set up to prevent adoption in any state of the Dworkin/MacKinnon ordinance which would allow women hurt in pornography to use civil rights law to take action against the pornographers. They are anti-censors, but whenever they were asked to debate the 'censorship' issue with feminist campaigners they stipulated that they would only debate if the feminists did not show pornography. They said it was manipulative to show pornography when you wanted to discuss it. An odd argument since one might have thought that knowledge was strength. I believe the reason for the ban was that they know that the majority of women when faced with porn in a context chosen by feminists are so horrified that they will listen to no arguments about how it is educational, only representation and so on. They will be angry.

Censorship does not just work to prevent feminists from showing pornography to women. The politics of radical and revolutionary feminists are routinely censored by the sexual liberal establishment. In the early days of revolutionary feminism in this country we were censored by methods such as the leaving of our resolutions off conference agendas, attempts to get our papers removed from conferences, being left off lists to chair workshops, and having our workshops or papers left off conference schedules. Such censorship was never acknowledged. It was always an 'accident'. If such censorship was and is operated even within the WLM, it should not surprise us that it operates in the academic world.

Over the last two years I have been censored in various ways at academic women's studies conferences that I have volunteered or been invited to speak at in the USA. At a New England Women's Studies Association conference I offered to speak on my work on feminist campaigners against male violence in the late nineteenth century. A FACT member who worked on how porn could be useful to women was found to be on a panel with me. I would have understood it had the organisers wanted me to share a panel with a historian with a very different perspective, but I was angry that they had selected a contemporary pro-porn campaigner to oppose my historical work. I refused to participate. Can we imagine that if a sexual libertarian historian like Linda Gordon or Judith Walkowitz volunteered to talk on her research, the conference organisers would scurry about to find a member of Women Against Pornography to set alongside her? Of course not. It is revolutionary feminist history which must be challenged at all costs by whoever can be found, whilst sexual libertarian history is accepted as 'truth'. My historical work is regarded by the sexual liberals who control the women's studies establishment in the USA as almost as alarming as actually showing porn to women.

In October 1986 I was invited to speak at a conference entitled 'Feminism, sexuality and power' organised by the women's studies departments of the five colleges in the valley in NW Massachusetts. The keynote speaker, i.e. she who set the tone of the conference, was Gayle Rubin, leading proponent of sado-masochism in the USA. I was asked to be the endnote speaker and decided to speak on the title 'Eroticising women's subordination: sexology from Havelock Ellis to Gayle Rubin'. The vast majority of speakers were sexual libertarians, opposed to radical feminist sexual politics. The only radical feminist speakers, apart from myself, were Janice Raymond and Julia Penelope. Rubin ensured that extra sexual libertarian speakers were recruited when she knew the title of my talk. I found out two weeks before I was due to fly over for a couple of days to speak that two libertarians including an editor of an 'erotica' magazine, had been put on immediately before me. To me, in England, this felt like intimidation. Was pornography, a hugely acceptable multi-billion dollar industry, really in need of so much protection against me? One of these speakers later compared me with the moral majority leader, Jerry Falwell, in a write up of the conference. Women's studies in the US is dangerous territory for radical and revolutionary feminist politics and I fear that women's studies in this country is going the same way.

These are but a very tiny number of examples of the way that censorship works against the voicing of radical or revolutionary feminist politics or the showing of pornography to women. Sometimes those of us who campaign uncompromisingly for the elimination of porn and men's abuse of women in the sex industry, sexual violence, child rape, feel entirely boxed in by the hostility of the supposed pro-feminist, liberal and progressive, academic, cultural and media establishment in this country and in the USA. I make a point of showing how this censorship works because, ironically, it is feminist anti-porn campaigners who are accused of being 'censors'. In fact we are often represented as terrifying moral majority ogres with huge political clout who are a threat to the liberties of artists, writers and creators of 'representations' and, of course, pornographers.

Just to put the record straight, it should be explained that feminists in Britain have never supported legislation against pornography in the form of censorship laws. USA feminists have supported the Dworkin/MacKinnon ordinance which does not empower the state to take any action against pornography, but only empowers individual women harmed by porn to take action under civil law. In Britain, civil law does not allow for such eventualities and, as yet, no legal formulation has been suggested which would thus empower women rather than the state. Anti-porn feminists are called censors in Britain for making, when they get the opportunity, a political critique of pornography. This critique declares porn to be both the propaganda of womanhatred and a guidebook to the abuse of women. It sees porn as a source of serious abuse to the women used in the industry and to all those women whose civil liberties are infringed by a product which silences all women by showing us simply as holes and pieces of meat which enjoy and lust after abuse.

What motivates those who would deny feminist anti-porn campaigners a platform? The anger and hatred which this feminist campaign has met with from men and women who see themselves as progressive is unparalleled when compared with other feminist campaigns.

One reason is that porn reveals the hatred of women built into the construction of male sexuality in a particularly clear way. The porn industry is massive and the values of porn are clearly derogatory to women in a way which does shock. The idea that so many men share such values is horrifying to women, and for those who do not want to face what porn reveals about male supremacy, the only solution is to make the feminists who show porn into the enemy instead of men. It is difficult to live with the knowledge of what the majority of men think about women. It can make life almost unbearable. For those women not prepared to take on the burden of such knowledge it makes sense to blame and fight feminists instead of male power.

Men who support the pornographic consumption of women have good practical reasons to oppose the feminist critique of porn. They have every reason to want to keep the sex industry under wraps, so that the abuse of women is available to suit their desires but not available to the prying eyes of other women. But the reason for the 'progressive' intellectuals, the sexual libertarians, to fight feminists on this issue goes further than that. The 'progressive' left sexual agenda for women has always been based upon more 'sexual freedom' for men, meaning more sexual servicing from women. The feminist agenda of the transformation of male sexuality from its present aggressive exploitative form to one more suited to women's health and safety fills such 'progressive' men with alarm. They stand to lose the agenda set in the 60s 'sexual revolution' before feminists got uppity. 'Progressive' left men have sought to gain women's support for their male sexual freedom agenda on the grounds that it was about our sexual freedom, too. Whilst men retain power and control under male supremacy and seek to act out unchanged a sexuality based upon objectification and the eroticising of women's subordination, sexual freedom for women can be only very limited in scope. It consists in effect of saying 'Yes, lovely' to anything men demand. Saying 'no' and 'we demand total change' is not seen as sexual freedom because of course it would restrict the freedom of men and interfere with their prerogative. Also feminist demands are not seen as amusing or fun, and sex is supposed to be both.

Behind the alarm of 'progressive' male opponents lies not just fear

of losing sexual prerogative, but anxiety about the maintenance of
the foundations of male supremacy itself. Male supremacy is
organised through heterosexuality. The foundation of the family in
which men are served emotionally, economically and through
·domestic labour, is sexual intercourse. This is not an option for
women, but a practice into which women are directed by restriction
of opportunities, punishment for erring, and propaganda from the
moment of birth. This intercourse is both a metaphor for male
dominance, a means of enforcing it, and a means of justifying it.
Questioning of the sexual system through which women's oppression is maintained threatens the basis of men's power. The
feminist critique of pornography challenges the notion that
women's subordination should be sexy for men and for women, too,
and so poses a challenge not just to men's pleasures, but to the·
organisation of the heteropatriarchy.

There are men who support the feminist sexual agenda, but their
opposition to the 'sexual freedom' lobby has been very muted up to
now. I hope that this is not because they fear the disapproval they
will face from other men if they make a public stand. It is important
that these men break ranks. Men who wish to express support must
not just do so privately. They need to get writing and speaking
out.

Women's opposition to feminist anti-porn campaigners is less
simple to explain. For some women it's a simple 'job's worth'
equation. Women do not progress in male-dominated worlds such
as academe, media, or left politics by challenging the basic
organisation of the heteropatriarchy or by being seen to have
allowed feminists to do so on their patch. They do progress by
adopting the male sexual agenda and saying that this is actually a
feminist agenda.

Another reason for women's opposition is that we have all, as
women, been trained to eroticise our own subordination and to call
that pleasure and freedom. The sexual liberals argue that if we have
a sexual response to anything then that must be good and positive.
This is clearly not true, since women can orgasm during rape and
sexual abuse, and men do so when torturing and killing women, as
in Vietnam. But some women who have a sexual response to porn,
particularly really degrading and humiliating porn, can persuade
themselves that their bodies and souls would not lie, therefore it
must be the feminists who encourage them to mistrust such
responses who are the problem and are to be fought.

There is another possible reaction to discovering that you are 'turned on' by porn. That is to recognise with rage the extent to which our deep emotions and sexual responses have been tuned to make us complicit in our own oppression and to take pleasure from it. Every woman grows up in a heteropatriarchal world. Every woman learnt her emotional and sexual responses in an unequal situation. We may respond sexually to the degradation of women in porn, fantasy, etc, to a greater or lesser extent, but we have the same problem. We need to reconstruct our own sexuality whilst forcing men to reconstruct theirs. The answer to being turned on by porn is not to attack the feminist campaigners who are revealing the problem. Women promoters of sado-masochism have been in the forefront of the anti-feminist backlash. They have decided to defend their sexual responses to the degradation of women through a frontal assault on feminism. Anti-porn campaigners have sexual responses to porn too, but we choose to fight pornographers. It is perhaps the greatest tragedy of our oppression that it can be from images and fantasies of that very oppression that we draw what we have been encouraged to see as empowering, and liberating, i.e. sexual pleasure. The fact that porn can turn us on should empower our rage not our complacence.

But what can be done about the censorship of revolutionary and radical feminism? Students should be critical of their booklists, audiences of the media, everyone should be suspicious of the politics of those 'progressive' men who seek to deracinate feminism by promoting the version that they see as most supportive of their interests. You will notice the satisfaction which it affords some left gay males to hold up lesbian sado-machochists as the 'real' feminists. These men are not at all keen on revolutionary feminists who demand changes which threaten their pleasures. We should all be asking 'Where is the rev/rad feminist viewpoint?', 'Where is the critique of the eroticising of power imbalance?', 'Am I getting a full picture of what feminists think of porn and SM?' Demand your right to know sisters. Help to end censorship today.

THERE SHOULD BE A LAW AGAINST IT . . . SHOULDN'T THERE?

Wendy Moore

If women are ever to be treated as equal members of society something must be done to change the way they are portrayed in the media. The media shapes our perceptions of each other. It influences our expectations and self image. It helps create a climate where women are treated as inferior beings and where our needs and desires — whether for freely available childcare or top careers — come second place to men's. It implicitly supports discrimination against women, which in turn is a major determinant in prompting violence against us. But what can be done since persuasion and education have achieved little success? The most common and often the most effective way of protecting vulnerable people from fear and injury is to introduce legislation. Surely then, there should be a law to protect women from the harmful effects of degrading images in the media. But such a suggestion is immediately greeted by allegations of censorship. Is this fair?

Censorship like freedom is an entirely subjective term (although we can strive for collective agreement on what is acceptable and non-acceptable censorship). All but the most far-right libertarians support 'censorship' when it suits them. All of us protest at attacks on our freedom when we are prevented from doing something we wish to. The arguments are all relative. But in Indianapolis, legislation which, for the first time, restricted the publication of pornographic material was overturned before it could even be used because the pornographers pleaded their right to free speech. Indianapolis city council accepted evidence at a public hearing that pornography could cause violence to women. But the publishers successfully argued that legislation which prevented them printing pornography amounted to censorship, infringing their right to free speech under the First Amendment of the American constitution. In Britain, moves to bring in similar kinds of legislation which would curb pornography and other discriminatory portrayal of women are now also being attacked as censorship. Such legislation would restrict the so-called freedom of the media, it is said.

Feminists must thoroughly debate whether or not the law could provide some improvement in the way women are portrayed in the media. But we should not be sidetracked by allegations that such a move would be of itself censorship. Legislation might prove ineffectual. It might be rendered useless by the male-dominated and often anti-women judiciary. It might conceivably be used against rather than for us to, for example, prohibit lesbian erotica which poses no threat to women, rather than prohibiting the pornographic and sexist material which poses a daily threat. If legislation were misused in that way, we might justifiably complain of censorship. But the principle of a law which would protect women against the fear and sometimes violence which can result from sexist or pornographic material — a law intended to safeguard the fragile rights of women — should not of itself be described as censorship.

Under British law, unlike in the United States, members of the public are not assigned specific rights. Instead the law lays down what is not allowed. All of British legislation, therefore, is censorious in that it prohibits people from carrying out certain acts. Much of our legal system, although obviously imperfect, is designed to protect the rights and the freedom of individuals, particularly vulnerable individuals. Therefore, it is against the law to murder, to rape, to injure, and to steal. Such laws are inevitably restrictive of individual rights — restricting the 'right' to kill, maim, rape and rob. But such restrictions are, of course, accepted because it is universally recognised that a free and democratic society entails abiding by laws which protect individuals, especially from those with more power, whether through strength, status or economics.

The same principles apply to legislation covering the media. The media does not, by and large, have specific rights under British law. Instead journalists are covered by the same laws as everyone else and work within the confines of those laws. Freedom of the press is a notion which is bounded by the laws which govern all society. The press in this country is 'free' under legislation only in as much as it does not contravene the law.

A wide range of legislation already governs what the media — or for that matter anyone else — can publish. Journalists are bound by, among others, laws of defamation; laws preventing the identification of rape victims or defendants, and of juveniles; laws governing the reporting of court cases and criminal charges; by the Official Secrets Act; the Rehabilitation of Offenders Act and by the Race Relations Act. They are restricted too from publishing what is deemed 'blasphemous' or 'obscene' material. In broadcasting specific regulatons apply which lay down standards of quality.

Quite clearly, then, legislation is by no means a new phenomenon to the media, and fairly heavy restrictions already govern what can be printed or broadcast. And even the most libertarian of civil rights campaigners would not oppose laws which restrict journalists from printing the names of women who have been raped or children who appear in court. Neither do they call for the repeal of the Race Relations Act, which, for all its ineffectuality, deters journalists or members of the National Front from printing overtly racist material.

Society also clearly accepts the need for laws to limit unproven allegations, despite their curtailment of free speech, because it is accepted that the press should not have unbridled freedom to print whatever it wishes about people, regardless of its inaccuracy or the damage it causes (although sadly the existing libel laws are far from effective in delivering this aim). Indeed a major complaint against the libel laws is that they are currently open only to the wealthy who can afford the huge costs of going to court. Some media campaigners would go further still and are keen to extend the regulations which govern the media, to introduce effective curbs on accuracy and distortion.

It is absurd, therefore, given all the existing restraints to suggest that introducing one more law with the aim of protecting the rights of women against attack in the media, is of itself censorship. Significantly, one of the few laws restricting journalists which has been described as censorship is the Race Relations Act, which makes it an offence to publish 'threatening or abusive matter likely to stir up racial hatred'. This protective law has been cited as a possible model for legislation protecting women's rights within the media. It is no coincidence that mainly white, male journalists and lawyers isolate the Race Relations Act and moves to adopt legislation curbing degrading images of women as threats of 'censorship'. They see such legislation in terms of restricting the 'rights' of the media, ignoring the existence of other restrictive laws which they deem as acceptable and denying the rights to protection for vulnerable groups such as black people and women. Laws which protect people's rights are an essential ingredient of a democratic society, whether or not they curtail the rights of the media. Indeed in some instances it is *from* the power of the media that such laws protect.

So, when we discuss the desirability or otherwise of using the legislative system to protect women, we need first of all to reclaim the language. Andrea Dworkin in her analysis of pornography 'Pornography — men possessing women',[1] rightly ascribes the 'power of naming' to men. The male-dominated media uses language to make women invisible, to make women possessions, to undermine women and the issues which matter to them and to reduce women to objects of sexual desire. But we must not allow the power of male language to stifle our debate on how to deal with sexism. In America it was the pornographers, the enemies of women, who contorted language to cite 'freedom of speech' as a defence for the publication of pornography. As women, we cannot accept such a definition of free speech. Under any democratic system of law, free speech is necessarily curtailed by restrictions.

As women we have been denied the most basic of civil liberties all of our lives, in the name of men's freedom — freedom to insult, offend, injure and possess. It is time we demanded our own definition of freedom. And in a society which sets down basic freedoms by law — by virtue of prohibiting activities which are accepted as anti-social — we are surely right to demand a law which would protect women from both the offensive existence and the effect of sexist and pornographic material in the media.

The principle of legislation must be a fair one. But before we rush to grab the nearest bill we must think carefully through all of the practicalities. The question we should be asking is not whether the concept of legislation is acceptable, but whether legislation can actually achieve what we want.

What kind of legislation might work?

Since we do not live in a perfect world, we do not get the laws or the legal system we deserve. Not all laws are designed to protect individual rights and freedoms — or for that matter to promote democracy. In addition laws do not always do what they set out to do. The most perfect of laws is only as good as the imperfect legal system which applies it. Thus the Obscene Publications Act is notoriously used by the homophobic police and court system to confiscate material which is deemed 'obscene' purely by virtue of its relating to lesbian or gay sex. Likewise judges have often misused protective laws, freeing a rapist because he 'only' raped his wife or excusing violence because it was 'only' directed against a woman. At the same time laws are brought in or are used to safeguard and extend the power of Government, regardless of their curtailment of individuals' or the media's rights. The Official Secrets Acts, with its catch-all Section II is used to prohibit, whenever convenient, the publication of any 'unauthorised' government material. This is an obvious example of a law which is used by the powerful to curtail both the freedom of the media to report and of the public to know.

To focus on the practicalities, rather than principles, of legislation, and avoid the pitfalls it is essential to set our aims into the context of both the politics of the media and our beliefs as feminists.

The way women are portrayed in the media is part and parcel of the politics of the media as a whole. The fact that ownership of the media in this country is concentrated in the hands of a few extremely wealthy men is a major factor in the way the media treats women. In such a system women are denied access at every level. Women join journalism in roughly equal numbers to men. But they drop out at a much higher rate and those who remain are largely excluded from positions of power or national influence. The male-domination of journalism means issues of interest to men dominate the media and that issues are seen from a male perspective. Topics of particular relevance to women or from a woman's point of view are mainly absent. The way that journalists are trained, usually by fellow male journalists or by college lecturers who are ex-journalists, reinforces this mode of working. It also means that negative images of women are not challenged, have become acceptable and indeed the norm. Journalists gather their news most commonly from the main institutions within society — central and local government, the civil service, the courts, the police — which are also heavily male-dominated. They scarcely approach the organisations in which women are organised — which are few anyway — except to ridicule. And women have little opportunity to seek redress. Their complaints, to the Press Council or Broadcasting Complaints Commission or direct to the media, are usually ignored or undermined.

The entire system, therefore, has to change in order to improve the way women are portrayed. A whole package of reforms is needed to introduce equal access to the media at every level for women (and for everyone else who has so far been denied access too). Such reforms would include restrictions on the monopoly ownership of the press, a statutory right to know, real media accountability, workers' participation, a strictly adhered to code of practice setting out journalistic standards, and an accessible, accountable system for people seeking redress. The media manifesto of the Campaign for Press and Broadcasting freedom sets out the recipe for reform in detail.[3] Some measures would be achieved through legislation — such as freedom of information act, limits on media ownership and a statutory right of reply to correct inaccuracies in the press or broadcasting, overseen by a Media Commission. The Media Commission would replace both the Press Council and the Broadcasting Complaints Commission with a representative and accountable body responsible for promoting good standards in journalism. It would lay down guidelines, based on the National Union of Journalists' code of conduct,[2] for the industry to follow and would issue specific guidance as necessary on topical issues. It would support and advise members of the public with media complaints. The Media Commission would be complemented by a Media Enterprise Board, dealing with the commercial side of the industry. The board would provide enterprise grants and loans to generate new and diverse publications. It could give priority to publications where gaps currently exist and should ensure new ventures promote equality in employment as well as through their publications. At the same time a greatly strengthened Advertising Standards Council could effectively regulate standards in advertising. Other changes would be achieved through longer term efforts of education and campaigning. All would contribute in some way towards improving the portrayal of women.

But what about specific legislation to restrict negative images of women and promote positive ones? Before setting off down this road we have to be clear about our aims and principles and not concentrate solely on end results. Allying with the moral Right for example might achieve the end result of banning some sexually explicit material. But at what price?

Lisa Duggan in this book argues that the Indianapolis legislation was the result of an alliance, though mainly unwillingly, between some radical feminists led by Andrea Dworkin and Catharine MacKinnon and a coalition of far-right groups. Duggan rightly rings alarm bells at the manipulation of feminist aims by strongly anti-feminist organisations whose main purpose in attacking pornography is to eliminate what they view as 'a threat to the sanctity and authority of the patriarchal family'. A similar alliance in Britain would be not only foolish but dangerous in the extreme. We should make no mistake that the aims and principles of right wing groups in this country, though keen to stamp out pornography, are entirely at odds with feminism. As feminists, our aim is to reduce unrealistic stereotypes and pictorial images of women which, because of the context they are shown in — portraying women as inferior, sexually available and inviting violence — both help create and reinforce inequalities in society. But we will fight to maintain our rights over our own bodies, to choice of sexuality, to unrepressed portrayal of equal sex and frank sex education. This is of course an entirely different standpoint from that of right wing moralists whose aim is to prohibit anything and everything which conflicts with their narrow view of acceptable society. Their perverse logic enables the Right to voice outrage at a scene showing sexual intercourse in the BBC serial 'The Singing Detective', while guffawing at serious attempts by MP Clare Short to introduce a ban on what Conservative MPs deem 'harmless' Page 3 pictures in newspapers.

If any doubt lingered about the intentions of the right, then recent moves by the Thatcher government make brutally clear their motives. Thatcher's plan to set up a broadcasting standards council, chaired by William Rees-Mogg, has been hailed as a bid to crack down on 'sex and violence' on television. But that stated claim is obviously not founded in logic since the worst portrayal of both sex and violence is undeniably in newspapers and the IBA and BBC governors already enjoy quite sufficient powers to curb broadcasting. The reality is that it is undoubtedly a move to introduce for the first time in this country a team of censors editing programmes for their political content. As a *New Statesman* editorial (20 May 1988) succinctly explained, it will be only such sexual material which offers an alternative view or which threatens the perceived idea of the nuclear family which will come under threat. '"Taste" is in fact a synonym for political and cultural controversy', the editorial right concludes.

The way to ensure we achieve what we want without either compromising our principles or playing into the hands of the right is to set down basic but strict criteria by which to measure any proposal for legislation. A great deal of work would have to go into drawing up adequate criteria. But they should include at least the following:
* Firstly, legislation would have to be universally accessible. That

means it must be simple to understand, easy to use (ideally backed up by specialist advisers) and not restricted by wealth (in other words open to legal aid).

* Secondly, it has to be effective. That means it needs to act as a real deterrent either through financial or other punitive means.

* Thirdly, it should aim to curb all types of degrading images and not just isolate one aspect, such as pornography. Most likely a number of different legislative measures would be the answer.

* Finally, it should hit its target squarely and not leave ambiguities which allow it to attack unintentional targets. That almost certainly means, at least until we get a sympathetic judiciary, it will have to spell out quite distinctly clear definitions of the images it seeks to prevent. It certainly means it will have to ensure that images are seen in their true context. It is gratuitous sexually explicit material which should be curbed and not that which is relevant in the context of education or public interest.

A further aim of legislation, which may not be immediately realisable, is to ensure the legal decision-making process is representative and accountable. That would mean appointing a body to oversee the legislation which gave full representation to women and which was appointed or elected in a democratic way. Such a body might be the Media Commission proposed elsewhere or a body set up especially for the purpose — perhaps a massively revamped Equal Opportunities Commission. In the meantime the existing tribunals system would be a generally safer bet than the civil or criminal courts.

It is unlikely that one legislative measure on its own would have much impact on improving the portrayal of women. A straight-forward ban on pornography, for example, might turn out to be the most ineffective way of tackling the pornography problem. Under such a law pornography might simply go 'underground', rendering it all the more difficult to fight. The purpose of any kind of reform, whether legislative or voluntary, should be to tackle the whole range of ways in which women are undermined through the media. Pornography may be the most shocking example of the media attacking women but it is just one extreme in a spectrum of degrading images. To focus solely on pornography as Andrea Dworkin does distorts the reality of the media's impact. The daily production in newspapers of pictures of topless women apparently making themselves sexually available to male readers, the ordeal of being confronted with unreal and offensive images of women on advertising hoardings and the way in which journalists regularly produce narrow and misleading stereotypes of women are at least as effective as pornography in perpetuating discrimination. So any legislation which is to be effective must deal with the whole range of ways women are portrayed and in all the different media.

Could legislation work?

We can draft our ideal form of legislation but would it work in practice? In debating whether the law can provide us with some solutions to the way women are portrayed in the media it is important to have realistic expectations. Even the most perfectly drafted legislation could not alone provide the solution. The limitations on legislation and its enforcement are substantial. Legislation may prove to be one element of a range of changes needed to tackle the problem. It may help achieve concrete changes and it may help to shape attitudes to contribute to other forms of change. But it cannot possible provide the whole answer. We should ask whether through legislation we can gain more than we would lose. In assessing this it is essential to understand how the legal system works and to learn from past experience of attempting to use laws to improve rights for women.

In her analysis of legislating for equality, *The Politics of Women's Rights*,[3] April Carter details the various problems associated with using the law. Legislation, she points out, cannot change deep-seated attitudes; pitfalls in legislation are exploited by those who wish to avoid its impact; and laws can promote lip-service to equality while failing to bring about any real change. She charts in particular the record of the Sex Discrimination and Equal Pay Acts, for which feminists fought hard but with often disappointing results. But she argues that passing a law instills moral authority, it influences public opinion and it empowers oppressed groups with the knowledge that equality is a right rather than a privilege. British society, she says, is particularly hesitant about using the law, compared to the trend in America, perhaps inspired by the US Bill of Rights. but the mood is slowly changing here with people proving more and more willing to assert their rights through the courts. One reason, she suggests, is the power of the European Court of Justice which has prompted extensions to equality legislation in this country. She concludes that using the law is a 'slow and frustrating process'. Nevertheless legislation has brought about real improvement for women in employment and even inadequate legislaton helps change general attitudes, influences women's own expectations and encourages them to fight for their rights.

If we aim to campaign for legislation to tackle portrayal in the media we need to acknowledge the likely limitations. We would be certain to encounter technical problems with the legislation itself. But this should not necessarily deter us. Almost all British law has benefitted from progressive amendments. Certainly the EPA and SDA both suffered initially from technical pitfalls, but later amendments and changes forced on the government by the EEC have improved their effectiveness. We would be bound to face problems with the offenders devising ways of avoiding prosecution. But again this need not put us off, since the law would still be likely to make their business more difficult, less respectable and, more importantly, more expensive. Perhaps the greatest drawback, however, is the way in which any legislation would be enforced. The issue is who controls the legislation. Obviously there must be major problems in expecting the establishment, which we are trying to change, to bring about alterations on itself.

Indeed it seems particularly curious that Andrea Dworkin ever contemplated using the male-dominated courts having so brutally condemned all men. Resorting to legislation, inevitably means expecting the male-dominated legal profession, government and judiciary to bring about changes which will work against them. This could have several results. It may mean, as in the early days of the EPA and SDA, that decisions will be clearly prejudiced against women. It may mean that the law we devise to improve our rights is used by men against us to limit our rights, by, for example, targeting lesbian erotica rather than anti-women pornography. It may be used by the powerful influences of the Right as a weapon to impose narrow concepts of morality. We must be honest and accept that almost certainly the existing structures of society will conspire to blunt any legislative instrument we can devise. We could therefore do two things. We could abandon all proposals for legislation on the grounds that a perfect world does not exist in which such laws could operate. But the logic of this approach would mean opposing all use of the law, whether general or specifically for women. It is unrealistic to oppose legislation on the grounds of spurious purity. So instead we could campaign for legislation designed as best we can to obviate its limitations. That could mean, for example, ensuring that women are financially and structurally backed in using legislation. It should mean ensuring women play at least an equal role in decision-making, perhaps by calling for equal numbers of women in tribunal hearings. It means avoiding the hierarchical legal system as much as possible by setting up or using an existing commission of appointed or elected members more likely to sympathise with our aims.

It would be foolish to expect miracles. The law is only as good, and usually much worse than, the rest of society. It would be naive to expect to achieve any of our aims under the current Thatcher regime. The perfect law has to be seen as a long term ambition. We must be as sure as possible of the legislation we want to introduce and how it will be controlled. But we must be aware too that legislation would not of itself bring about dramatic and concrete change. And any effect it did have would be slow to emerge. But it would give official state backing to women's fight to improve the way they are portrayed in the media. It would almost certainly achieve significant changes in society's attitude towards images of women in media. It would provide women who have campaigned against such images with a new weapon to tackle them. It would give women who have quietly suffered under degrading images a new confidence to oppose such discrimination. And surely, after all, it is these things we are trying to achieve.

Footnotes

1. *Pornography: Men Possessing Women*, Andrea Dworkin, The Women's Press, 1981.
2. NUJ Code of Conduct, Clause 10 states: 'A journalist shall only mention a person's race, colour, creed, illegitimacy, marital status (or lack of it), gender, sexual orientation, age or disability if this information is strictly relevant. A journalist shall neither originate nor process material which encourages discrimination on any of the above-mentioned grounds.
3. *The Politics of Women's Rights*, April Carter, Longmans, 1988.

SHOULD IT BE UNLAWFUL TO INCITE SEXUAL VIOLENCE?

Sona Osman

Can there be legislation to create an offence of incitement to sexual violence/hatred against women in the same way as there is an offence of incitement to racial hatred against Black people? This is a topical subject, as a group was recently launched supporting the introduction of legislaion to outlaw certain kinds of pornography on the grounds that it is sex discrimination. This group then split into two different groups: the Campaign Against Pornography (CAP), supported by *Everywoman* magazine, and the Campaign Against Pornography and Censorship (CPC), which includes Cathy Itzin, a member of the Women's Rights Committee for the National Council of Civil Liberties, and a chief instigator of the original group.

The idea for this kind of legislation came from the States, where Itzin saw various attempts being made to pass anti-porn ordinances (discussed elsewhere in this book). Itzin envisages that a Bill would work in the same way as, she seems to postulate, the Race Relations Act 1976 and the Public Order Act 1986 have made racism illegal.[1] She has made such a statement without realising the implications of it. The race relations legislation *has* attempted to make discrimination on the grounds of race illegal, but we must all be aware that this is not the same as making racism illegal. No law can do this. Racism is a subjective process by which an individual or group of people have been influenced by the way that society has conditioned them. Britain was an imperial power: she once ruled territories around the globe. It follows that British history and culture have been imbued with a British colonial view — white supremacy. Racism has definitely not been made illegal or eradicated by the Public Order Act.

In assessing the viability of modelling an offence of incitement to sexual hatred on that of incitement to racial hatred, there are two things to point out initially. Firstly, there are two particular differences in the legal systems of the US and the UK which relate to the current discussion: the sources of law, and the existence of class actions. In the US, federal, state and local governments can pass laws, but they can also be challenged in the courts on the basis that any law is unconstitutional. Britain does not have a written constitution or a Bill of Rights, so the same situation could never arise. Also in the US, class actions are used in civil and civil liberty cases, where one person acts as a representative for the group of people bringing the action. Class actions are hard on the representative, who needs a lot of time and money to survive the case. In Britain class actions do not exist; an individual can bring a case on their own behalf only.

Secondly, there are the differences, in the UK, between the civil and criminal courts. Civil actions are those which deal with the rights of individuals and give rise to the awarding of damages where for example, an individual proves negligence, breach of contract, unlawful discrimination or dismissal. Criminal actions are those brought by the state; its sanctions are penal. The Race Relations Act is a civil law, whereas the Public Order Act is a criminal law.

Itzin has been heavily influenced by the US radical feminism of Andrea Dworkin and Catharine MacKinnon, the latter a lawyer. During the course of the passing of the Minneapolis ordinance, pornography was defined by them as a violation of women's civil rights, and as such women were entitled to claim damages from the manufacturers of porn in the civil courts.

In Indianapolis however, publishers and distributors of pornography banded together and obtained an injunction preventing the operation of a similar law as soon as it was passed. The case went to the US Supreme Court, and they ruled that 'free speech' as practised by pornographers had to be safeguarded. Itzin refers to this ruling as being a statement about the status and value of women, not unlike that of 'negroes in the USA in the 1850s'. At that time 'the US Supreme Court felt it was more important to safeguard the constitution by keeping negroes in slavery than to recognise their full citizenship. The analogy of slavery and racism with pornography and women is appropriate.'[2]

Then suddenly, in the same article, Itzin makes a transatlantic leap and begins to point to British legislation, referring particularly to the offence of incitement to racial hatred, which 'through the publication, distribution or use of threatening, abusive or insulting words , behaviour or written material is recognised as resulting in race discrimination and the mistreatment of black people (including violence). It is illegal: legislated against in the Race Relations Act 1976 and the Public Order Act 1986.'[3]

Can the UK Race Relations Legislation be Used as a Model?

The inspiration for Itzin's views has been the US experience, but how far can this be transferred to Britain? Although I agree with some of what she has to say about the universality of women's oppression, I disagree with how she draws a direct analogy between the position of women and Black people. Importantly, our experiences as Black people are so different that any attempt to blanket us into one group is simplistic and lacks analysis. The experience of the slaves in the US is totally different from the experience of the Black immigrants to Britain who arrived in their 'mother country' after the Second World War. Any attempt by a white woman to band Black people from the US and the UK as one group sharing a common history is dangerous and disrespectful. In short I do not think it is right to draw an analogy between 'the Black Triangle' (i.e. the slave trade) with the history of Black post-war immigration to Britain.

My second area of contention with Itzin is that, judging from her interview in *Everywoman* (May 1987) and her article in the *London Daily News* (24 April 1987) she appears to be somewhat confused between the Race Relations Acts and the Public Order Acts. She states that 'race discrimination and the mistreatment of black people (including violence), has been made illegal in the Race Relations Act 1976 and the Public Order Act 1986'. Yet these two Acts have been passed along two very different tracks and to draw them together as Itzin is attempting to do is very misleading and confusing.

The Race Relations Legislation

There have been a series of Race Relations Acts, which have been passed just before or just after the passing of an Immigration Act restricting entry for Black people, particularly those from the Indian sub-continent. A cynical view would be that although successive British governments want to control the influx of Black people into this country to appease their racist voters, they also have to offer something in return to the emerging British Black population. Thus successive governments have offered us the Race Relations Acts with their sections outlawing race discrimination, and with the Commission for Racial Equality, which is supposed to be working away towards the elimination of discrimination.

And yet, as Black people who live and work in the UK, we have the day-to-day reality of knowing that those aims and objectives are not even half met. Sure we know, if we have access to the information, that we have a legal redress if we can prove that we were directly or indirectly discriminated against on the grounds of race. But what if we do not know that vital information or where to go for help? What if we are so worn down by living in a racist state that we do not have the energy to pursue a claim, or are sceptical of its value? Passing a law, in itself, could potentially be a good thing, but it is not enough to pass a law and then imagine the problem is solved. All the factors which oppress people, including society's attitudes, need to be considered, so that other measures which are required to make the law effective and to remove oppression are not neglected.

And of course the Race Relations legislation does not take on board the subtleties of racism. Sometimes it is very difficult to pin down a statement, a comment, a posture as racist if it is made by a sophisticated person. (It could also be pointed out how totally ineffectual the existing sex discrimination legislation is, for very similar reasons.)

Incitement to Racial Hatred

This offence is very different from anything contained in the Race Relations Acts, although confusingly, the first reference to incitement to racial hatred was created by the Race Relations Act 1965, as previously contained in Section 5a of the Public Order Act 1936. Before these acts were passed, there were other ways of penalising such conduct, under the common law offences of seditious libel, public mischief or criminal libel. The 1936 Act was passed to appease the Jewish Establishment's fear with regard to the rise of the British Union of Fascists and to deal with the battles in the East End of London between the Union and the Jewish community. 'The major areas on which public opinion had been crystallising were the desirability of banning provocative marches, measures to deal with racial incitement and the banning of political uniforms.'[4] The most important provision was Section 5, which made it an offence for any person, in any public place or at any public meeting, to use 'threatening, abusive or insulting words or behaviour, with intent to provoke a breach of the peace or whereby a breach of the peace is likely to be occasioned.' The maximum punishment for a breach of section 5 was three months imprisonment or a fine of £50, and offences were triable only at summary level, that is, they could only be tried in the Magistrates Court.

Historically, there is a dispute as to whether this section had any impact, and if so, what? The official view was that despite the moderate level of these penalties, Section 5 achieved an immediate result, with police shorthand writers regularly attending meetings of the British Union of Fascists in search of threatening, abusive or insulting words and finding them.[5] The first conviction for insulting words was against a speaker in London's East End who referred at an open-air meeting to 'dirty, mongrel Russian Jews' and declared that 'Jews are the lice of the earth and must be exterminated from the national life.' He was bound over for six months in the sum of £50 and threatened with imprisonment if he committed a further offence.[6]

There were also other prosecutions. However the Jewish working-class community in the East End began to lose their confidence in the police. 'As the year of 1936 drew to a close, he [the *Jewish Chronicle* special correspondent] claimed that the police had consciously or unconsciously supported the fascists. Through their failure to check slanderous and inflammatory statements it was, he concluded, "safer to be fascist than anti-fascist".[7]

The Act became law in 1937. In that year, there was a British Union of Fascists meeting in Hornsey, where many antisemitic statements were made and the stewards treated any opposition to the BUF in a brutal way. The Jewish community leaders were forced by these events to take a more sober view of the Act; for them 'the most discomforting feature was the apparent indifference of the police'.[8] Until then they had agreed with the official view that Section 5 was an unqualified benefit for the Jewish community.

Section 5 was considered to be effective mainly because of the key phrase 'threatening, abusive or insultng words', which was also used in subsequent legislation. These words were supposed to give the courts wide discretion in applying the law. But, of course, this discretion was used to maintain the status quo; during the Second World War, it led to the suppression of views which were critical of the government. In one case a man was imprisoned for two months for saying 'This rotten government is holding 390 million Indians in slavery' in the course of a speech.[9]

After the War, pressure increased for a change in the law and in particular for the creation of a specific offence of incitement to racial hatred. The Labour Party, committed to anti-incitement legislation, passed the first Race Relations Act in 1965. Section 6 of this Act said: 'A person shall be guilty of an offence under this Section if, with intent to stir up hatred against any section of the public in Great Britain distinguished by colour, race or ethnic or national origins, (a) he publishes or distributes written matter which is threatening, abusive or insulting; (b) he uses in any public place or at any public meeting words which are threatening, abusive or insulting, being matter or words likely to stir up hatred to that section on grounds of colour, race or ethnic or national origins.' The maximum penalty was imprisonment for six months and/or a fine of £200 on a summary conviction in the magistrates court. This offence could also be tried in the Crown Court. There, the maximum penalty was two years imprisonment and/or a fine of £1000. Prosecutions could only take place with the consent of the Attorney-General.

Many prosecutions would fail because of the need for proof of intent to stir up hatred. The first conviction under the 1965 Act was in 1966. Britton, a 17-year-old white labourer, stuck a leaflet printed by the Greater Britain Movement reading 'Blacks not wanted here' on the door of Sid Bidwell, MP. He was convicted at Middlesex Sessions in October 1966.[10] The conviction was later quashed on appeal, on the grounds that his actions did not amount to 'publication or distribution in terms of the provision'.[11] In 1967 there was the first prosecution against a Black person, Michael Abdul Malik, a prominent member of the Racial Adjustment Society, addressed a meeting at Reading. He was convicted of inciting racial hatred and sentenced to 12 months' imprisonment. His appeal was refused.[12] In the same year, four members of the Universal Coloured People's Association were also prosecuted for using words which were said to have stirred up hatred against white people at Speakers' Corner, Hyde Park, and were fined a total of £270.[13]

In sharp contrast, four members of the Racial Preservation Society were tried in March 1968 for incitement to racial hatred for distributing copies of the Society's *Southern News* in East Grinstead. It referred to the dangers of 'race mixing', attacked politicians as 'race levellers', and contained speculation about genetic differences between races and the dangers of racial contact. The defendants asserted that their broadsheet was an educational enterprise aimed at educating politicians with regard to prevalent immigration practices. They denied any attempt to attack Black immigrants. All the defendants were acquitted.[14]

Since the Tories came to power in 1979, there have been no major prosecutions for incitement to racial hatred. The last important prosecution, which took place after the repeal of the 1965 law and its replacement by the Race Relations Act 1976, was of John Kingsley Read for addressing a meeting on 12 June 1976, at which he said, 'I have been told I cannot refer to coloured immigrants, so you can forgive me if I refer to niggers, wogs and coons.' He then refused to the recent murder of Gurdip Singh Chaggar in Southall and said, 'Last week in Southall, one nigger stabbed another nigger. Very unfortunate. One down, a million to go.' The first jury could not come to a verdict about his comments, so there was a retrial. Judge McKinnon, who presided over this second trial, made his views known when he spoke to the jury. As far as he was concerned, the term 'niggers, wogs and coons' was jocular and he told them that when he was at school he was called 'nigger'. Not surprisingly, with a summing up like that, the jury acquitted Read. At the end of the trial McKinnon said, 'He is obviously a man who has had the guts to come forward in the past and stand up in public for things he believes in.'[15] The importance of this trial is that it demonstrates that even while supposedly effective legislation is on the statute book, somebody can still get away with making such blatantly racist comments.

Public Order Act 1986 Part 3

Part 3 of the Public Order Act 1986 (ss 17–28) (which is printed as Appendix II of this book) is an attempt to cure these defects. It creates new offences, for example, Section 18, which combines from previous legislation the two tests of intent to stir up racial hatred and the likelihood of racial hatred being stirred up. But legal and other restraints on prosecution still exist, and it remains to be seen whether the creation of new offences will increase the prosecution rate. The Attorney General must give his consent to a prosecution, but successive Attorney Generals have publicly expressed their reluctance to do so. It is said that this is because unsuccessful prosecutions do more harm than good to racial equality.

What About Passing a Law Against Incitement to Sexual Violence?

Having looked in some detail at the anti-race hatred laws which

Itzin is suggesting would provide a model to help women fight sex hatred, it becomes obvious that considerable problems remain. For a start, is there any likelihood that if such a law were passed, it would be used in women's interests any more than the existing laws have been used in Black people's interests? Then there is the problem of exactly what the offence of incitement to sexual violence would consist of. What does it actually mean? Ask any feminist, any woman, and the responses will be extremely varied, stretching from actual physical violence, through sexual harassment at work, to day-to-day sexism.

The next difficulty is whether such an offence would be tried in the civil or the criminal courts. It seems that the CAP and CPC have decided to move away from putting this offence into the criminal courts, preferring to make it actionable in the civil courts, just like the Dworkin–MacKinnon ordinances in the US. But this still ignores some fundamental differences in structure between law in Britain and the US.

Whenever someone thinks up a Bill which could become law, they do have to consider the political climate of the day. We are, at this time, surviving Thatcher's Britain, with its destruction of the trade unions and its onslaught on the working class in every possible way. The Social Security Act 1988 has just come into force, and the Housing Bill is currently going through the Houses of Parliament. Attacks against people who are different from the majority are increasing — homosexuals and lesbians are being attacked by the infamous Section 28 of the Local Government Act, and the new Immigration Act effectively removes the right of appeal against deportation unless a person has been here for more than seven years. Given all of this (and more) it does seem incredible that there are women who feel that their energies are best put into a legal campaign against pornography and that they seriously seem to believe that the powers-that-be would even consider any shift in the balance of power to give women any more control over their lives. Thatcher's government has already made considerable inroads into women's rights. You only have to look at the hugely regressive changes in Maternity Benefits in 1987. How many feminists did anything about that, despite a campaign set up to fight against it?

I am not dismissing out of hand the idea of introducing legislation against pornography at some stage. That would not be fair to my sisters and to the development of this debate, but I am worried about the implications of such a campaign in the immediate future. What will happen if a man wants to claim damages on the basis that a feminist publication promoted sexual hatred? We cannot make the law women-only, we cannot forget that we live in a patriarchal society!

As a lawyer I am concerned that not enough thought has gone into the framing of this offence. How will we be able to prove causation? How will it be proved in a civil court that a woman has been harmed by pornography and that because of that 'harm' (the definition of which I do not know) she is entitled to damages? If the offence is pursued in the criminal courts, how would it be worded? Like the present Public Order Act? Having followed the history of the law dealing with incitement to racial hatred, it seems that not many prosecutions would be brought, and of those, few would succeed. For the foreseeable future, the status quo would always be adhered to, and under patriarchy, it seems highly unlikely that such an inroad into its power would be allowed. Why should men give women anything?

There are no easy answers to these new campaigns. I only hope that more thought goes into what is being advocated. It is disturbing that the women in the campaigns think it useful to use as a model the offence of incitement to racial hatred, when it has quite clearly failed to serve Black people, and that they believe that racism has been made illegal by the 1986 Public Order Act, as well as by the Race Relations Acts. The campaigns have been useful in putting pornography back into feminist debate, but they have raised all the questions we have argued out among ourselves before. I wish that the women involved would confine themselves to that arena and not make comparisons with other areas of law which have so clearly failed, and are inappropriate for a variety of reasons.

Footnotes

1. *London Daily News* 24 April 1987.
2. ibid.
3. ibid.
4. *Facing up to antisemitism: how the Jews in Britain countered the threats in the 1930s* by David Rosenberg, Jewish Cultural and Anti-Racist Project, 1985.
5. Lester and Bindman, *Race and Law*, Penguin 1972.
6. ibid.
7. Rosenberg, op. cit.
8. ibid.

9. Lester & Bindman, op. cit., p. 351.
10. *The Times*, 20 December 1966.
11. (1967) 2QB 51.
12. (1968) 1A11 ER 582
13. *The Times*, 29 & 30 November 1967.
14. Lester & Bindman, op. cit.
15. *The Times*, 7 January 1978.

Postscript

I could not have written this article without the help and support of Gail Chester, Sue O'Sullivan, Pratibha Parmar, Rod Blake and Rick Scannell. If there are any legal inaccuracies then they are, of course, my fault.

SNAKES AND LADDERS

Julienne Dickey

My progression from an anti-media sexism, anti-pornography campaigner who favoured legislative restrictions with uncomplicated certainty, to someone who feels confused and uncertain about how best to proceed — and my witnessing of the confusion of most feminists on the issue — has led me to an interest in the reasons both for this confusion and for the rigid divisions that separate us. A parallel shift in emphasis has been from concern for short-term solutions to a longer-term view of how best to bring about changes in society.

There seems to be a fairly universal agreement among feminists that we do not like the way we are portrayed by the media, that media sexism and pornography are the unacceptable expression of an obnoxious, destructive, wasteful, reactionary ideology. But what to do about it? In particular the debate which concerns many contributors to this book has centred around the extent to which we support some form of state censorship of sexist material in principle, and the degree of offensiveness we are prepared to tolerate. Our disagreements often become heated, not to say virulent. So why does the subject evoke on the one hand such passion, even hostility, and on the other hand an incapacitating confusion?

I intend to explore some of the factors which I believe obscure clear, rational thinking, both about pornography itself and about possible solutions to it, and make it difficult for us to engage in constructive debate.

To begin with, sexual mistreatment of children is widespread in this society. This ranges from severe sexual abuse, through inappropriate touching and kissing, to unaware, disrespectful handling of genitals, innuendo-laden stares and name-calling and other invasions of a child's personal space. All this is exacerbated by an appalling lack of correct information and ethical discussion, within the family, in sex education in schools, or elsewhere; a

superabundance of ill-informed taboos and harmful misinforma-
tion, including sex stereotyping and pornographic images; and the
virtual non-existence of children's rights. Throughout our lives
society lays enormous stress on sex as a means of getting close, of
achieving happiness and fulfilment, of scoring points, and of
distracting us from all ills.

Thus it is small wonder that people grow up obsessed, confused
and 'warped' about sex, and that they pass this on to succeeding
generations. Small wonder also that many of those who would right
what they perceive as society's evils have concentrated on sexual
activity. Yet it is difficult for us to imagine what a rational, truly
human sexuality would be like, so damaged are we all in this area.
Of course, many people think they already know; certainly Mary
Whitehouse does, as do some 'sexual libertarians'. I doubt if any of
them are right.

For feminists, intervention in the areas of sexuality and the
transmission of ideas about it have always been important, because
we recognise what harm the present system does to us. But feminists,
like everyone else, try to develop strategies of intervention through a
haze of confusion. We may understand that Victorian notions about
sexuality and human bodies are repressive, but we are not immune
to feelings of distaste and puritanism ourselves. Sex is still a
relatively taboo subject within the women's movement; it can still
make us embarrassed and uncomfortable. We all have contradictory feelings of arousal and outrage at many sexualised images of
women — and because of our past mistreatment and our resulting
confusion we find it difficult to think rationally about solutions.

In addition, we often try to work out strategies for dealing with
offensive material without any real understanding of why (some)
men consume these images. To say that it is because men hate
women is simplistic in the extreme. To say that it is irrelevant to
understand men's responses is like a general saying he can plan for
a battle without any knowledge of 'the enemy'. Some feminists have
espoused a philosophy of despair that men — indeed society — can
ever change, and thus repressive measures are seen as absolutely
necessary.

Our thinking is also affected by, and has to fit into, society's ideas
and practices concerning the control of representations. The debate
about censorship of offensive material has to date been largely
dominated by the right. The left has in general been reluctant to
support anything but a libertarian approach to 'free sp :ch', for the

historically perfectly understandable reason that the left has traditionally been dominated by men. And of course arguments about freedom of expression have often seemed academic to women, since we've seldom enjoyed the privilege; women have often been more immediately concerned with freedom from sexual harassment and violence.

The monopoly of the debate by the right has meant that it is the right who are seen to be those most concerned with the moral question of the treatment of 'women and children'. More importantly, it has allowed them to frame the debate in their own terms, in other words in terms of 'morality' and 'decency'. This means that men like Churchill and Howarth can pontificate about the evils of pornography without the least regard to the fact that they fully support the kind of social mores that spawn it.

Once the debate has been framed in these terms, it is very dfficult to shift them, to change the agenda, to redefine the problem in our political terms. Our concern is that it is the imbalance of power relations between men and women in every aspect of society that is the root of the problem, and until that is eliminated its manifestations will not disappear. As long as the right does not accept or act on this analysis, inevitably they will favour more and more stringent attempts to curb the symptoms (in the same way as they call for tougher and tougher law and order measures as their answer to the disaffection of unemployed youth).

Yet as feminists, we are far from clear about the distinction between 'moral' and 'political'. We too have moral values, and sometimes, for some of us, these happen to coincide with those of people on the right. To find ourselves agreeing on moral grounds with those who have such antithetical political opinions to our own is confusing; how do we reconcile them? A common reaction is to refuse to accept that there can be any common ground, to refuse to listen, to come out strongly in the opposite direction, and to criticise anyone who appears to be 'allying' herself with the wrong 'camp'.

Not only do we need to locate our arguments within a broad political overview, we also need to understand how media institutions work, and the history of attempts to control them. Yet when the CPBF women's group conducted a questionnaire about these things, it became clear that very few feminists had any real knowledge of existing statutory or other controls, or of the bodies which implement them. This is, of course, typical of the prevailing ignorance throughout society of the institutions which control our lives — an ignorance designed to keep us feeling powerless and to minimise the risk of our taking effective action to change things. But while this may not be our fault, it is surely dubious to call for solutions if we have little understanding of how exactly they would operate, and their probable consequences.

It is not only ignorance of media and legislative institutions that makes it difficult for us to make informed decisions. There is also very little reliable, incontrovertible data available and accessible on the effects of media sexism and pornography. Of course many women believe that it is not necessary to quantify mistreatment and prove specific causal connections; common sense or the balance of probabilities are sufficient. And in one sense, actual harm and representations of harm are inextricably entwined, all part and parcel of the confused morass of sexual attitudes and behaviours.

But on the other hand, I believe it *is* important that we distinguish between how pornographic material makes us (women) *feel* and how it may make them (men) *act*. There can be no doubt that many women *feel* offended by media sexism and pornography, though there would be a wide diversity of opinion about the degree and nature of the offence. But because we feel offended by certain material, is this sufficient reason to have it removed? Certainly, one of our feminist tenets is that our subjective experiences as women are as valid as the supposedly objective, scientific (male) rationality. But what are we to do with Mary Whitehouse and all those others who *feel* (just as strongly as we do) that any expression of lesbian sexuality is wrong? Are some feelings more rational than others? Who decides?

There can be no doubt that media sexism contributes to our feelings about ourselves and our expectations, inevitably placing limits on our achievements and our enjoyment of life. But if we were to ban things on the grounds that they contribute to women's lowered expectations and negative self-image, then surely we should ban anything which presents women in stereotyped roles. The portrayal of women as engaged solely in the service of men — at home, at work, at play — is all-pervasive, and arguably more damaging to women's self-estimation than the (statistically rarer) instances of explicit pornography. Do page three pictures and pin-ups teach us any more about our role vis-a-vis men than the more common clothed representations of heterosexuality? Can we really say that pornography is more damaging to women than romantic pulp fiction, advertising billboards or *Dallas* and *Dynasty*? A major problem with making 'unacceptable' images subject to legal sanctions, is that it legitimises everything else: all other images remain, by definition, 'acceptable'.

The effect of media sexism on men, as indeed on women, is difficult to estimate in isolation from all other influences in society. After all, sexist attitudes existed long before the mass media and the ready availability of pornography. Feminists often operate on the assumption that common sense tells us that media sexism and pornography reinforce, even cause, men's attitudes towards women. But even if we want to base our arguments on positive proof of harmful effects, then the truth is that research has produced contradictory and mostly unsatisfactory results.

The doctrine of the centrality of pornography, as espoused by Andrea Dworkin and others who argue that 'pornography is the theory, rape the practice', is based on a theory, not on sound evidence. In the absence of such evidence, this may not be a bad thing, but it must be recognised for what it is. Unfortunately, few feminists actually make the effort to study what research there is in detail, and are often satisfied with hearsay accounts of 'proof'. I know that I have frequently quoted snuff movies to make my point about how bad things are, yet Carole Vance, in her article in this book, claims that no-one has ever actually produced one, and I certainly have no real proof for my former assertions. It is also possible to manipulate results of research to fit particular theories, as Alice Henry describes elsewhere. I do not think we are doing a service to our cause by being less than rigorous about our methods, particularly in the present political/moral climate where 'common sense' and hearsay are the excuse for all kinds of repressive legislation: witness Clause 28.

There are also other dangers in espousing a centrality of pornography position. Focussing so strongly on sexual imagery can lead to feminist struggle being co-opted by the right, thus defusing the very real threat that feminist ideas and practice pose to the patriarchal structures of society. It can divert feminist attention, resources and energy away from other sites of struggle, such as socio-economic problems, women's inequality in every sphere — and the appalling but non-pornographic content of the rest of the media.

Devoting huge amounts of attention to pornography can also have damaging psychological effects on those who do it, as I have found to my own cost in the past. If you go for a walk looking for dog shit on the pavement, you'll certainly find a lot of dog shit — but you will also miss seeing the trees, the buildings, the other human beings . . . Some women committed to ending pornography believe that women must be constantly reminded of how awful it is by forcing themselves to watch it, and that women must be constantly vigilant for anything that could be construed as a pornographic image. Yet why must we fill our heads with disturbing images? It's hard enough anyway to rid our minds of extraneous rubbish. Thinking clearly about how to deal with any problem demands some psychological distance, so that the problem can be acknowledged while still recognising that the world is also a wonderful, inspiring place. Otherwise we become swamped by the problem, letting it define our lives and our responses.

In trying to think clearly about solutions to the problem, we encounter the question of short-term versus long-term solutions. These are, of course, not mutually exclusive, nor would most feminists concern themselves with one to the disregard of the other. But I suspect that there are all kinds of reasons why many women seem to come down, however reluctantly, to measures such as legislation.

It is very uncommon in our society for people to have consistently before them a vision of how things should or could be, and work pro-actively towards that. It is far more common to react negatively to what exists, to feel a sense of urgency and impatience. And the truth is that in trying to think about long-term strategies to deal with media sexism and pornography, we run up against a tremendous amount of hopelessness: about men's 'nature', about the inadequacies of the education system, about the sexism, heterosexism, racism and all the other oppressions that underpin society in general and the media in particular. We may know that the only way to effect the permanent elimination of pornography is to change utterly the conditions under which people develop — to create a non-sexist world — but we have been struggling to do this for decades with insufficient success. Unfortunately, I see in the 'women's movement' of the late 80s too much resignation and too little analysis of why our strategies have so far not worked. We seem to have lost any sense of a shared vision and espoused a doctrine of individualism and despair. But that's a whole other article.

One aspect of the problem, seldom acknowledged, is our relationship to creativity. The media we have is a product of human creativity — or its lack. If our educational system devoted itself to developing our creativity, rather than squashing it out of us, it seems likely that we would have media of a far higher quality, that we would not tolerate the rubbish that we are currently served, and that there would, in any case, be a lot less of it about — we would be too busy living life at first hand. I'm sure a relationship exists between pornography and the suppression of human creativity. Like the call for a more enlightened sex education and the teaching of a more critical awareness of both the working of the media and women's role in the world, thinking about creativity involves long-term strategising.

The debate about solutions, legislative or otherwise, to media sexism and pornography will continue. Ideally we will see this as a strengthening process, refusing to allow it divide us, but rather committing ourselves to listening respectfully to one another's arguments. It will mean remembering that we largely agree on the objectionable nature of pornographic images, and neither over-estimating our differences nor over simplifying nor distorting the position of these who argue for different strategies. At the moment we fall short of this ideal, and again the reasons for this are the subject of another article. But, in any case, it is essential that we face up honestly to what it is that makes it difficult for us to think clearly, instead of assuming that our present position is unassailably rational, and the only correct one. We need an open, ever-enquiring mind. And we need to stop limiting ourselves to piecemeal protests and to develop effective, long-term strategies to win allies and change the whole picture.

WOMEN, EROTICA, PORNOGRAPHY — LEARNING TO PLAY THE GAME?

Elizabeth Carola

If you go into almost any women's or gay bookstore in the United States, you'll be confronted with an array of new publications and audio-visuals. This material is not the latest in feminist/alternative thought. No, it's pornography produced by women, and ostensibly 'about' and 'for' women. *On Our Backs*, *Bad Attitude*, *The Power Exchange*, *OW!* — *Outrageous Women: A Journal of Woman-to-Woman SM*, *Noni*, *Eidos*, *Yellow Silk*.

This, the issue of the 'lesbian sex revolution' and more generally, of the trend towards sexual libertarianism in the women's movement (as distinct from Women's Liberation Movement, a term which indicates more consciously feminist politics), is what, more than any other arena in alternative publishing, is being marketed. This is what is selling. This is what's being presented to new feminists and lesbians as 'women's culture'.

A similar phenomenon exists in women's communities in Holland, Denmark and Germany. But because it is so much more developed in the States, and because the material being produced is what tends to be imported to Britain (and to provide a model for like-minded women here), I'll focus on this phenomenon in the States.

Analysing this trend has meant some reproducing of the language of pornography. This, I've been sorry to do. However I thought it unavoidable: if we are to understand the underlying messages and ideology of this material: and if we are to bring informed pressure to bear on booksellers here in Britain to refuse to stock it. I want to stress that the fact that this should even have to be argued, that it is even a question, is an indication of how deeply feminist principles have been eroded by sexual libertarianism and its promotion of 'individual freedom' — irrespective of racial, class or sexual oppression. But more on this later.

Like all porn, this new 'woman's' porn is neither about nor for women. Like all porn it is, in a most basic sense, *against* women and *about* male fantasy — the basic male fantasy of Woman as Wholly Sexual Object whose Purpose is To Be Fucked — which feeds men's egos, fuels their violence, and keeps their wretched patriarchy rolling smoothly along. *Unlike* straight porn, this material is about how this basic fantasy has infected our sensibilities and sexuality. But like all pornographers, female pornographers are still fully responsible for exploiting the vulnerability and confusion of women,[1] including their employees, their readership and the larger women's communities whose values they subvert. And of course, like all porn, lesbian porn represents itself, when convenient, in proto-political terms, as a defiant, revolutionary outlaw force bravely struggling against the censure of powerful, reactionary moralistic prudes, puritans and feminists.

In fact, it is the existence of this porn — from the 'softest' to the most violent stuff, which is contributing towards the censorship of women, and not the other way around; it is as an agent and not a victim of censorship that this porn, like all porn must be understood. It subordinates women's lived reality, our intelligence, our integrity, our totality, to a fetishised and masochistic sexuality. It furthers a dangerous political escapism, capitalising on political distress and anxiety about social/economic problems by distracting women. Feminists have been called 'patronising' for pointing this out, and charged with 'not crediting women with the ability to choose. After all' (goes the argument) 'we are free agents.' The fact remains, however, that pornographers, advertisers, corporate publishers and mediamen, even when female, do aim to influence/mould a populace. And the fact remains that their messages — which are the reactionary ones (sexist, racist, heterosexist, imperialist...) of the dominant culture — do serve to manipulate and disempower oppressed groups. Lesbian porn may be selling in some quarters as briskly as Mills and Boon is in others. People, including women, will consume what's on the market. But we have had little real choice about the images and values purveyed there.

* * *

These publications, in particular, are not just about 'lesbian sex', as publicised. They're about the sexuality of eroticised male dominance and eroticised female submission, and this ideology they promote with great vigour. *On Our Backs*, in particular, is full of adverts for phalluses and endless verbiage about (and imagery of) extremely masculine 'Butches' introducing large objects — fists, bottles, phalluses — into the bodies of 'Femmes'. A common theme, as in all porn, features a feminist or a strong, competent woman surrendering, after much initial resistance, to the aggressive advances of a surrogate man, ultimately giving into her 'true' nature, which is the insatiable 'desire' To Be Fucked. Its columns are lined with adverts for sex shops and strip clubs, tattoo joints and 'piercing parlours' for the growing interest in the piercing of nipples and labia. One issue of *On* carried a lengthy piercing photoessay, with how-to demonstrations by a 'piercing artist' who 'took pride in announcing' that she had 'pierced over one hundred virgins' at a recent women's festival. Another featured child porn — a photoessay called 'Girls' Cunts' displaying the naked torsos and genital areas of pre-pubescent girls. Prostitution-related agencies advertise here for fresh, unbroken flesh, alongside adverts for the products of the 'lesbian sex revolution' itself — videos produced by women with names like *Fun with a Sausage* and *Private Pleasures*, 'sex tapes' (cassettes ostensibly of heavy breathing) with names like *Hot Women For Hire, Be My Good Bottom, Lipstick & Lace Femme*. Here's an excerpt from a story called 'Cry Baby' — *a piece written and narrated by a woman*, describing an ostensible lesbian sex scene — from *On Our Backs* no 4:

> I snatch the knife and cut the beautiful silken blouse off you, tie it for a blindfold for your eyes. I rip out my little dick and rape you out of your wits. I make you kneel impaled rising up and down on my dick. You then plead with me not to move so I move abruptly, jerk it out of you into your mouth to make you shut the fuck up. I watch your lips pull along and suck my dick. It's so hard now that I make it spill empty inside your mouth. You just about gag.

This excerpt is by no means an isolated example. Yet what I find even more dangerous than the overt sexual hostility in these publications is the subtle co-option of feminist ideas that pervades them; the manipulation of the anger, revolutionary desire for change, and deeply creative culture that has emerged out of lesbian/feminism in the past 15 years. In each of the publications I saw, the feminist ideas alluded to were consistently sexualised, depoliticised, burlesqued. The name *On Our Backs*, for example, is a parody of the strongly feminist American women's newsjournal *off our backs*. Its motto, 'Lesbianism is the lust of all women condensed to the point of explosion', plagiarises a phrase from the famous essay on radical lesbian/feminism written in 1973 by Anne Koedt, substituting 'lust' for the original 'rage'. Feminist concepts like 'women-only space' are exploited by female entrepreneurs in the organising of 'lesbian strip shows' in clubs rented out from male pornographers; several such 'women-only nights' are advertised in *On*, presumably so that customers can enjoy an evening ogling young incest survivors and Philippino refugees.[2] And, of course, there is a surfeit of prone feminists peopling the pages of *On Our Backs*.

It is not only tattoo parlours which advertise in these publications. Because these mags are selling, women are advertising in them. Ads for feminist bookstores and businesses; women doctors, accountants and therapists appear calmly amidst the copy and notices for peep shows as if in a mass, unspoken resignation to porn as the medium of the 80s.

On Our Backs represents the 'middle range' of lesbian porn. The harder core publications like *The Power Exchange* feature half page adverts for surgical scalpels for 'unparalleled cutting and piercing' interspersed with litanies of young women being violently fist fucked, whipped and pierced and, of course, gratefully licking their 'mistresses' boots in return. The softer core publications like *Noni*, *Eidos* and *Yellow Silk* are less sadomasochistic in orientation. They carry the same ads as the others and, like the more violent stuff, reduce women to wholly sexual creatures whose main purpose is Sex. The damage that these publications (which call themselves 'erotica' rather than porn) do to women is subtler, lying more with their promotion of alienated sexuality in a neo-feminist format designed to appeal to far more women than the strongly sado-masochistic material will.

At this point a discussion of 'erotica' is important, since it is often seen by feminists as acceptable, non-exploitative sexual representation, distinct from, and in no way continuous with pornography. Nonviolent, consensual material which 'merely' objectifies without harming. As such, there is much interest in 'women's erotica' in Britain at present. Sheba Feminist Publishers, for example, are bringing out an anthology of British Lesbian Erotica, and there is interest in several quarters in producing women's journals of erotica.

And yet, even if woman-produced erotica *were* an entirely different entity than men's pornography (a premise I don't think is tenable) I believe that the act of producing and consuming it in itself destroys the conditions helpful to women fighting for genuine change. Preoccupation with recording our sexual activities and fantasies dissipates anger at real sexual oppression, and deflects attention from the material conditions in which our activities and fantasies have been constructed.

Fantasy being the key word here. Many feminists feel, and I would agree, that it is crucial to talk and write about sex: our real desires, responses, ambivalences and fears. But this is neither the purpose nor the function of erotica, which is essentially about fantasy. What it *does* do is temporarily palliate — while ultimately feeding — the real and widespread emotional and sexual frustration created by patriarchal alienation. I believe that the purveyors, and would-be purveyors, of porn/erotica for women are aware of the extent of these unmet needs and the potential for their exploitation.

An incident at the 1986 London Women in Publishing Conference on Censorship was telling in this respect. At the conference, keynote speaker Andrea Dworkin testified as to horrifying — and real — developments in the porn industry. In the ensuing discussion, several proponents of pornography for women criticised her. One in particular claimed that Dworkin's speech was 'manipulative'. She said, 'We need to open discussion on women's relation to pornography. . . . My relationship to pornography is important to me.' I found her words chilling. She felt no need to even attempt to refute anything Dworkin had said about humiliation, torture and death of women in pornography. No, she liked porn, and that was that. To hell with real women and their lives and death.

Of course, dependence on porn/erotica can indeed become a 'relationship' as (if not more) important as relating to other people. By separating sex from the rest of lived experience and offering fantasy instead, erotica entrenches a vicarious response to external information, rather than encouraging a direct connection with oneself/another. It fosters a dependence on alienated imagery. In a culture of patriarchal alienation, fantasy can supersede reality for women as well as men. And sexually 'relating' to a fetishised image is far easier than sexually relating to another human being. But feeding this relationship is inimical to the aims of feminism: challenging male power, working for material social change, and interacting *as real women with one another*.

Now, sexual libertarians would argue that 'sexual freedom' (orgasms more easily, more often and however obtained) — and not social change — *is* the main aim of feminism. Unfortunately, in their defence of such freedom they tend to enlist the most traditional ideas — including the most reactionary tenets of psychoanalysis.

In 'Daring to Speak Its name: The Relationship of Women To Porn' (*Feminist Review* No 24), the writer, Marion Bower, bemoans the lack of feminist interest in the early psychoanalyst Melanie Klein, though she cedes that it is

> ... not surprising. A female sadism with women as its object — and which exists in its own right — is hardly an attractive idea. It has been more comfortable for us to identify and attack this unattractive aspect of ourselves in men. By projecting our aggression on to men, we attempt to maintain an illusion of innocence. I do not think it is ultimately to our advantage to be dissociated from this aspect of ourselves.... If pornography gives expression to something which already exists then eliminating it will not eliminate male sadism or violence towards women.

The gist of her article is that porn affects women and men in identical ways and serves the same function for both, and that sadomasochism is innate in the human psyche, an expression of 'repressed infantile hostility' and the 'desire to devour the mother'. Violent pornography is 'a symbolic representation of early painful mental experiences'.

Infantile longings and trauma become here direct, causal analogues to the porn industry, female sexual slavery and rape culture in general. Capitalism and patriarchy don't come into it. In any case, the fact that 99.9% of the former infants who rape, pimp, torture and kill for sexual gratification are *men* goes unmentioned. Finally, in a stunning denial of male violence, the writer 'doubt[s] if women *or men* find murderous porn such as snuff movies titillating'. (Italics mine.) Through articles like these, publications like *Feminist Review* and (sadly) the once-radical *Spare Rib* have been at the forefront of the libertarian lobby attacking feminist efforts against pornography.

In view of widespread misrepresentation, it's important to restate certain basic facts. Feminists are not denying the potential seductiveness of pornography for women. What we are saying is this: that women do not choose to sexually respond, still less to become habituated, to images of our own powerlessness and degradation. This 'preference' is pounded into our heads from the moment of birth. Masochism is not innate but political. It's in men's basic interest to keep us powerless, and one of the most effective ways of keeping us, not only powerless, but colluding in our subordination has been to eroticise it to the point that objectification/ humiliation feels basic to our sexuality. It is central to women's oppression that it is our sexuality which is most attacked, distorted, turned against us and offered back to us by men at a price — that of our human dignity and integrity. This specifically sexual opp- ression, from which no woman escapes, has been the most effective over the millenia in dividing us from ourselves and each other. Ultimately, I think there is a sexuality which could embody our original sense of self-respect and integrity, sexuality which could originate in self love and acceptance and allow for a total, directly experienced connection with ourselves and others. There is no reason to believe this could not be so.

But this is not the kind of sexuality that the libertarian lobby is interested in. *Spare Rib*, for example, ran a forum on sado- masochism in 1986 as a 'debate', illustrating *each* of the four articles (two pro, two con) with the same graphic of a woman being fist fucked. (Other issues, like economic sanctions against South Africa, or the desirability of a Labour government, are not seen as 'debatable' by *Spare Rib*, though there is undoubtedly as much dissension about these issues among women as a group as there is about the practice of sadomasochism.) Here, too, women are employing the political language of feminism — 'Choice', 'Freedom', 'Power', 'Repression' — to argue for women's 'right' to produce/ consume porn and, above all, to 'explore our sexuality', with their main claims coming down to the following:

— 'Some Women like it.'
— 'Women should be Free to Read / Do what they want to.'
— 'Feminism is about Choice, isn't it.'
— 'I Want to feel Powerful in my sexuality.'

These assertions are generally uncomplicated by any critique of the social process by which women come to like and want what we 'like' and 'want'. And once we return to thinking in terms of the political realities for women in a patriarchal world, they become meaningless. For any true exercise of 'rights' or 'choice' must come out of a context of real social power. Sexual libertarian women 'feel' powerful indeed. And as educated, mostly professional, white, western women they have both more access to (token) power, and more prospect of 'feeling' powerful than most women. Sexual libertarians may exhort other women to also 'feel their power' via exploring their sexuality, but the facts remain: Men control culture. They regulate technology, create the Image, define what is sex and what is not, what constitutes violence and what does not; what is 'obscene' and what is not. They determine who shall own less than 2% of the world's wealth and less than 1% of its land. They decide who shall be 75% of the world's poor, 80% of the world's illiterate, and 99% of the world's raped. And the fact remains, 99% of the world's women are more concerned with the right not to get raped, battered, starved, worn or worked to death by men. They are more concerned with the right not to be assaulted with sexual degradation at every turn than they are with the 'choice' to read porn and the 'right' to explore their sexuality.

* * *

It's in this context that censorship needs to be understood. Censorship is the systematic control, regulation and repression of a populace by those with social and institutional power. The ability to effect it presupposes that power. But the looseness with which the term censorship is used by liberals and libertarians — as meaning everything from disagreement or disapproval through to torture and genocide — is a deliberate attempt to obfuscate who has power. It is men, and in particular, powerful white men like pornographers, police, the judiciary and state who censor women's lives and 'choices' — and not the other way round. (Andrea Dworkin analyses this at length in her essay 'Against the Male Flood: Censorship, Pornography and Equality', *Trivia* no 7). And it's here, around the preservation of their 'rights' to unlimited access to images of female humiliation, that there is the strongest bonding between right-wing women, left-wing men and male-allied sexual libertarian women. During the screening of BBC-2's *Open Space* on May 11, 1987, some members of the *Spare Rib* collective came out as vehemently in their opposition to Labour MP Clare Short's bill to ban Page 3 as did Tory MPs during the parliamentary hearing of the bill. The reasons may have been different, but the effect was the same — the defeat of the bill and the continued abuse of girls and women via Page 3.

It's long been in men's interest to present the merest feminist challenge to their power as 'censorship'. But with the advent of sexual libertarians as a force in the women's movement, and particularly in women's publishing, some women are increasingly in a position of upholding male values by proxy, defining the issues, setting the terms of debate, controlling the exchange of ideas. The now defunct literary monthly *Women's Review* is one example. WR

published Kathy Acker and other 'avant garde' female pornographers and enthusiastically reviewed art exhibits like L'Amour
Fou (Mad Passion — a surrealist exhibit at the Hayward in Autumn
1986 which featured photos of mutilated, seductively displayed
women's corpses). Yet with two or three exceptions WR systematically avoided publishing any feminist critique of pornography or
radical feminist perspective. Their editorial policies, like those of the
new women pornographers, represented a more indirect form of
censorship than that which men/the state effects. But it was control
nonetheless, the exercise of power by women whose avoidance of
challenge to male values has gained them some access to and token
authority within the media. Women who name men as perpetrators,
and pornography as an agent, of women's victimisation have
continued to have little or no access to the media and have remained
largely silenced. (This is not to deny the women's presses and
publications who remain committed to publishing radical women's
work.)

It is crucial to name this power relation between women, for it is a
minority of radical feminists who have been most frequently
charged with being 'censors' when we have challenged the influx of
pornographic/sadomasochistic values into our communities. The
content of what has been challenged (bookshops' stocking of the
pointedly sadistic American SM manual *Coming to Power*, the
prospect of bondage displays at the London Lesbian and Gay
Centre, public whippings and fist-fucking of women at a defunct
London lesbian SM disco) has been ignored and 'debate' has
focused wholly on the iniquity of 'repressing' any form of
expression. The very framework of debate has been false —
pornography as politically defiant speech integral to the free
exchange of ideas in a democratic marketplace; radical feminists as
a powerful, reactionary lobby — and has allowed any and all
opposition to porn/sadomasochism to be neatly denounced as
'censorship'. This charge has functioned as a powerful silencing
tactic.

Meanwhile, the issue continues to control and divide us. In
December 1986, several other radical feminist lesbians and I
organised a slide show and discussion on lesbian pornography to
air the issues and air our perspective. As on other occasions where
women have clashed over these issues, the conflict was intense and,
as on other occasions, those of us who knew exactly where we stood
— pro and anti — were most vocal. On this occasion, I was trying to

explain the effect of these images on me as an incest survivor. Yet there was so much hilarity found in the images we were showing, that soon I had to stop trying to explain. I just couldn't go on — the laughter undermined my reality too much. The tone of the porn supporters (I realised that evening) echoed the tone of the porn itself — glib, parodying, burlesque. If I can't talk to other lesbians about my struggles as a survivor of sexual abuse (abuse in which pornography has played a large role) no trust or further communication is possible. I was deeply divided from my sisters that night by the mechanistic, alienated values embodied in those magazines. Their existence in the women's community helps create a climate of alienated fantasy which precludes any serious discussion about the confusion, ambivalence about sado-masochism, and frustration we've experienced as lesbians — surely an important part of our sexual *reality*. At the same time it nullifies the passionate tenderness and love we experience with each other.

Reading through the material to do this article was a depressing experience. I felt a deep sense of futility, as if my vision of helping create new values and a new sexuality for women had been eclipsed. I experienced the aggressive emphasis in the mags on women getting violently penetrated by surrogate men as more an anti-lesbian aversion therapy than 'entertainment for the adventurous lesbian'. I like to think of women being encouraged to be adventurous, but all I got out of *On* were images of women being tamed, subordinated, enslaved, and submitting to 'It'.

Forget it sisters. The censorship of women's lives, our spirits and our sexuality won't end until we have obliterated this propaganda completely — by any and all action that we take against 'straight' porn — first from our bookshelves, then from our consciousness.

Footnotes

1/2 Women don't just happen to find themselves in porn/prostitution. We are systematically driven into it by economies which offer us few other choices — especially when we're poor/Black/migrant/incest survivors . . . The 'option' to work in porn is merely a logical extension of the low self-esteem, sexually objectified self-image, and vulnerability brought on by prior sexual abuse. According to research now being done, 90% of women in the prostitution/porn industry were sexually abused as children. It is also a function of the international traffic in women whereby thousands of primarily Third World women each year are bought/kidnapped/procured and shipped to large urban prostitution-based economies (see Kathleen Barry, *Female Sexual Slavery*, 1979).

SAPPHO WAS A RIGHT-*OFF* WOMAN

Barbara Smith

The term 'lesbian pornography' usually refers to the particular *visual* brand, produced by heterosexual men for heterosexual men, which portrays two or more women in a sexual situation with each other. Since pornography always leaves a space in its fantasy into which the 'audience' might step in order to 'participate' vicariously, and since porn is usually produced for straight men, this means that such portrayals are really an extension of male heterosexuality. Lesbian sex is thus depicted in such a way as not to threaten heterosexual male sexual hegemony and is thereby co-opted by it. The women are not lesbians — they are having 'lesbian' sex, which is a male heterosexual fantasy. Since it is a fantasy it is not 'real' sex, and since it is portrayed as a sub-category of the pornographic genre, lesbian sex itself is seen as pornographic. It is a *menage à trois* where only the male and the male orgasm are real.

Even when a woman consumes such material, the presumption is that 'lesbian' sex is also perceived as part of *her* heterosexuality, in that she is still presumed to be relating sexually to a man as her prime sexual relationship. As in the past with 'romantic' friendships, female emotional and sexual relationships are seen as either an aperitif to, or bolster for, the heterosexual one. So pornography's 'lesbians' are in fact little more than sexually rampant, rock-bottom *heterosexual* swingers, easily and ultimately available to heterosexual men. Interestingly, it is never automatically presumed that *lesbians* might also consume such portrayals. But if it were, think of the implications. Straight men and women find 'lesbian' porn exciting. So do (some) lesbians. Presumably gay men do not. Therefore the false presumption is that there are only two sexualities: male *heterosexuality* — which subsumes *all* female sexuality — and male *homosexuality*. Really, women cannot win!

One of the many criticisms levelled at straight male pornography is that it reflects, feeds into and thus perpetuates power imbalances between the subject and object, whether these be based on gender, age, sexuality, race, class etc., and this power imbalance comes about because the two sides of the equation are dissimilar: the subject is always superior to the object. In the same way that 'lesbian' pornography is not for or about lesbians and lesbian sexuality, so 'black' porn is not for black people, and 'kiddie' porn is not for children. Pornography does not describe sexuality, it describes sexual *acts*. It solidifies white, male, heterosexual fantasies, and then commoditises them. Because of this, however, there is a conflation of sexual fantasy, sexual deed and sexual identity. Since all these portrayals revolve around white, male heterosexuality, who and what are depicted are marginalised and controlled by who is at the centre.

Straight male pornography is therefore 'pure' fantasy, and absolutely requires a distancing technique for its power to work. Distancing means that heterosexual males can disown the problematic aspects of their sexuality by relegating them to the pornographic realm and 'visiting' them like tourists in their own country. However, instead of accepting that their fantasies are part of *them*, they are externalised, stereotyped, and become icons in their sexual pantheon. In this way, everything *bar* white, male heterosexuality is problematised and becomes a 'demon' when placed outside the pornographic context, that is, outside of male control. Precisely because such sexual acts and sexual identities are confined to pornography, pornography itself is a form of censorship.

Pornography is the graphic representation of sexual acts carried out by stereotyped fantasies masquerading as real people. It is complete in itself, and requires only the passive presence of the observer. Nothing is left to the imagination, everything is described in detail. Because it is thus seen to have an existence separate from the observer, it can be disclaimed. The observer can step in or out at will because it does not 'belong' to him. Erotica, on the other hand, merely begins the process of sexual imagination. It hints at, but never fully describes or reveals, it is skeletal and needs the *active* participation of the observer's imagination to flesh it out. Thus the outcome can never be completely disowned because it is a direct reflection of the observer's sexuality. This is still a crude and simplistic distinction, but I think it is closer to the truth than, for example, saying that erotica is sexualised Art and pornography is sexualised Capitalism. In this sense, the second type of lesbian pornography is not pornographic at all: it may be pornographic in content, but I would say it is erotic in form. However, to avoid confusion, I will continue referring to it as pornography.

This second type, then, is produced and consumed by lesbians, where the participant observer is presumed to be not only female but lesbian — a radical step in itself. The women portrayed are also presumed to be lesbians, and although the sexual acts might still be fantasies, lesbian sex per se is a reality. It is a sexuality in its own right rather than an extension of someone else's. Pornography for lesbians stands representation theory on its head, because here the gaze is *not* male or masculine, there is no sharp distinction between object and subject because, being female and lesbian, the participant observer can either inhabit the 'gap' or directly participate in the proceedings, but in either case she cannot completely be detached from what is portrayed. It self-consciously speaks to and of her sexuality. There is no need for alienation, detachment or distance for the power of erotica to work.

To a large extent the representation of lesbian sex and clarification of what we *really* do in and out of bed, is part of a wider debate over general representations of lesbians — and the lack of them — in all kinds of media. Think how many lesbians are portrayed on TV, radio, in film and how many times these images are positive. Think also how many times lesbians are only defined by what we do in bed, rather than how we earn our living, by what we do with our lives when we're not fucking. This is what we mean by the invisible lesbian. Finally, think how many *lesbians* deny the reality of lesbian sexual activities by attempts at sanitisation. The times I have read that lesbians rarely use dildoes, that women do not ejaculate, leaves me wondering whether it is men or women, heterosexuals or lesbians who know less about us and our bodies.

The current round of obscenity debates and definitions threatens to make lesbians even more invisible. The Obscene Publications Bill, engineered by Gerald Howarth, recently failed to become law. However, the Tories will try again, having been returned to power. The proposed re-definition of obscenity will again be anything that 'a reasonable person' finds 'grossly offensive', and this can and will be used to cover (up) not only depictions of lesbian sex but also *any* image that presents lesbianism in a positive light. Both types of lesbian porn will be deemed the same — will the 'reasonable person' care for fine distinctions? — so any lesbian who advocates further state invasion of privacy and control of sexual representation (not just 'how' but also 'if') will end up discriminating against herself. Our twenty-year progression from *The Killing of Sister George* to *Desert Hearts* will be swallowed up in an instant and we will find ourselves again drowning in *The Well of Loneliness*, because you can be sure that the 'reasonable person' will not be lesbian or lesbian-positive.

When Thatcher says she wants a return to Victorian values she means literally that — back to the hypocritical moralising, a retrenched sexual double standard, superordination of the family at the expense of women, a bourgeois triumph over working-class culture. And the threat of such a regression has seen both left-wing politics (the costly 'lesbian and gay issue') *and* some feminists retreating to a right-tending Victorian opposition, with frantic attempts to sanitise and make respectable the very people they claim to represent. The 'good' woman/'fallen' woman syndrome of the *first* wave of feminism is a legacy with which we are still grappling. During that period, lesbians were also invisible. My reading of this is that, in the main, white, heterosexual, middle-class women, appalled at the prospect of VD invading the newly emerging nuclear family unit, either campaigned against what they perceived as prostitution, or tried to reform such 'fallen' women. Few took into account that because the majority of alleged prostitutes were working class women, economics and a different sexual and moral code might be at play. Some realised that male sexuality was also at fault and attempted to regulate it with social purity movements — but the whole thing boiled down to various groups trying to censor the sexual activities and sexual identities of others — without dealing with all the issues at once, and without once looking to themselves as one of the problems.

The present debate becomes even more complex when we consider the lived *reality* of lesbian sexuality and *self*-censorship. None of us becomes lesbian in a vacuum. We are as much sexually conditioned by society as the heterosexuals we criticise. It is therefore no surprise that what is called pornography for lesbians, at present, *appears* little different to straight male pornography, in that we still seem to be objectifying women and our bodies. But if we see such representations as the words of a visual language, then obviously we have to speak the language with which we are familiar. And just as real words, such as cunt, have been at least partially reclaimed, so can symbolic language if we are given the time to explore, change and make our own.

Unfortunately, not only is the Tory government and the right-tending opposition trying to clamp down on our sexuality, but so are those we thought were on the side of reason. There is a brand of feminism — an odd amalgam of revolutionary and radical feminism as practised by women such as Andrea Dworkin or Sheila Jeffreys — which bases its theories and most of its practice on woman as powerless victim. On the one hand it argues *against* biological destiny for women, as regards traditional gender roles of wife and mother, and on the other — and at the same time — argues *for* biological determinism as regards the 'innate' nature of both male and female sexualities. Male sexuality, whether heterosexual, homosexual or bisexual, is regarded by them as innately and immutably murderous. Male sexuality is seen as predicated on the combination of sex and violence so that we have slogans like 'Pornography is the theory, rape is the practice'. Female sexuality, on the other hand, and if male sexuality would leave it alone, is seen as innately and ultimately gentle, nurturing, empowering. One would therefore suppose that lesbianism is the epitomous expression of autonomous female sexuality, as in 'Feminism is the theory, lesbianism is the practice'.

However, what is seen as ruining this Utopian vision, besides those infuriating women who persist in sleeping with the 'enemy', is the vocal and active emergence of lesbian sadomasochism, which has since ben made the scapegoat and symbol of (some other) women's repressions. If heterosexual women fuck the enemy, then SM dykes fuck *like* the enemy. SM dykes loudly proclaim that we are into sex and power, both physical and emotional, because many of us reject images of powerless women. There is nothing intrinsically wrong with power, but with what you do with it and why. SM dykes use power to increase, not deplete, the overall power of women. If lesbianism proves that women can be and are actively and autonomously sexual, then lesbian SM should prove that we like it hot and raunchy. You'd think that lesbian feminists especially would latch onto lesbian SM as the perfect expression of women's power — but not so. It seems to have further problematised it. And the fact that the majority of the little porn that does exist for lesbians is also SM, or at least seen to be SM, has irrevocably compounded the felony. Far from being saviours, we are the Fifth Column. To make matters worse, we will not be silenced.

Few 'reasonable' people would today assert that lesbians, because we fuck women, want to be men. Additionally there may be some who see butch-femme as mimicking traditional masculine and feminine roles, and heterosexual sex and relationships. At the same time, though, there are those who see lesbians, and butch-femme, as potentially radical and subversive of the way in which both sexuality and gender are constructed in our society. There are also those who think using dildoes demonstrates classic Freudian penis-envy, though there are others — like me — who do not see them as penis-substitutes (i.e. attached to a *man*), but as extensions of *female* anatomy and *feminine* sexuality, so that they can also be potentially radical and subversive of the biological status quo. The problem with our society is that anatomy, sexuality and gender are all subsumed by compulsory heterosexuality. Everything is reduced to reproduction. All this is to ask, therefore, why pornography for lesbians, or being into SM, or using dildoes, are *automatically* deemed by some to be reinforcing traditional male- and hetero-sexually-defined stereotypes? Why are some lesbian activities automatically male-identified and others not? Why do we bemoan the apparent powerlessness of women, and then moan even more when women *do* have and use their power? And why is power considered male?

Of course, it is not necessarily true that when women do something they are better than men. At the same time, though, it can also never be exactly the same — especially in sexual matters. Pornography can be, and often is, racist, misogynistic and class-divisive — of which women are also guilty. But misogyny is not the same as sexism — they start from different power bases, such that men can be both misogynistic and sexist, but women can only be misogynistic, since they do not possess the male power that discriminates against women as a sex, though they *can* feel self-hatred — and the racist and classist imagery of pornography is predicated on the ability to wield purely *male* sexual power first. The white male plantation owner who sexually terrorised his black female slaves wielded an entirely different kind of power to the likes of Lady Chatterley — *in a sexual context*. Overriding all other considerations is the assumed dominance of male over female. Was working-class Mellors the defenceless victim of Lady Chatterley's aristocratic lust? Was she totally dominated by his male lust? Or was there an interesting tension between the two different kinds of power each wielded? And was that why *Lady Chatterley's Lover* was deemed obscene?

Pornography for lesbians is unique in that it presumes a *female* gaze, and a lesbian one at that. It presumes active female sexuality. It celebrates autonomous female sexual enjoyment. It still presents women as objects, but through the eyes, and to the eyes, of other women as *subjects*. It takes stereotyped images and, with some humour at times, utterly subverts them in both intention and context. Pornography for lesbians at least portrays us in our true light as the spectrum of womanhood — strong, sexually demanding and fulfilled, active, passive, and always assertive. No one is going to take that from us — most especially other lesbians. Sappho, thank God, was a right-*off* woman.

TELEVISION AND CENSORSHIP: SOME NOTES FOR FEMINISTS

Mandy Merck

I. Storm Over Video Nasties

In May 1983, a current affairs programme made by an all-woman production company became the focus of a paradoxical controversy. 'Storm Over Video Nasties On Channel 4' headed the *Mirror* preview of 'A Gentleman's Agreement?', the *Broadside* team's sceptical examination of a newly-announced code of practice issued by the British Videogram Association. The programme featured scenes of a Leeds distributor 'just delivering *Nightmare in a Damaged Brain* for the Speights and their five children'; children's descriptions of particularly gory sequences ('All sick came out of his mouth and all white out of his ears, and then they chopped off his head'); a spokesman from the NSPCC comparing 'strong videos' to loaded shotguns; a mother's defence of hiring such fare ('It's much cheaper than going to the pictures'); Labour MP Gareth Wardell discussing the inefficacy of voluntary regulation 'on people who basically are not gentlemen'; and an interview with a member of the feminist anti-pornography campaign, Women Against Violence Against Women. The programme also included sequences from two video titles which had been forfeited by Magistrates Order under the Obscene Publication Act during the previous summer, *I Spit on Your Grave* and *S.S. Experiment Camp*. The first clip showed, in the words of the *Daily Telegraph*, a 'naked woman in a speedboat plunging an axe into the back of one of her victims', the second 'a woman's naked body being put into a furnace and consumed by flames, along with other naked women'.

The argument of this programme was unmistakable, even to the British press: this harmful material would continue to be seen by children until legislation replaced the trade's cynical self-regulation. Nor was the programme's implicit narrative any less clear: an historically suspect fictional genre — horror — with its traditional linking of sex, violence and special effects — touted by ungentlemanly profiteers — condoned by neglectful working-class parents ('a simple sort of family', noted Nancy Banks-Smith in the *Guardian*) — was being consumed by ominously *blasé* working-class boys ('some of it were boring', one complained) — via a new media technology dangerously out of state control.

In condemning what had already come to be known as 'video nasties', *Broadside*, with its explicit political commitment and women's liberation logo, added an important feminist voice to the chorus calling for greater regulation of home viewing. And yet, in what Banks-Smith saw as 'a nice irony', even this programme elicited a stiff protest from Mary Whitehouse. The illustrative extracts were from titles subjected to forfeit under the Obscene Publications Act (OPA). No matter that the *Broadside* producers chose relatively mild sequences with a view towards transmission. No matter that these sequences were placed in a clearly condemnatory context. (Mrs Whitehouse has never been a respecter of context. Indeed, the provisions in this regard within the OPA are among those she wishes to amend.) The opportunity to shift the blame from the smallfry of video rentals to mainstream television proved irresistible. Channel 'Swore' was condemned for broadcasting violent scenes. The OPA was condemned for exempting television. The Independent Broadcasting Authority was condemned for not demanding cuts in the programme under the 'taste and decency' provisions of the Broadcasting Act.

Programmes demanding censorship may themselves fall foul of the censor, if only because they tend to publicise or display that which they criticise. But on Wednesday, June 8, Channel 4 transmitted the disputed edition of *Broadside* uncut, albeit at the unusually late hour of 10.15. One year later, the Video Recordings Act was passed into law. Its contents, and the clamour which accompanied it, transformed not only the future of video, but of broadcast television, cinema and censorship generally in this country. The Act's main provisions were to raise the British Board of Film Classification from an industrial advisory body to legally empowered censors; to outlaw the sale or hire of any cassette not approved by those censors; to police particular images (of genitalia, excretory functions, acts of sex or gross violence, or anything which 'might stimulate or encourage' such acts) rather than moral harm; and to extend a system of classification designed for public exhibition into the privacy of the home. Its passage marked the end of the liberal climate which had prevailed in British sex legislation since the Obscene Publications Act was passed in 1959.

II. Obscenity and Indecency

Passed on the impetus of extensive lobbying by the Society of Authors (after Secker and Warburg, Heinemann and Hutchinson were all tried for obscenity in the bumper year of 1956), the OPA established far-reaching criteria for educational and artistic merit. In determining whether material 'tends to deprave or corrupt', juries can be asked to consider the total work, the target audience, and any extenuating contribution to 'the interests of science, literature, art or learning, or of other objects of general concern' (the 'public good' defence). Subsequent appeal rulings have further established that shock or disgust by itself does not indicate obscenity, since works which provoke such feelings might discourage depravity; and have replaced the 'average', 'reasonable' or 'most vulnerable' reader with the one most likely to encounter the material.

As part of the wave of legal reform which followed publication of the 1957 Wolfenden Report, the Act was premissed on the report's division between a public sphere in which greater regulation was deemed necessary to protect non-consenting citizens from offence (from solicitation by homosexuals or prostitutes, indecent displays, etc) and a private sphere in which consenting adults were entitled to make (im)moral choices (acts of homosexuality and prostitution, the consumption of pornography, etc).[1] In distinguishing crimes of 'obscenity' from those of 'indecency', British legislation has tended to reproduce this dichotomy, defining the former as a matter of personal moral corruption and the latter as one of public offence. Obscenity implies an act of individual choice — indecency the nuisance or affront occasioned by unchosen contact. Where the former requires an objective demonstration of debasement, the latter appeals to subjective experience — 'anything', in Lord Denning's 1976 judgement, 'which an ordinary decent man or woman would find to be shocking, disgusting or revolting'.

Such legislative zoning is framed according to the ethical geography of nineteenth-century utilitarianism, concerned to maximise personal freedom while minimalising harm to others. But both the technology and the politics of recent years have redrawn the utilitarian map, merging the separate spheres of the Victorian social order. The feminist conviction that 'the personal is political' will not abide the legal dispensation which makes domestic

violence, divorce settlements, or the division of state benefits private
matters. Nor has Mary Whitehouse and her National Viewers and
Listeners Association ever regarded 'the home' as a domain
properly exempt from political jurisdiction.

Where feminists and the far right have, until recently, disagreed is
over the desirability of state regulation in the area of sexual
representation. Thus Ruth Wallsgrove's argument in a 1977 issue of
Spare Rib:

> I don't want to choose between Mrs Whitehouse and the producers of
> *High Society*, between two equally unacceptable alternatives —
> between censoring all mention of sex through vaguely worded laws
> that will be applied by men, and allowing pornography to invade my
> life at an ever-increasing rate, on Radio One and in packets of
> bubblegum, and even in the radical press. I believe we should not
> agitate for more laws against pornography, but should rather stand
> up together and say what we feel about it, and what we feel about our
> own sexuality, and force men to re-examine their own attitudes to sex
> and women implicit in their consumption of porn. We should talk to
> our local newsagents — many of whom feel pressured into stocking
> porn — or picket porn movies, or walk down Oxford Street with our
> shirts off.

This sceptical anti-statism persists in some British feminist
quarters, but it has been widely superseded in others by vocal
campaigns in favour of parliamentary or local council intervention
(against video nasties; Page Three pin-ups in the tabloids; against
the screening of particular films in the London Borough of
Camden). Such agitation may merely reflect an intensification of
feminism's historical belief in the ideological effectiveness of
representations — a conviction heightened by the writings of US
anti-porn campaigners like Andrea Dworkin and Susan Griffin,
whose influence began to be felt in Britain in the early '80s. Or it
may, as Australian feminist Lesley Stern has argued, indicate a
significant transfer of political attention from *acts* of sexual violence
to their *representation*, as feminists losing ground to the Right search
for a unifying theory of sexism and its causation: 'If rape is the grand
metaphor of oppression, then porn is the original sin.'[2] The new
enthusiasm for legal intervention may also owe something to the
arrival of individual feminists in local and national government,
and the general decline of 'abstentionist' politics on the British left.
And it is undoubtedly affected by changes in the mass media
themselves and in social attitudes to them.

III. Regulating Home Viewing

Television, with its peculiar combination of public transmission and private consumption, has always been a difficult medium to regulate, all the more so as recent changes in technology and exhibition patterns transform the box into the major outlet for mass media in Britain. With one of the developed world's highest per capita concentrations of video recorders, and one of its lowest rates of cinema attendance, the British now subject their home viewing to vastly contradictory demands. Where one consumer clamours for 'serious, adult' programming, another insists upon the protection of children. Paradoxically, the assumed presence of minors, who legally cannot grant consent, transforms the home from a private site of consensual consumption into a public one of unchosen encounters.

During the 1986 debate on the Churchill Bill to amend the OPA, Conservative MP Nicholas Fairbairn expounded enthusiastically on the theme of television as what sociologist Laurie Taylor calls the 'Uninvited Guest', equating the medium with the telephone as 'the only two intrusions into private homes that anybody can make without permission'. (More ambivalently, the Annan Report on the Future of Broadcasting noted in its 1977 deliberations, 'Our country should not be one of the many countries in the world in which Socrates would be put to death. But Socrates never bearded people in their homes.') And repeating the erroneous argument that visual images are immediately legible in a way that written words are not, Fairbairn argued that this trespass is unavoidable. Since television, in his phrase, 'requires no intellectual effort to absorb, translate, comprehend or interpret', it's always too late to turn over — the damage is done.

The idea of television created by such notions resembles a billboard more than a novel or a film, and its regulations borrow appropriately from the general stipulations against public indecency. Formulated to govern commercial broadcasting in 1954 (inaugurating a continuing relation between private ownership and moral regulation in the mass media), these strictures were voluntarily adopted by the BBC in 1964. Now embodied in the Broadcasting Act of 1981, they prohibit material 'which offends against good taste or decency or is likely to encourage or incite to crime or to lead to disorder or to be offensive to public feeling...'.

There is no legal definition of indecency as such, but programme guidelines for commercial television single out potential problem areas, including the use of offensive language, the representation of sexual behaviour, and jokes based on racial characteristics. The prohibitions against encouraging crime or disorder are elaborated in terms of interviewing criminals or individuals who advocate criminal measures for political ends, conveying detailed information about criminal techniques, encouraging crime through TV coverage, and gratuitous displays of smoking and drinking. The offence against public feeling provisions are applied to invasion of privacy, intruding upon bereavement and interviewing subjects without informed consent.

Noting the extent of these provisions, and the even greater self-censorship practised by programme-makers, the Annan Committee actually admonished broadcasters to risk giving offence — 'to show their audience what they believe to be the truth even if the truth shocks'. And the same Committee laid the groundwork for the establishment of a Fourth Channel required by law to 'appeal to tastes and interests not generally catered for by ITV' and 'to encourage innovation and experiment'.

In recognising a diversity of viewers' interests, as well as the possible desirability of offence, the Annan Committee challenged 'broad'-casting's aggregation of many disparate audiences into one unified public. This placed the nascent Channel 4 in an awkward legal position, whereby its legally enjoined attempts to address minority audiences — by, for example, a ten-second commercial for a gay newspaper after a programme aimed at homosexuals — have been banned by the IBA as offensive to public feeling.[3]

Channel 4's gay programming seems also to have spurred the first of two recent attempts to extend the more severe penalties of the OPA to television — Winston Churchill Jr's 1986 Bill with its notorious 'laundry list' of forbidden representations, including acts of 'sodomy, oral/genital connection and oral/anal connection'. The Bill's opponents, including Labour MP Jo Richardson, noted an anti-gay bias in these prohibitions, which Churchill and his co-sponsor Sir Nicholas Bonsor were happy to confirm. Churchill repeatedly expressed concern about Derek Jarman's *Sebastiane*, screened on Channel 4 some months before the Bill's publicaton, while Bonsor singled out 'explicit homosexual acts' for banning.

Churchill's Bill sank under the weight of opposition from broadcasters and civil libertarians, and its own ludicrous drafting, but within months another attempt to revise the OPA was promulgated from the Tory backbenches. Like its predecessor, Gerald Howarth's Bill was supported both by the NVLA and members of the government, including Mrs Thatcher and Home Secretary Douglas Hurd, and much more strategically phrased. Again it extended the OPA to broadcasting, but instead of an *a priori* list of forbidden positions, the measure added to the '59 Act's 'deprave and corrupt' clause a new test of obscenity: any representation of violence, cruelty, sex, genitalia, drug-taking or 'incidents of a horrific nature' which 'a reasonable person would regard as grossly offensive'. Going with the grain of existing television regulation, Howarth's Bill collapsed obscenity into indecency by way of 'offence', with the 'reasonable person' clause designed to allay fears of what the law amusingly refers to as 'perverse' judgements. Howarth's claim for the test was its flexibility, 'producing a definition capable of moving with changing social values of what is acceptable and what is not'.

And indeed, as Mrs Thatcher waved to a watching Mrs Whitehouse at the Bill's second reading last April, it was apparent to at least one commentator that social values had changed. The *Independent*'s Media Correspondent, Maggie Brown, attributed this transformation to Conservative pressure on the BBC, rising concern about the effects of television violence, the imminent increase in television output via cable and satellite, and 'clamour, from both the right and the left, for improved access to, and influence over, the media'. Other writers have cited AIDS (and the related changes in the representation of sex by both TV programmes and advertising) and — more recently, with its tremendous impact on the popular perception of 'copycat' effects — the Hungerford killings.

Gerald Howarth's Bill ran out of parliamentary time in a session cut short by the June '87 General Election, but the Tories went to the country with a manifesto commitment to bring television under the Obscene Publications Act. Since, as both civil libertarians and Mrs Whitehouse agree, nothing currently broadcast would fall foul of its 'deprave and corrupt' test, the Government must either amend the '59 Act along the lines of the Howarth Bill or introduce a new regulatory system in the broadcasting legislation promised for 1988 or '89. The feminist response to this initiative could be of critical importance.

IV. The Hungerford Effect

The turn in British censorship away from legislation predicated on objectively demonstrable harms — depravity and corruption — to subjectively perceived offence is paralleled by a reduction in the use of research which seeks to demonstrate that particular representations give rise to predictable psychological or behavioural effects. Many media scholars have criticised the design of this research, its inappropriateness to lived experience, and the uncertainty of its conclusions, on empirical grounds — children who hit toy dummies after watching cartoon violence do not necessarily hit people. Media analysts who employ semiotic and psychoanalytical approaches would further insist upon the instability of meaning, arguing that a given TV programme may generate a host of possible readings, which will vary between audiences and over time, and whose range may be difficult to predict or limit. (Such convictions, it must be admitted, rarely restrain those who espouse them from enthusiastically offering their own interpretation of particular works — but it would be fair to say that analysts working from these perspectives have generally been loathe to support legislation which would ban specific representations as *inherently* harmful.)

Interestingly, the Right has moved first to jettison 'effects theories' as unhelpful to the case for censorship. As Tory MP Douglas Hogg admitted during the debate on the Churchill Bill, the need to add a 'laundry list' of automatically proscribed images to the deprave and corrupt test constituted an admission that 'a causal connection between violence on television and the commission of violent offences . . . has not been certainly established. (However) society is entitled to say that certain matters are so offensive that they should not be published, even if we cannot establish that they have a prejudicial effect.'

This move away from effect arguments was given added impetus by the Hungerford killings in August '87. Rather than attempting to *prove* that 'the Rambo killer's' attacks were caused by his consumption of particular representations, commentators began to argue that such demonstrations were rendered unnecessary, almost callous, by the magnitude of the horror. Mary Whitehouse's denigration of media research just before this year's Conservative Party Conference was not wholly unexpected: '. . . you've got to get away from this silly business of having to prove things. We've got to start using our common sense and human experience, then we might get somewhere.' The cross-bench chorus to the same tune later that week on the BBC's *Question Time* (with Labour's John Prescott echoing Mrs Whitehouse's invocation of 'common sense' on the issue of TV violence) was rather more surprising. But what about *New Statesman* journalist Sarah Benton's remarks in that magazine after Hungerford?

> No one will ever know whether or not Ryan was influenced by TV portrayals of murderous men but that may not be the point . . . it was a film portrayal of causal male violence which immediately provided the name for Ryan's act . . . I for one felt relieved that TV was pulling off violent movies . . . I do not speak as a responsible citizen who believes that Michael Ryan, unlike me, is going to be incited to murder by violent movies; I speak as someone who does not want her citizenship to be continuously undermined by paranoia about male violence.

A number of feminists have warned against the siren call to outlaw offence.[4] A controversial, if aging, politics has little to gain from restraining outrage. Nor is it likely to find many allies among those the courts might deem 'reasonable'. But should we legislate against fear? Would the civil rights of women be enhanced by not broadcasting films about disturbed Vietnam War veterans who run amuck (*Rambo*)? The USA city ordinances drafted by Andrea Dworkin and Catharine MacKinnon include similar wording about *pornography* 'restricting women from full exercise of citizenship and participation in public life', and are currently under consideration for possible application here.

Even if we discount the extensive American feminist opposition to this legislation — which argued against its conflation of sexual explicitness, violence and sexism; and against its assumption 'that sexuality is a realm of unremitting, unequalled victimisation for women'[5] — it would be difficult to translate to British television. Dworkin and MacKinnon's civil liberties argument depends upon a definition of pornography which is both sexually explicit *and* violent or 'dehumanised'. The targetted material has to be characterised in very extreme terms to warrant the ordinances' description of it as 'central in creating the civil inequality between the sexes'. Since, however, 'there really isn't much explicit sex to be seen on public service television', as Colin Morris noted recently on Radio 3's *Drawing the Line*, it seems an inappropriate object of this legislation. The everyday diet of British broadcasting, however oppressive or frightening, fits awkwardly into such a sexualised definition of sexism.

V. Future Strategies

Many feminists within the Labour Party now argue that the moral ground must be seized from the Right on the question of media regulation. Faced with succesive private members' attempts to revise the law on broadcasting and obscenity and the prospect of government intervention in the near future, they call for the legislative equivalent of a pre-emptive strike. Can we reassure the 'decent people out there' without reverting to the language of indecency, of a regulatory tradition more concerned with sexual than sexist expression?

The Missing Culture, a Labour Party discussion paper published in October '87, offers one startegy in its critique of the limited opportunities available to women in the arts and media. Noting the marginal participation by women in television at both the programme-making and managerial levels (no woman in the BBC's Board of Management, only one woman Controller) and the similar marginality of their on-screen presentation, the paper calls for improvements in recruitment, training, childcare and maternity leave, as well as detailed monitoring of employment practices. A vocal commitment to enforce such policies in television would signal Labour's intentions towards women more positively than any amount of continued tinkering with the products of a male-dominated medium.

It would also begin to address one of the underlying causes of the current concern about television — a widespread sense of exclusion from its practices and policies. This discontent, which as Maggie Brown noted, results in political demands from both the Left and the Right, is now voiced most vigorously by Tory populists like the MP for Eastwood, Allan Stewart:

> I believe that many people feel that we are often subjected to metropolitan and permissive values emanating from an elitist attitude in parts of the London media.

Faced with a Conservative government eagerly pursuing a partisan programme of managerial appointment and direct censorship (*Real Lives*) against a more liberal television bureaucracy, Labour has often felt forced to side with the programme-makers in the name of democracy. Indeed, it executed an acrobatic *volte face* in regard to the BBC's 1987 election coverage, first claiming political bias, then backpeddling to offer better co-operation in pursuit of more accurate reporting — because, as party spokespeople admitted,

Labour can't be seen to do a Tebbit.

This effectively locks the Party into an alliance with a broadcasting system which *is* elitist in both its personnel policies and its programming presumptions. In response to this dilemma, Labour could follow the predictable strategy of its own partisan appointments when in power, replacing retiring members of the IBA and the BBC Board of Governors with its own great and good, or it could seek wider public support with a commitment to a devolved and elected broadcasting administration, a demand which feminists would be wise to raise.

A similar opportunity presents itself with the imminent establishment of a new Broadcasting Standards Council, which will have a wider remit than the Broadcasting Complaints Commission. The BCC, set up in 1981, may only take complaints about unfair treatment or invasion of privacy from directly involved parties, people who have been the subject of TV programmes. The Broadcasting Standards Council is designed as a response to current concerns about programme content. Although its Tory origins warrant a cautious approach, it has not yet been given terms of reference. Labour should join with feminists to argue that these should not simply reproduce the traditional canons of taste and decency, but formally refer to the representation of disadvantaged sections of the population. It is time to put the representation of women onto an agenda dominated for far too long by the gender-blind considerations of British censorship.

Postscript

This article was completed in January 1988. Since then Sir William Rees-Mogg, the former *Times* editor and BBC Governor who opposed the screening of *Real Lives* has been appointed chair of the Broadcasting Standards Council. As of Summer 1988, the powers of that body were still unclear, but Rees-Mogg's appointment, and his newly awarded life peerage, were widely hailed as a Right turn for television regulation.

Footnotes

1 See Annette Kuhn 'Public versus Private; the Case of Indecency and Obscenity', *Leisure Studies* 3, 1984, pp 53–65.
2 Lesley Stern, 'The Body as Evidence', *Screen* November–December 1982, vol 23 no 5, pp 38–60.

3 See Geoffrey Robertson and Andrew G.L. Nicol, *Media Law*, London, Sage, 1984, p 375.

4 See, for example, Jean Seaton, 'Pornography Annoys', in James Curran, Jake Eccleston, Giles Oakley and Alan Richardson (eds), *Bending Reality: the State of the Media*, London, Pluto, 1986, pp 157–168.

5 Lisa Duggan, Nan D. Hunter, Carole S. Vance, 'False Promises', *Caught Looking*, New York, Caught Looking Inc, 1986, p. 85. (Extracted in this book — see page 62.)

6 Quoted in Julian Petley, 'Power to the People', *Independent Programme Producers Association Bulletin*, August 1987, p. 15.

RED ROSES FOR ME: CENSORSHIP AND THE LABOUR PARTY

Teresa Stratford

The Labour Party's attitude to censorship has been, on the whole, ambiguous. As an opposition party, it has usually advocated disclosure, but when in power, has used legislation as competently as the Conservatives in order to prevent it. The Wilson and Callaghan governments in the '60s and '70s, in particular, developed a history of censorial prosecutions, using various pieces of legislation. Section 2 of the 1911 Official Secrets Act was used successfully to prosecute Crispin Aubrey, John Berry and Duncan Campbell in 1976–77 (the ABC trial),[1] and unsuccessfully in an attempt to suppress the Crossman Diaries in 1975. Harold Wilson used the libel laws to sue the Move, a band who featured him nude on a postcard to promote their latest recording; the lawsuit secured them the desired publicity. In 1977, *Gay News* was fined £1,000 for blasphemous libel, because of a poem which featured Jesus Christ. This prosecution, the first such case for 56 years, made Mary Whitehouse a household name.

The notorious Section 2 of the Official Secrets Act, under which it is an offence to pass on unauthorised information, has been used against civil servants by the present government, in several cases which have been opposed by Labour MPs, despite Labour's earlier poor record. When Sarah Tisdall was imprisoned for giving Ministry of Defence information to the *Guardian*, Gerald Kaufman, then the Labour Home Affairs spokesperson, described the prosecution as being 'dangerous to freedom'. Labour MP Tam Dalyell has waged what has often been a lonely campaign to obtain information about the Malvinas/Falklands war, and the prosecution of Clive Ponting, who supplied him with unauthorised documents, was condemned by many others in the party.

The government's recent attempts to suppress individual programmes and publications have, on the whole, been opposed by the

Labour Party. Kevin MacNamara, Labour's Northern Ireland spokesperson, condemned the attempt to stop the IBA allowing transmission of Thames TV's *This Week* programme on the Gibraltar killings as 'ministerial arm-twisting'. Neil Kinnock supported the *Guardian* and the *Independent* in their attempts to publish extracts from Peter Wright's book, *Spycatcher*, even communicating independently with Wright's lawyers in Australia, much to Mrs Thatcher's wrath. Yet it came as a disappointment to many Labour supporters when Kinnock agreed with the Prime Minister that transmission of Duncan Campbell's 'Zircon' programme, in the *Secret Society* series, would constitute a risk to national security.

This position is reminscent of the days of the Wilson and Callaghan governments when, in several decisions, fears they expressed for national security took precedence over deference to citizens' rights to information. This preference is perhaps most clearly expressed in policy towards the reporting of Northern Irish issues. Roy Mason, for example, who became Labour's Northern Ireland Secretary in 1974, wanted a complete blackout on reportage of what he termed terrorist activities, and accused the BBC of providing a 'daily platform' for the Provisional IRA.[2] In 1977, he joined Tory spokesperson Airey Neave in condemning the BBC for transmitting an interview with Bernard O'Connor, a Catholic school-teacher who alleged ill-treatment by the RUC at Castlereagh prison.[3] Although Labour politicians would argue, correctly, that the party's position is different now, this past attitude of denial and hostility has given the present government more than lessons in rhetoric for the likes of Norman Tebbit. The Criminal Law Act, passed by Wilson's government in 1967, enabled the RUC to seize film from the offices of the BBC Belfast in early 1988. Had Thatcher not decided to use this little-known Act, she could have used the Prevention of Terrorism Act, which has a section on withholding information. This Act, passed by the new Labour government in 1974, was originally conceived as a temporary measure, renewable every six months. In 1986, the Conservative government made it renewable annually, and this year (1988) it has been made permanent.

Sex and Violence

It has been the Tories who, especially in recent years, have linked these two words, which many of us consider should not belong together, and used the tabloid press to excite public concern about their damaging effects when relayed via TV programmes, films and videos. The Labour party has, so far, resisted the populist appeal of blaming most of the society's shortcomings on screened material. Graham Bright's Private Member's bill, which became the 1984 Video Recordings Act[4] was opposed by the majority of Labour MPs. So was Winston Churchill's Private Member's bill of 1986, to extend the 1959 Obscene Publications Act to television; most Labour MPs found that the infamous 'laundry list' of items likely to 'deprave and corrupt' was far too all-encompassing, and some individuals, like Jo Richardson, objected to the intentional anti-gay bias. The Obscene Publications Act is, however, another Labour legacy to the Tories. Passed under Macmillan's government in 1959, it had been sponsored by Roy Jenkins, at that time in the Labour Party.

Some Labour politicians are unhappy that the responsibility to administer the Obscene Publications Act lies with the police. They would prefer to see this handled by an independent commission but there is not, as yet, a policy on its reform. The lack of consensus in the party on this is perhaps most evident in issues affecting lesbians and gay men — people who have had reason to feel particularly aggrieved by the use of this Act. Section 28 of the 1988 Local Government Act is feared by many to adversely affect gay representation in the media. Yet although a Labour MP, Joan Ruddock, is trying to bring a Private Member's bill to repeal the section, when it was first introduced as a clause, it was not opposed by the Labour front bench.

The People and the Media

Labour Party policy on censorship is summed up in these words from the 1974 report *The People and the Media*, produced by a group chaired by Tony Benn: the group 'absolutely rejects any policy for the mass media, or any system for operating it that is based on government censorship or central control'. The desire to preserve individual rights, which is expressed in this report, is still a strong motivating factor behind Labour Party policy. It is a particularly influential factor behind the 'Democracy Section' of the 1988 Policy Review. The group who worked on this section made the preservation of individual freedoms a priority. The group's Chair, Roy Hattersley, has repeatedly expressed his concern about individual rights and freedoms in his journalism. Yet, as Stephen Howe has argued,[5] this report may actually represent a missed opportunity to empower those sections of the community whose access to resources is more limited than Roy Hattersley's. In contrast to the Tory interpretation of democracy as a free market, Labour has traditionally been the party which has tried to help more vulnerable members of society to participate as fully in our democratic system as the more powerful ones. The Race Relations Act of 1968 and the Sex Discrimination Act of 1975 were both designed by Labour governments to do this. And, although Harold Wilson stopped Leo Abse in his first attempt to introduce legislation legalising 'consenting adults' acts of homosexuality', the bill was passed in 1966 (applying to men, over 21, in private).

But it is obvious that a policy of total non-interference in the media will greatly benefit multinational magnates, whose commercial interests alone predispose them towards the Conservative Party. The closure of three left-wing newspapers in the 1960s, and the consequent takeovers in the print industry[6] (despite legislation passed by Harold Wilson in 1965) have left the Labour party with only two advocates among national newspapers: the *Mirror* and the *People*. (Some might argue that the *Guardian* can be added to this short list, but although individual articles support Labour policies, its editorial advice at the 1987 election was to vote Alliance.) In reaction to this, Frank Allaun's Media Committee (set up in 1980, comprising MPs, union delegates and CPBF representatives) proposed a franchising system for publications, with grant aid in certain cases, and a right to distribution for small, poorer journals and papers. (These proposals were strongly influenced by Michael Meacher's Plan for the media.)

Another expression of the Labour Party's willingness to acknowledge the need for some kind of media regulation is found in its consistent defence of public sector broadcasting. Labour opposed the two acts which established ITV and Channel Four, and Mark Fisher, Shadow Minister for Arts and the Media, currently chairs a Broadcasting Committee which has, as one of its tasks, to work out the best way of opposing current government attacks on public sector broadcasting.

Our Bodies Our Selves

The example of other countries (France, Germany, Sweden) shows that government intervention in ownership and control of the media can produce more diversity. This tends to benefit groups which are constantly misrepresented in both press and broadcasting, notably black people and ethnic minorities, lesbians and gay men, and women.

Members of these groups have repeatedly expressed their disbelief that present media arrangements can provide them with fair representation. This disbelief has been expressed in the launching of their own publications, the making of their own films and videos, and the broadcasting (often illegally) from their own radio stations. Labour Party proposals on franchising, grants and distribution rights would help often impoverished publications like *The Voice, Caribbean Times, Gay News, The Pink Paper, Spare Rib* and *Outwrite* and broadcasting media; the proposed Right of Reply bill, which has been unsuccessfully introduced on several occasions by Frank Allaun and Anne Clwyd, would give individuals and groups a guaranteed means of response to misrepresentation.

But arguments have come, particularly from feminists, for legislative intervention in order to achieve fairness of representation. Suggestions have been most coherently organised, and in the USA and Canada, actually realised, behind the demand for pornography to be controlled. Feminists have been complaining about the degrading and often violent misrepresentation afforded to women through pornography for over a decade; the arguments are set out elsewhere in this book. Their campaigns have not, as yet, made a difference to Labour Party media policy, but they have had an impact on individual MPs.

Clare Short has introduced a bill to ban Page Three images from newspapers twice, and the bill has passed its first reading both times. The reason it has got no further is lack of committee time, but, as she points out, its value lies in enabling women to vocalise their dislike of pornography, and give their feelings a political focus (and the hundreds of letters she has received testify to widespread support). She is setting up a consultative committee to work out the most effective next step.

Jo Richardson, the Shadow Minister for Women (although she has no-one to shadow) is a member of the Campaign Against Pornography, which campaigns for legislative action against porn. She is optimistic about getting pornography onto the Labour Party agenda, asserting that there is 'a much higher profile in terms of outright opposition in the party to soft porn', and she points out that a number of male Labour MPs helped Clare Short in the queuing system to secure a place for her Page Three bill.

Mark Fisher's Press Committee has not, as yet, devoted time to the

issue of pornography and its control. This may well be due to the
absence of either of the above MPs on it, a situation which Jo
Richardson is determined should change. But he has paid attention
to the general problem of women's misrepresentation, in a
discussion document which drew on material from Equal Opportunities Officers in unions, and from feminist research: *The Missing
Culture.*

The participation of union officers in this document is significant,
for it has been in unions, and specifically at the Women's Trade
Union Congress, that the connection has been made between
pornography and sexual harassment. TUC guidelines on what
constitutes sexual harassment include 'the offensive use of pin-ups
and pornographic pictures',[7] and women active in trade unions feel
that the use of pornography to declare a territory 'male' disastrously
undermines the efforts we are making to increase women's work
possibilities.

Policy Reappraisal

Editorial freedom is under attack from the present government. So
are workers' rights. So are the institutions which protect the
vulnerable from exploitation and hardship. It is evidently hard to
formulate any policy when the opposition has publicly defined the
terms of reference. This is, however, what the Labour Party has to do
to create an effective strategy for the media. For what is needed is a
policy which will prevent government political censorship, but
protect vulnerable groups in society from media misrepresentation.
The only way to redefine the terms already set by the right is to treat
them as separate issues. The constant misrepresentation of certain
groups by the media is a civil rights issue: no-one should have to face
repeated degrading and intimidating images of their race, sexuality
or gender. When MPs discuss personal freedoms, they need to
recognise the limitations of those which exist, and the subjectivity
which they bring to the discussion.

The present political situation demands that Labour organise a
confident and well-informed opposition to the government, which is
pushing ahead with its own plans for the media. To be effective, the
opposition needs to be informed by the experiences of oppressed
groups, but be clear about the limitations and disadvantages of
legislative intervention on their behalf. It needs to exercise some
cunning, and be prepared to use piecemeal measures to effect
gradual changes, in order to prevent proposals being taken over and

transformed by the right. Recognition that concern about media misrepresentation is as much a part of the attack on capitalism as opposition to multiple ownership would be a constructive step towards redefining the terms which the Tories have set, and, as Clare Short justifiably points out, would find sympathy with large sections of the electorate.

Footnotes

1. *Taking Liberties*, NUJ, 1982.
2. *Ireland and the Propaganda War*, Liz Curtis, Pluto, 1984, p. 138.
3. Ibid, p. 374.
4. See *Video Nasties*, Martin Barker, ed., Comedia, 1984.
5. Article in the *New Statesman*, 15.4.88, pp 10–12.
6. *Power Without Responsibility*, James Curran and Jean Seaton, Pluto, 1984, pp 107–117.
7. *Images of Inequality*, TUC, 1984, p. 8.

LIBERALS, FEMINISM AND THE MEDIA

Elizabeth Sidney

For as long as it remains a separate political entity, the Liberal Party will remain pledged to work for a society in which '... none shall be enslaved by poverty, ignorance or conformity'. The phrase is enshrined in the Party's constitution. Liberals could be expected therefore to take a position regarding the imposition of conformity upon women by the media. Supposing the Party were in power, would it legislate to control sexism, pornography or stereotyping in the media? Without power, what influence can its parliamentarians be expected to exercise on this topic? In the political situation, about all that can be done to answer such questions is to explore the existing (1986–87) Liberal standpoint and to describe how Liberal policies, which might become legislation, are currently developed.

Party policies derive from resolutions passed at Assembly and at Party Council. Resolutions are the outcome of work undertaken by various bodies within the Party and of debate in Party publications. All this material guides the policy drafters, forms the basis of the election manifestos and indicates our priorities for legislation. Of all the resolutions the Party has passed over the last twenty years, only one contains a direct reference to women's image in the media. In 1984, a resolution on Action to Improve the Status of Women recognised that 'the media play a major role in influencing opinions and attitudes: and urge(d) that both women and men (be) presented in programmes, articles and in advertising in a manner which avoids detrimental sex stereotyping.' The Party has long been committed to equality for women, and between 1967 and 1986, passed nine resolutions to this effect in various policy areas. Thus, a Liberal Government would undoubtedly consider legislation where appropriate.

However, other resolutions show that the Party would probably not legislate to control the media directly, at least not by stronger censorship. Indeed, a 1973 resolution viewed 'with concern the activities of puritanical pressure groups who wish to introduce legislation to limit freedom of expression in literature, the theatre, the cinema, painting and other art forms by imposing new and more restrictive definitions of what is obscene, shocking or offensive' and proposed that 'under no circumstances should harder or more illiberal legislation be introduced. Rather, existing censorship should be examined to see where it can be abandoned . . .'

The free movement of information has been an abiding Liberal concern and remains a major concern today, with our commitment to repeal Clause 2 of the Official Secrets Act and introduce a Freedom of Information Act. A paper on Reform of Information Law in the United Kingdom (June 1986), prepared jointly by Liberal and SDP lawyers proposes that:

'— Everyone has the right to seek, to receive and to impart information and ideas of any kind, by any means and through any media of his or her choice.

— Public bodies . . . have a duty to make information available . . . (and) to ensure that adequate and appropriate media of communication are available . . . and that there is non-discriminatory access to them . . .'

Since 1953 the United Kingdom has subscribed to the European Convention on the protection of Human Rights and Fundamental Freedoms. The convention affirms 'the right to freedom of expression (and) to receive and impart ideas without interference by public authority and regardless of frontiers.' The United Kingdom has also been bound since 1971 to support the International Covenant on Civil and Political Rights which affirms this right and states that it covers transmission orally, in writing or print, in or on any other media.

All human rights must, of course, be limited by the need to protect other, (possibly conflicting) rights. The ICCPR itself proposes a prohibition on dissemination of war propaganda and on any advocacy of national, racial or religious behaviour. Various other proposals from the ICCPR and the ECHR would limit dissemination of information which might damage public morals, lead to disorder or crime or endanger public safety. But when drawing up the paper, the Alliance lawyers looked hard even at these limitations. They rejected the constraint on material which might lead to disorder and chose to restrict it to material which might incite people to (their quote) 'crimes carrying a high degree of social stigma'. They expressed grave reservations about limiting material which might damage public morals, since this potentially creates almost infinite censorship powers. They preferred to confine the constraint to materials which 'could give grave offence to a substantial majority of the community'.

None of this necessarily precludes the Party from introducing legislation to strengthen control of pornographic or sadistic materials, particularly if this business develops, as it may, with the growth of cable television and modern methods of printing. In America, according to NAPCRO the (U.S.A.) National Anti-Pornography Civil Rights Organisation, over 2 million households now subscribe to cable pornography and the magazines *Playboy*, *Penthouse* and *Hustler* each have a larger readership than *Time* and *Newsweek* combined.

Pornography (defined by NAPCRO in their analysis of American legislative findings as 'the systematic practice of exploitation and subordination of women (including) the harms (of) dehumanization, sexual exploitation, forced sex, forced prostitution, physical injury and social and sexual terrorism presented as entertainment') clearly violates the freedom of many, without bringing any compensatory enlargement of knowledge or vision. On these grounds, the Party might at some time decide to increase constraints on the presentation of both pornography and gratuitous violence. But Liberals hold strongly to the view that present day Britain is too closed a society, that much information is kept unnecessarily secret and that far too many ideas are suppressed. It is not a view which is easily reconciled with putting legislative constraints on the media.

The view of Women's Groups in the Party

Until the early 1980s Liberals appeared content simply to affirm commitment to sex equality. The Women's Liberal Federation (which had been a major force at the turn of the century) enjoyed a decent respectability which frustrated feminists and some WLF members. But in the 1980s things changed. The Party's central governing body set up an Ad Hoc Women's Group, major resolutions on women's status were passed at the 1984 and 1985 Assemblies, the WLF began to publish much more vigorous and precise demands and the party appointed a Training Officer with special responsibility for women's training. The Party has also declared itself an Equal Opportunities Employer and requires constituencies to interview at least one woman and one man when selecting a Parliamentary candidate. A Women's Local Campaign Pack and a WLF publication, *The World We Want*, outlining national issues, have also been produced.

Although this seems a fairly comprehensive list, it does not include specific comment on women's representation in the media. The basic assumption in Liberal thinking relating to women is that their power base must be strengthened, which would include, once in office, being committed to 50% representation of women on all public bodies within a decade. The logical outcome of such a power shift would be a shift in media representation, since the media are highly responsive to power structures. Regardless of immediate issues, the most effective long-term way of tackling media mis-representation surely lies in improving women's status generally and so rendering denigration harmless. It would then appear comic, rather than as reinforcing an unjust status quo.

Short-Term Legislation

Is there an argument for more direct or short-term legislation? There is no doubt that Liberals would subscribe to the objectives of the Women's Media Action Group. These include eliminating the portrayal of violence against women as acceptable or enjoyed by women; ending stereotyping of women, including the presentation of heterosexual marriage as women's only normal sexual state and the portrayal of women as sexually available and subservient to men; and preventing the use of sexist and belittling language and the inclusion of irrelevant sexual details (such as appearance or marital status) when reporting on women.

The question is whether and how legislation would reduce these undesirable features. The general function of the law is to underpin shifts in public opinion and to change what are clearly seen as socially damaging practices. Could a case be made out for legislating against stereotyping? or against hard porn and sexual violence? or against sexual innuendo in advertising?

Sexual Stereotyping

This case seems the weakest. The feminist complaint is that women are stereotyped in particularly limiting/constraining and out-of-date ways to a degree that handicaps our efforts towards achieving equality. It is, however, questionable whether media stereotyping is as out-of-date as the Government's (as reflected, for example, in taxation and social security policies), or the views of parts of industry and the trade unions, or the major professions. In some respects, indeed, the media stereotype advances on reality: in parts of the media we are allowed to run businesses, to dominate in a profession and to achieve public recognition to an extent which borders on fantasy. Do these enlarging fantasies further our cause? But damaging stereotypes do, of course, remain, notably in the consumer ads. Since the housewife with young children is the archetypal consumer, we are often portrayed as smart little nest builders, coping with a dumbo cockbird and a collection of fledglings, in thrall to the washing powder salesman and dependent for happiness on a cornflakes packet.

While this is irritating and demeaning, it seems doubtful whether legislation is the weapon with which to oppose it. Much more powerful and effective would be complaints from large numbers of consumers' and women's groups. The complaints would have to be to the advertisers: the Advertising Standards Authority is not likely to see family ads as indecent, dishonest or generally offensive.

Hard Porn and Sexual Violence

For many people, hard porn has some initial curiosity value before the reaction turns to boredom or disgust. A minority do not lose interest and there is some evidence that they include a high proportion of those who commit violent and sadistic sexual crimes. Whilst it cannot be argued that without access to hard core pornographic material these criminals would not have turned to violence, the possibility is strong that it stimulates aggression and helps translate fantasies into action. On these grounds society should and does introduce measures to control it. Yet attitudes are ambiguous, even in response to hard porn and sadism. Why do women help to create these materials? It is just that too many of us are culturally conditioned into accepting the unacceptable?

In the absence of any clear understanding of the attraction of sadism and its probably multiple causes, any direct legislation to eliminate production of sadistic materials is likely to be futile. On the other hand, there is sufficient concern about its effect on young people to suggest that more should be done to keep such materials from them. Stronger penalties might be imposed for admitting the under-age to films; video hire shops should display the implications of video classification more prominently; the Indecent Displays Act could be toughened (hands up who knew we had one).

But overall, more appropriate action is probably for women's groups to campaign vigorously against specific materials. There is some evidence that environmental pressure group campaigning, in particular, has succeeded in shifting public opinion. The targets would have to be specific, so that the right people were attacked, and the campaigns would need to be skilful to avoid charges of overzealous puritanism. The Women's Rights Unit of the National Council for Civil Liberties set an example when it complained to both the publishers and the unions involved regarding the new porn magazine, *Sunday Sport* (WRU Newsletter, October 1986).

Sexist Ads

Finally, sexist ads. Of course, we do not want advertisements which imply that sexual favours from women will accompany men's purchase of particular products. But alas, any complaints against such advertisements immediately involve arguments about what is truly derogatory.

Women's Media Action Group (WMAG) complained to the Advertising Standards Authority about the ad for the male perfume Bel Ami, which featured an erotic sketch of a woman lying in what could be a post-orgasmic stupor. At their meeting with the ASA, WMAG had some of their complaints accepted while others (including Bel Ami) were dismissed on the grounds that the ads were more silly or fantastic than offensive. Indeed Sir Ian McGregor (Chairman, ASA) confessed to a liking for fantasy and himself dreaming of strapping a diamond on a beautiful girl's thigh. Which sexy ad you complain about is often a matter of taste, as are the watch dogs' judgements. For this reason, it is an area where legislation could as well be harmful as helpful: we could have factual advertisements for condoms rejected and Bel Ami still allowed.

More objective complaint could be made about the imbalance between the amount of female cheesecake, designed to titillate men, and the paucity of male cheesecake for us. If women's sexual needs can be earnestly discussed in the women's magazines, and any shortcoming in our sex lives accepted as a suitable case for treatment, it could be argued that the next step toward equality should be equal display. Equal representation of male and female figures in advertising, including equality of roles, is one of the few measures on this subject which might be enforceable by law. But I doubt if the Liberal Party would ever hasten to bring in this piece of legislation.

A Bill of Rights

One piece of legislation which could greatly assist women in dealing with the media, as with other inequities, would be a Bill of Rights for the UK which would incorporate the European Convention on Human Rights. This is high on the Liberal agenda. With regard to the media treatment of women, such a Bill of Rights would include an important clause (Article 3) enabling the individual to demand the prohibition of degrading treatment. Much that is dangerous and distasteful in the portrayal of women in the media might then be challenged more easily.

The Government currently recognises the competence of the European Commission on Human Rights to receive petitions from anyone in the UK and also accepts the compulsory jurisdiction of the European Court of Human Rights. But until these rights are incorporated into our own laws, recognition can be rescinded by whichever government is in power. Moreover, taking a case to the European courts requires even more time, resources and persistence than going to court in the UK.

The Problem with Censorship

There is a fundamental problem for feminists over the question of censorship. On the whole, the women's movement has greatly benefitted from such freedom of information as Britain currently enjoys. Much of the force of the campaigns for women's equality derives from the evidence produced by the public and private research institutions. Imperfect and controlled as this information certainly is, so far, it is still accessible and discussed in a relatively free press. We should be extremely cautious about supporting any legislation which might provide a license to curtail that freedom further.

Proposals to introduce stronger controls on obscene materials are regularly considered in the press and the Conservative 1987 manifesto included a pledge to extend to broadcasting and television the controls which now exist over obscene publications. The proposal may have some surface logic, but in my view, feminists should view all extensions of censorship with extreme caution. We should fear repercussions on artistic expression, on what social statistics are released to us and ultimately on our own freedom of behaviour. Worldwide, we have seen reactionary regimes limit expression of 'unpalatable' ideas, constrain awkward behaviours and, above all, suppress women's attempts at emancipation. Censorship has alarming side effects. Not only does it give some banned activities a remarkable pseudo vitality; much more seriously, it becomes a habit. Governments find it increasingly easy to suppress information which they deem bad for other people to know. Individuals find it increasingly easy to suppress ideas and information rather than acknowledge the discomforts some ideas bring. Freedom of information and ideas does make us free; inevitably, from time to time, it does so at the cost of some personal pain.

EXCLUSION IS CENSORSHIP

Kirsten Hearn

'What!' said I, clutching wildly at the front passenger seat as the driver swerved violently. 'You can't have a feminist anthology without a disability input! That's censorship, by default... How long did you say I've got to write it in?... Two weeks!'

As I flopped back on to the car seat in stunned silence, my mind revolved with nagging thoughts. I wondered why we had not been asked earlier, pondered the difficulties of getting a group together or getting the message around to likely women in the three weeks I had been given. The 'Oi, what about us!' compunction is upon me. No time now to be democratic, better just get on with it. I worry about the future credibility of this book, and decide, honestly for once, that it is not this which is so upsetting, as the old feeling of being left out. Some sisterhood, huh, I muse. Will anyone even notice the omission if I don't get my act together fast?... probably not, but I'm not going to even give them a chance. It bloody well isn't going to happen again... Over my dead body.

'Exclusion is censorship,' I mutter, fag in mouth, as I grope around for brailler, typewriter and tape recorder. This whole episode is a fine demonstration of exclusion in progress among feminists. Need I write more? I suspect so, since I have little faith that my eight or so years of wild verbal gesticulations have really been taken seriously. I battle with the internalised oppression: 'I'm not really worth it anyway, don't worry about little me,' and then decide that, damn it, I and all my blind sisters bloody well are. We are not going to shut up even when faced with a ridiculously short time to put forward our arguments.

My exclusion is not confined to the feminist world. As a blind person, discrimination, myths, stereotypes, lies and refusal to take on my own and our collective needs and rights, have barred me from full participation. The world is full of print, it is full of visual things, obstacles, environments and people that refuse, yes refuse, to accept that not everyone is sighted. I don't know where 'ABs' got this stupid idea that they are the sole inhabitants of this planet, but it seems to have got under the skins of feminists too. Because 'ABs' refuse to acknowledge our existence (except when dipping into pockets for the charity collecting bowl or remembering to oppress us), they expect us to constantly apologise for our existence by making us ask for our needs and rights to be met. It's always for us, 'Excuse me, but I can't read that,' or 'I'm sorry but I can't see.' We didn't ask to be born blind, but there we are, large as life and twice as wonderful, blind and beautiful. The refusal to acknowledge our 'difference' as equally important to the liberation of women as a whole excludes us, thus censoring our participation in the women's movement. It is nothing short of blatant ableism.

I first became active in disability politics in 1980, when I came across a radical group of people with disabilities. For the first time in my life, I learnt that my experiences were similar, if not the same, as thousands, even millions of other people. I learnt that I was no three-headed monster from outer space, inconveniently placed on this planet for the sole purpose of suffering for a 'sin' I was not aware was wrong — the 'sin' of existing and and daring to live, love and be happy without sight. I got angry about my exclusion from socialism. (I was at this time a right-on socialist.) With other blind people I decided to get organised. We formed the Alternative Talking Newspapers Collective (ATNC) in order to start our own tape magazines and campaign for access to ink print information in the socialist and feminist movement. Our first tape, a monthly digest of the weekly and monthly alternative press, was appropriately called *Left Out* since that was what we were.

I had joined my college women's group and learnt that the sisterhood's umbrella had holes in it. There was nothing, absolutely nothing, feminist on tape. If we thought the situation was bad over socialist material, we soon realised how comparatively lucky we were. The powers-that-be in charge of taping and brailling information (the RNIB, the Talking Newspapers Association of the UK, the Talking Book Library) occasionally did something socialist-ish. They were resolutely obstructive on the feminist front, but that was hardly surprising, considering the patriarchy of the organisations in control. The women's group within the ATNC started a women's monthly tape of the feminist press. We called it, optimistically, *Women's Tapeover*.

It was through reading such 'nasty, evil, blind-person-perverting propaganda' that I found myself challenging my lifestyle. I learnt so much about women that had been hidden from me. For instance, I thought that lesbians were a female version of the heavy mob in drag — cigars in mouth, twirling invisible moustaches, leering lustily through the smoke-filled haze of the twilight world of the cellar lesbian club at sweet little femmes in frocks and lipsticks. (Radio 4 had broadcast Radclyffe Hall's *The Well of Loneliness* during my first year in sixth form at blind school, which, with D.H. Lawrence's *The Fox* were the only two pieces of lesbian-orientated literature I had ever read. No, not for me the tentative and generally homophobic studies which occasionally appeared in the non-feminist women's magazines, or the more positive images portrayed in the new range of women's and yes, even lesbian, magazines, produced by the WLM. I knew nothing of these until the ATNC. It was hardly surprising that shortly after my first exposure to 'tell it like it is', real lesbian life stories, carried in such magazines as *Cat Call* and *Scarlet Women* and even *Spare Rib* that I recognised my lesbian leanings and popped right out of the closet. My mind wanders back to the pre-*Women's Tapeover* days and shudders at the thought of what I might have been confined to, before my pleasurable awakening by the sisterhood in print and then on tape. A lifetime of hetero-sexuality. Talk about exclusion!

Pondering only briefly my lucky escape, I tumbled headlong into lesbian feminism. Here, in the world of true sisterhood with women-loving-women and all that Greenham jazz, I confidently hoped for, nay even expected, acceptance, welcome and inclusion. My hopes were short-lived. *Women's Tapeover* was already waging war with the feminist magazines. Our efforts got *Spare Rib*, the *Radical and Revolutionary Feminist Newsletter* and *Lysistrata* on to tape, with some difficulty and quite a lot of bumbling around by sighted women. But what about all those books? Not just feminist theory, which could, after much battling, occasionally find its way on to the Students' Tape Library list. What about the wealth of lesbian literature that was emerging? There was nothing for it, something had to be done!

Feminist Audio Books (FAB) was born in 1983. It's purpose — to provide on tape books and pamphlets of interest to women about all manner of women's writings. The halcyon days of the GLC were upon us. After much agonising, we went for a grant and eventually got it. With workers and an office the operation would have slid along very nicely thank you if it hadn't been for a whole series of problems, some political and most practical, to do with liaising with the GLC's funding-body successor, the London Boroughs Grants Scheme (LBGS).

Some women (sighted, mainly) on the collective wanted to restrict our operations to lending to women only. They thought that as a women's organisation, this was legitimate. However, our solidarity as blind people had not deserted us. We felt that the argument was about access to information and that blind men should not be excluded if the literature we were offering was ordinarily available to sighted men (as all feminist literature which is sold in leftie bookshops, such as Collets, is). We had learnt in five years of activity in the women's movement that even sighted women were not to be totally trusted around understanding the politics of the oppression of blind people in general and women in particular. Some of the sighted women left and FAB carried on. But the LBGS were not into us. Call it disorganisation or call it discrimination, the fact of the matter is that the LBGS insisted that all our lending records, kept in braille for the convenience of blind workers, be produced in print, and then totally refused to believe that they were accurate. It is also true that the changing political climate under a third term of Thatcher helped this process on. The more recent introduction of Section 28 into the Local Government Act 1988 has been a firm indication of this. The end result was that FAB lost its funding in December 1987, having received not a penny in payment from the LBGS since April that year.

FAB has gone voluntary now, but the pressure is not off the women's movement. *Women's Tapeover* survives and its collective are nothing if not persistent about the issue of access to information within our sisterhood. But we are still being left out. On the Monday after the Lesbian Ball in 1987, all my lesbian co-workers were sitting around the office saying how great it had been — who had been dancing with whom, what colour frock so-and-so had been wearing, the fantastic dance routine performed by the Women's Softball Team. It was the main topic of conversation in the office for five days. I hadn't even known it was going on and felt really angry and upset at being excluded. If the London Women's Liberation Newsletter had still been in existence and available on tape, I would have known about this and many other activities I never hear about until afterwards. This is pretty ironic, considering that women with disabilities were one of the groups who were mainly blamed for its demise. (But that's another story!)

Posters and leaflets in bars, women's centres, on demos, etc, are one of the main ways of communicating about all alternative activities. I never get to find out about the content of the beer-soaked pieces of paper which litter the tables unless a sighted person tells me, and I'm never aware of posters on walls unless they fall on my head!

Spare Rib is still on tape, and so are other magazines. But we always have to remind women of our existence. It has not become the reflex action we had hoped for way back in 1981, when we first started getting angry in public. Taping information is not difficult. The technology even exists to copy cassettes in the home on those groovy double-cassette numbers that were undreamt of in 1981. There are a number of guides to how to put stuff on tape, and the users are still here and growing in number.

Imagine my surprise at the ignorance of leftie organisations such as Lesbians and Gays Support the Print Workers when they stole the name 'Left Out'. Did they think that blind people would not support the print workers — or did they just not think at all? By choosing our name it made me, for one, reluctant to get involved, even though it was around the issue of access to information, which I would normally wish to participate in. Imagine further my wrath when I discovered that the campaign to stop the latest abortion bill calls itself 'FAB' (Fight the Alton Bill). I went purple in the face and spat to think that I didn't even hear about the meeting that stole that acronym from blind women, because it was only advertised in the printed media. I very much suspect that had *either* campaign actually heard of us, they certainly experienced no qualms about stealing our names without giving a thought to what it might mean to us. Exclusion is collusion is censorship. Thank you sisters.

Resources:

Alternative Talking Newspapers Collective 01-318 2002, also the contact number for *Left Out*

Women's Tapeover, 72 Alpine Road, London SE16 2RD

Feminist Audio Books, 52–54, Featherstone St, London, EC1., 01-251 2908

Guides to putting material on tape.

ATNC has a short one called *Taking Taping By the Spools*. There is a much more comprehensive one (which also considers braille and large print) available from London Boroughs Disability Resource

Team, Room 92–95, The County Hall, York Rd, London SE1 7PB.
For trade unionists, there are *Taping & Brailling Guidelines For Trade Union Material* available from CAMBRA, c/o Braille House, Goswell Rd, London, EC1

Students' Tape Library, Braille House, Goswell Rd, London EC1

RNIB (Royal National Institute for the Blind) 224 Gt Portland St, London W1

Talking Newspapers Association of the UK

Talking Book Library c/o 224 Gt Portland St, London W1

OPENING THE GATE: MAKING A CASE FOR BALANCED COMMENT

Melba Wilson

I learned a good deal of what I know about the basics of journalism and news reporting in the United States. Much of the syllabus for myself and other budding American journalists concerned the legal rights of reporters to ask for and receive information from a wide range of individuals, groups, and government officials. An American Civil Liberties Union handbook, *The Rights of Reporters* was required reading for everyone doing a university course in journalism. It was the heyday of Watergate and everybody wanted to be an investigative reporter.

The First Amendment to the US Constitution clearly established the freedom of the press; so we all knew of our unquestioned right to pursue 'Truth'. That was the theory, anyway.

The reality and practice — since much of my work to date has been in Britain — is Section II of the Official Secrets Act; the Parliamentary Lobby System, which is designed to give a privileged few the illusion of power; and a generally accepted view by those in power that journalists are adversaries; to be thwarted if possible.

'To be a keeper of secrets,' writes Donald Trelford, in a recent *Observer* article, 'confers status and identity'. He adds that if a government's job is to keep secrets, part of a reporter's job is finding them out [and that is the job of an editor to] decide whether to publish them or not'.

In my own work there is not such an immediacy of risk of censorship from government. Once, however, when working for an electrical trade journal, I wanted to describe the wiring done by an electrical firm on the Queen's estate at Sandringham. I was surprised to be told by my editor that I had to ring up the Lord Chancellor's office to check whether we could print what I considered to be a completely innocuous statement.

It seemed, however, that my story was not so harmless. I was informed by the Lord Chancellor's office that I could not write the story as intended, and furthermore had to amend it, making fewer references to the work that was actually done at the estate — in the interest of state security.

That is the disturbing thing about being a journalist in this country. While this instance of censorship was relatively mild, compared with some of the constraints placed on journalists pursuing their trade, it nevertheless is a hallmark of the kind of attitude and climate which prevails. That is, one which assumes that the public is entitled to know as little as possible, for its own good.

Thus, if your job is the dissemination of information for public perusal, whether it has to do with electrical wiring or the Zircon satellite, it is not such a rare situation to find yourself in direct conflict with the state and its perceived interests. In this sense, the notion of a free press is only illusory at best; and non-existent, when all the punches are pulled and there is, as in the case of the blanket warrants obtained (under Section II of the Official Secrets Act) to invade the BBC offices in Scotland, outright interference and muzzling of the press and the media.

On the whole, however, I am not often confronted with such overt censorship. Usually, there is a polite (sometimes, not so) tug of war with a sub-editor or editor over the emphasis of a piece or a story. This is a much more subtle form of censorship and one which is not so easily pinpointed. In any discussion between editor and journalist, there is a certain amount of give and take about a story when it is commissioned. If, however, when the final product is turned in, the two viewpoints do not quite jibe, it is most often the writer who gives ground.

This form of censorship can either be based on differing political views or it may involve considerations of house policy or worries about how the readership will take to a particular idea or set of ideas as presented by the writer. This last point is more often the case on specialist publications. I have worked on magazines like these, which cater to a specific readership group. It means in fact that the publication's life blood partially rests on its antagonising as few readers as possible. Care is taken not to rock the boat with a too radical or too political approach, lest the reader is left behind. The lowest common dominator is the norm.

It is in the arena of *political* differences of opinion between writer and editor that the censorship debate is more finely drawn, however. If, in the course of writing a story, what I unearth does not support an editor's original hypothesis, I have found a marked reluctance amongst some (though not all) to publish and be damned.

As a black woman journalist (who is also a feminist), with the particular perspective that this allows me to bring to my work, it is within this political domain, regarding crucial points of emphasis, where I most often come into conflict with editors. Whether I'm doing a book review or a profile; a conference report, a feature article, or whatever (depending upon the subject matter, of course) I often have a political point to raise regarding black and Third World people (particularly women) and their situations in this country and elsewhere. It is important to me to be able to do this, in my capacity as someone with access (however limited) to society at large.

Most of the time there is agreement between an editor and myself on how these pieces should be handled. If, however, in the course of writing a story, my position does not coincide with the editor's initial impression when the idea was first mulled over, there is the inevitable phone call wherein we 'just have to clarify a few points'.

Two instances stand out particularly. One concerns an interview I did with the writer Toni Cade Bambara. The editor at a well-known weekly asked me to do a profile piece centred around her written work. It sounded straightforward enough at the time, but having done the interview, it seemed to me to make much more sense to mould the article around work she was doing, in regard to the killings of black children in Atlanta; and to emphasise what she had to say to aspiring young black writers.

Both areas of treatment would have had more interest and relevance for black people and the black community generally, than the set-piece basic interview that was originally requested. This happened to be around the time of the deaths of the 13 young people in New Cross, and I knew, from work I was involved with in the community at the time, that there would be more interest in and insight gained from the article the way I wanted to do it.

Unfortunately, the editor did not agree with my emphasis and the story never saw the light of day. Similarly, a review I did of an Angela Davis book was rejected (by the same publication, incidentally) for being 'too political'. (This is a publication which prides itself on the political nature of its content.) In both cases, the editor was a white, middle-class male, who was convinced (in the way they are) of the rightness of his approach. This, despite the fact (I assume anyway) that I had been asked to do the piece in the first place because of my empathy with or line into the very community with which both these authors were concerned.

In the instance of the Davis review, the book was about her view of feminist perspectives. I felt it had some very pertinent things to say, particularly with respect to all the nuances which come into play between black feminists and black and white feminists. Again, I felt that my active involvement in a black feminist group made me well-placed to offer what I considered was relevant and useful comment, given that frame of reference.

It can be argued, of course, that these instances merely amount to a difference of opinion over how a piece should be written, but the fact remains that it is the editor (and in some instances, the publisher directly) who has the final say-so when it comes to such matters, and if no consensus can be reached, it is the writer who loses out. Particularly, if that writer happens to be black and female and attempting to advance an alternative viewpoint. That amounts to political censorship in my book.

Also, I think the two instances illustrate the problem that black people have generally in this country. That of having our ideas, thoughts and perspectives filtered through the white 'norm', to make them more acceptable to mainstream society. Thus, as a black journalist, I must always be mindful of the fact that my work may be judged not simply on the merits of what it has to say, but on how well it can be re-interpreted to make it more palatable for a wider, white readership, and its ideas about what I *should* be saying.

There is also unintended censorship. That is what happens when a writer's copy is red-lined by a sub-editor whose main concern is making the words fit the available space. (In all honesty, I have to say I have not directly experienced this type.) I say unintended because in many cases a sub-editor has no axe to grind, but is mainly concerned with meeting his or her deadline. That is something we can all understand (deadlines, that is). Nevertheless, a copy editor who works with little regard for the copy in their care or the intent behind it can cause damage and distortion.

The final point I want to make concerns self-censorship. The 'gatekeeper theory' was one other thing I learned about in that college journalism course. In plain language it means that there is no such thing as an unbiased story; only ones tempered by the composite experience of the writer. How much or how little of this experience is injected into a particular story or article ultimately rests with the writer. It is impossible to write a story — any story —

without this influence coming into play. It cannot be otherwise since few of us are blank slates. Nor, in my opinion, should we be expected to be; without this subjective interpretation most literature would probably make very dull reading.

Given this framework, therefore, as a journalist I feel a responsibility to my sources, to my readers and to myself to accurately and fairly write any story with which I am involved. I will not knowingly write a lie or mis-quote a source. Nor will I subjugate myself or my craft to allow others to do so. Within that framework, however, I do feel a sense of responsibility to try and correct the negativism which characterises how black people and women are depicted within the mainstream media. In practice, this means that I will almost always give the benefit of the doubt. For instance, if I'm interviewing a black woman, who presents a view which I may personally be uncomfortable with or she gives a good (in media terms) but politically 'iffy' quote, I will not use it. Usually, I will ask her to explain or clarify further, i.e., 'Do you mean . . .'; in other words, ask a leading question, which might help to focus thoughts more clearly, or, if that doesn't work, I will just ignore the point and concentrate on something else.

When blackwomen/people, are quoted in the mainstream media, even if what they have to say is not intended from a 'speaking for the race' perspective, it is likely to be used in that way to draw whatever conclusions fit the bill. There is too much misinterpretation and outright distortion of facts, as things now stand. So, I have no qualms in sacrificing what an editor might consider 'good copy' if in doing so I am able to help redress, in an effective way, the imbalance of lies, misquotes and inaccuracies which mainly characterise the way black women and black people are handled. I am not out to score career points at the expense of black people.

I do not see this as selling out the reader, or as being in conflict with what I said earlier. To do otherwise would, for me, be a betrayal. A betrayal of what my experience as a black woman has taught me are the realities for black people and black women. If I did not draw on and make use of that experience in a positive way, then there would be no point in my doing the work that I do. It becomes my responsibility to do what I can to try and turn the tables. My job is to help ensure that alternative voices are heard.

Thus, I suppose I am coming down on the side of the readers exercising the ultimate censorship by rejecting what a journalist or writer has to say. With the important proviso, however, that that readership must not be pandered to in such a way as to subvert the rights of others. An editor will generally be guided by vested interests — either advertisers, or the publisher's particular brand of politics (usually conservative).

I am guided by my commitment and a life being lived as a black woman. Black women are alternately cast as emasculating matriarchs, neglectful mothers or as sexy, insatiable nymphs. I regard my work as that of reverse censorship, if you will; being to cut out or disregard those bits which I know will do harm, and instead to advance a more informed and informing viewpoint. In the process, not only will the cause of black people/women be better served, but society at large will be better equipped to move away from the entrenched tunnel vision that is applied to people, ideas and concepts which fall outside 'the norm'.

Anything other than this invites interference from those with a vested interest in stifling what remains of 'the free press' and foreshadows control not only over what we write for publication, but more importantly, what we think, as individuals in a constricting society. A society which must have a few (at least) unfettered voices if its disparate elements are to be heard.

THE FATE OF *OUT FOR OURSELVES: THE LIVES OF IRISH LESBIANS AND GAY MEN*

Noreen O'Donoghue, Women's Community Press

In June 1986 Women's Community Press, in keeping with its declared aim of promoting and facilitating disadvantaged groups' access to the printed medium, published *Out For Ourselves: The Lives of Irish Lesbians and Gay Men*. The book was compiled and edited by the Dublin Lesbian and Gay Men's Collectives.

Initially it was believed that such a book — the first of its kind in Ireland — would be explosive and would create an atmosphere which would allow the oppression and silence of lesbians and gay men to be aired.

That we were naive is putting it mildly. Having adequately informed the press of the launch of *Out For Ourselves*, only one reporter — a part-time trainee — appeared at the launch and no photographer. Admittedly the launch took place in the middle of a divisive divorce referendum campaign and the newspapers were fairly stretched for staff, but other launches and events were covered that same evening and even the trainee reporter's write-up was discarded and never appeared. It was the first time for Women's Community Press that at least some of the media failed to attend one of our launches.

Slowly the evidence began to build up as to what was actually going on. The trade representative we had at the time was palpably uncomfortable when we introduced him to *Out For Ourselves*. The trade representative (the person who seeks orders for our books from booksellers) was what we term 'mainstream' because there aren't enough alternative presses in Ireland to allow a sympathetic representative to make a half decent living out of the job. The orders were down on the subscriptions we normally expect from book-shops because a number of bookshops didn't order any copies of *Out For Ourselves*. In the case of some bookshops the reaction was — 'No one would be interested in that topic' and in other cases, in fact easier to deal with — 'We wouldn't stock that kind of thing.' I say easier to deal with, because at least their position was declared and their power to withhold the book from a local audience was manifest.

The former attitude we found extremely difficult to cope with. Here was prejudice and censorship hiding behind the guise of commercial decisions. To be fair, we now realise that some traders, especially in rural areas, did genuinely believe that no one from their community would be prepared to walk in to their bookshop and openly buy *Out For Ourselves*. To some extent what they believed was accurate enough, but at no point did they realise that their own attitudes were contributing to the precise situation they so blandly rhymed off to our trade rep. While refusing to recognise it, the bookshops and their communities were colluding with each other on censorship. And they weren't even censoring *Out For Ourselves* as a book, they were censoring the fact that such a person as a lesbian or gay man could possibly exist in their midst. At the risk of being racist, it was easier for them to believe that religious statues moved, many of which did around that time!

Another insidious example of the power that lies behind censorship was in our dealings with individual stores which are part of a larger chain of outlets. When approached by our trade rep. some of them refused to stock *Out For Ourselves*. When asked by a daily newspaper (on whose double standards, more later) if they actually refused to stock the book, they denied they had refused it in the first place. Despite their protests, what they told the newspaper was false. At that stage they had hurriedly received a small number of *Out For Ourselves* from their wholesale service. Although Women's Community Press embarrassed them into stocking copies of the book, the chain store was regarded by the media as having more credibility and integrity than Women's Community Press. The following piece from (unfortunately) a woman journalist will bear this out:

> There seems to be a great deal of confusion surrounding the availability of the new Women's Community Press publication, 'Out For Ourselves', which deals with the lives of Irish lesbians and gay men. Controversy over alleged refusals to stock the book might be seen as a clever publishing ploy to get the £4.95 paperback moving off the shelves ... but Noreen O'Donoghue, of the Women's Community Press claims that getting the book onto the shelves in the first place is the real problem.
>
> But the real confusion arises over Eason's position on the publication. According to the Women's Community Press, the

Dublin branch of the leading store has accepted the 'usual order' of several hundred copies, but the Cork branch wouldn't touch it ... 'Absolute nonsense', said Eason's Cork book buyer briskly. 'The book was bought in wholesale so we are naturally stocking it here. I didn't know there was any problem until I read it in the papers. We have no objections at all!'

There was nobody available for comment from either the Workers' Party or Sinn Fein bookshops yesterday evening — but perhaps they could cast some further light on the alleged 'suppression' of the book. 'The only thing we can put it down to is blatant homophobia ... if that's the right word', [Women's Community Press] says of the Workers' Party and Sinn Fein bookshops decision not to stock the book ... 'we would have expected so-called progressive shops like that to accept it without hassle'.

Irish Press.

Whatever about mainstream bookshops reacting badly to *Out For Ourselves*, we were dumbfounded when the two self-styled radical political bookshops, as mentioned in the above newspaper extract, refused to allow the book onto their shelves. When asked by *Women's Community Press* to comment on their refusal, the first said their customers wouldn't be interested in that particular book. It appears that certain members of the editorial board of *Out For Ourselves* and the party the bookshop represents are political enemies. Consequently, even though the issues raised in the book are beyond and outside political ideology in the narrow sense, these differences were allowed to stifle any 'lefty' unity on the issue of lesbianism or gayness in Irish society.

As for the second bookshop, an extreme degree of confusion as to the meaning of 'radical' became obvious. The buyer in their shop 'certainly wouldn't stock it, nor would they review it in their newspaper either' ... We know that this attitude was not shared by all members of the bookshop collective but internal differences are irrelevant to Women's Community Press when a book is rejected by a bookshop.

What our experience with these two bookshops shows is that lesbianism and gayness as a political issue or concern is so low in their list of priorities as to be non-existent. And it's not that they don't recognise the silence surrounding the debate in Ireland, but they know that the issue is potentially internally divisive and most of them feel that it's not enough of an issue anyway to create divisions over. More self-imposed censorship hiding behind the screen of 'It's not a big issue anyway'? Of course it's not a big issue because no one will allow it to become one ...

More and more it was becoming clear to Women's Community Press that power and censorship are closely aligned. We telephoned a large booksellers in Dublin to enquire if their stock of *Out For Ourselves* needed to be topped up. The buyer we spoke to refused to discuss the book and it seemed from her tone that she had relegated *Out For Ourselves* to the level of pornography.

When this encounter was published in the popular *In Dublin* magazine, our trade representative was summoned to the bookshop to immediately explain where this story had come from. Our trade rep. then sent us an ultimatum, saying that if we didn't publicly deny that this exchange had taken place, he would have no 'option' but to resign as our trade representative. His explanation from the booksellers was that the buyer we had spoken to was not dealing with *Out For Ourselves* at all and that it was management policy to stock progressive books. Managament policy, it seems, hadn't been made clear to important members of the staff! We refused to retract our statement to *In Dublin* and our rep., knowing where the real power and money lies, and obviously needing to earn a living, terminated his contract with us.

Although by now, *Out For Ourselves* was enjoying a certain notoriety, it was the idea of the book in an Irish context that was doing it. The content of the book and the political and social issues raised in it were almost entirely ignored. The big selling daily newspapers were to some extent happy enough to print reports of censorship on the part of booksellers, while at the same time not arranging for the book to be reviewed in their book pages. Having delivered a couple of copies to each of the book editors, we finally contacted them to discuss the possibility of a review. One of them said *Out For Ourselves* was not 'suitable' for reviewing and the others put us off by saying the book had not come to their attention! We heard through the grapevine that another newspaper, a weekly one, had been interested in reviewing the book but couldn't find a reviewer!

One of the Sunday newspapers did cover *Out For Ourselves* in some detail. The article, although sympathetic and supportive, was part of a newspaper that treats women as edible objects and regularly prints stories which suggest that lesbianism and gayness is some 'moral' disorder. The readers of the newspaper must have been very confused by the conflicting presentations of lesbianism and gayness, as on the one hand, 'unnatural' and 'dangerous' and on the other, as ordinary people who are outrageously oppressed by society. Women's Community Press hasn't as yet been able to articulate our own attitude to *Out For Ourselves* appearing in a context such as this. Are we ourselves contributing to exploitation and censorship by allowing the book be used by newspapers like this? Does the dominant tone of a newspaper mute any different presentations of a topic that appear in it from time to time? How does this compare with the many other newspapers that didn't cover the book at all?

It has to be said that *Out For Ourselves* was reviewed and welcomed by a number of alternative newspapers and magazines. However, in the overall context of the larger newspaper and magazine public, they represent a very small percentage of readers.

Finally, to prove that circular thinking produces circular results and that breaking out of that mould produces other results, I want to cite the example of a bookshop in Dublin, Books Upstairs, where many people felt free to purchase a copy of *Out For Ourselves*. This bookshop sold more copies of the book than all the other Irish bookshops totalled together. Why? Because people felt the prevailing attitudes didn't follow them into the shop and the sense of being 'seen' buying *Out For Ourselves* was absent. People didn't shop there unless they felt that, after all, the 'non issues' were really only 'hidden issues'.

INTRODUCING OUR SIMILARITIES AND DIFFERENCES

Diane Biondo, Florence Hamilton, Debbie Licorish

> We have destroyed this book because it is woman-hating. By selling
> this book in Sisterwrite you are not only condoning violence against
> women but more dangerously putting it forth as legitimate feminist
> sexual practice...

On a shelf near the window in Sisterwrite there is a notebook for
women to write in. The idea is to give customers the space to say
what they think of the shop. The entries in the book range from
single word superlatives to political commentary pages long. The
subjects cover the decor of the shop, the moods of the workers,
reflections on international sisterhood. But most of the comments
are about Sisterwrite's stock.

As the comment above shows, some women took offence at
Sisterwrite's decision to stock a certain book on lesbian sadomasochism. They took 'censorship' into their own hands and
destroyed the shop copy. Yet the absence of the book caused anger as
well:

> ... unfortunately, Sisterwrite spells out a very oppressive note of anti-
> S&M ... I refuse to be challenged on my sexuality by other
> lesbians.

It seems that what Sisterwrite stocks or censors will incite either
criticism or praise, depending on the politics of the commentator. In
the same way, Sisterwrite will arrive at its stocking policies through
the politics of the individuals on the collective. At present we are a
group of working class/Black/lesbian/white/heterosexual/middle
class/able-bodied women with different national backgrounds. Our
politics and priorities reflect this diversity, yet in making stocking
policies we begin by outlining the principles on which the collective
all agree:

1. Sisterwrite is a specialist feminist bookshop stocking books by

and about women. Therefore we will select and censor any titles which do not meet the collective's definition of a feminist criteria.

2. We aim to offer a wide range of opinions within the Women's Movement. Therefore it is impossible for the collective to agree with all the views put forth in all books in stock.

3. Decisions, once made, are never final (as was the case with the S&M book — for a few years we stocked it, now we do not). This is because previous decisions are often reviewed when the staff changes, so that the views of new members can be considered.

4. Because we are a non-profitmaking co-op, we cannot afford to take financial risks with stock. We turn down quite a few titles (especially imports) solely on the basis of their cost.

Points of Contention

Nonetheless, even in agreement, the process of deciding what not to stock is often arduous, involving reading, discussion and argument. In just the phrase 'books by and about women' there are many contentious areas. To insist that every book in the shop be written by an actively anti-racist anti-heterosexist feminist would be absurd. Even a book that portrays women in a positive and liberatng way does not guarantee that the author would not say 'I'm not a feminist, but . . .'. Fortunately, Sisterwrite is not concerned with large profit margins and is therefore able to censor mass market pop fiction which also claims to be 'for women'.

Of course, feminist literature is not free of prejudices and should not be assumed to be otherwise, as complacency poses a threat to any movement. But if a book by a socialist feminist offends a radical feminist, do we censor it? Likewise, books by well-known academic writers (are there too many books by white academics?) which might provide inspiration for many, often include anti-lesbian views. As said earlier, Sisterwrite does not agree with all views expressed in our stock, but in these instances freedom of information as regards feminist theory takes precedence. What about work by the Victorian ladies who used their power and privilege to publicise their 'pioneering in the British Empire'? Are we encouraging the assumption of white supremacy by stocking books about colonial women? One customer writes:

> I am disappointed to see that you stock Isak Dinesen . . . who in no way conforms to your stated policy re racism.

Writers such as Dinesen are not censored for their colonial existence, but are stocked for their historical importance in the emancipation of women. Another customer agrees

> Isak Dinesen's views would not be considered right-on today, but in her day they were courageous.

Are we also breaking the cultural boycott by stocking the work of South African women writers? Literature by or about South African women which presents the struggle against apartheid has a definite place in the bookshop. The experience and writing of Black South African women is largely suppressed in their country and is powerful in persuading readers of the desperate need for change. Likewise, the writings of white South African women are equally powerful in their exposure of the brutality and hypocrisy of such a regime. A white writer who supports apartheid would not be stocked.

There are occasions when the collective feel that the stocking policy should be waived. The children's section provides literature which aims to discourage sexist and racist assumptions. So a book about a boy knitting is equally valid to one about a girl who wants to be an engineer. We do stock children's books which are merely 'inoffensive', but the search for actively anti-racist and anti-sexist material does take precedence.

The dearth of literature concerned with Black British history led us to stock two books on the subject which are neither specifically for women nor feminist. The problem is whether we should relax our censorship of general black political literature, as the racism within the Women's Movement is surely symptomatic of the racism which is endemic in British society. Hopefully, such literature will be succeeded in the shop by feminist works which seek to reclaim this neglected heritage.

Traditional Censorship

None of the stocking policy decisions discussed above were made without considering what censorship has meant historically. Traditionally, official censorship has been used by right and left wing governments for different ends. Notorious examples can be found in the Nazi burning of Jewish literature in Germany, the seizure of lesbian and gay books at customs in England, and, in America, the emergence of the Harlem Renaissance as an effect of indirect censorship by the white literary establishment.

Many people believe that to censor anything, from pornography to fascist propaganda is opposed to libertarian ideals, that to prevent pornography is to infringe upon the rights of individual liberty. But whose liberty? And at whose expense? Mass market pornography and the question of censorship are still being debated by moralists, politicians, the church. In feminist circles, we are opposed to pornography because it degrades women, but we are also opposed to censorship being used as a weapon of oppression against other feminists. This means we must try to represent as many points of view in the women's movement as possible. At the same time, we cannot condone a book which portrays or depicts negative images of women.

Perfection

When Sisterwrite decides not to stock a book, we are not denying women access to this work, nor are we suppressing the work or silencing this writer. In most cases the book can be obtained elsewhere with great ease. We are carrying out what we feel is our political responsibility to promote positive images of women through feminist writing.

Perhaps in the end, we will find ourselves going back to discuss the roots and definitions of feminism. Whatever the debate, however, it is crucial that the discussion remain open — between ourselves on the collective, between the customers and the workers, and between women generally.

The Comments Book on the shelf near the window seems to be just as good a way as any to do this. Where else can a woman write 'Anyway, I expect perfection in sisterhood' and get away with it?

WHAT IS A FEMINIST PUBLISHING POLICY?

Susanne Kappeler

Since the beginning of feminist publishing in this wave of feminism, questions of editorial policy have stood in the foreground. Magazines, journals and newsletters like *WIRES* defined themselves as 'by women and for women', and endeavoured to introduce a less autocratic policy for accepting contributions by women. There was a recognition that editors, even if collectively organised, occupy an important position of power which regulates what is and what is not published. There was therefore a commitment, written or unwritten, not to exclude anything, not to invoke the power of veto which would disable a woman from expressing her views.

Trouble arose quickly, however. Magazines were accused either of publishing anti-woman views, or else of having rejected some contributions on political grounds — feminist or otherwise — as in the notorious *Spare Rib* dispute which centred around Palestinian and Israeli politics. Editors who rejected contributions for publication were accused of censorship.

The word 'censorship' is increasingly being used to indicate the silencing and suppression of women's voices. However, in the context of publishing, the law, and the freedom of expression, we should retain the precision of the term and honour the distinctions between different practices. Censorship is a term which applies to state interference in a society's freedom of expression: it designates certain *views* or *kinds of information* which may not be publicly articulated. Andrea Dworkin in 'Against the Male Flood' has drawn attention to the fact that censorship, as well as the practice of writing, mean something very different in western democratic states or police states respectively:

> In South Africa and the Soviet Union, for instance, writing is treated entirely as an act, and writers are viewed as persons who engage in an act (writing) that by its very nature is dangerous to the continued existence of the state. The police in these states do not try to suppress ideas ... They go after writers as persons ... and they persecute,

punish, or kill them ... Censorship is deeply misunderstood in the United States ... Censorship, like writing itself, is no longer an act.[1]

As women and feminists, our problem has been and is the suppression of women's views, rather than censorship proper. The two practices — suppression and censorship — are not the same, and we need to understand their respective mechanisms precisely if we want to fight them. If we misidentify the practice of suppressing women's, and especially feminists' views as censorship, we are likely to seek redress in the wrong quarters, i.e. through legislation around freedom of expression and censorship.

The suppression of feminist ideas in western capitalist patriarchies is achieved not through legislation, but through control of the market. Access to public opinion has been managed, historically and structurally, by men, and in the private sector is moreover determined by profit. Women's contributions have been *excluded* on a massive scale, rejected for publication or republication and preservation; they have not been censored as such.

In recognition of the general exclusion of women from public expression, feminist publications have virtually unanimously decided to exclude contributions from men, whatever their politics, as a policy of positive discrimination. However, beyond this, feminist publications may have more than one objective: to provide access for women's views, or to provide space for *feminist* ideas. The two have not always been explicitly separated, but they result in markedly different policies. The former would require no decision to exclude, whereas the latter, i.e. a *feminist* publishing policy, has the difficult task of analysing and selecting contributions on the basis of feminist politics, and of rejecting what is anti-feminist.

It is no help that in recent times, the *meaning* of the term 'feminist' seems to have gradually slipped away from us and become almost synonymous with 'woman' — not without the help of the malestream media. Because there is debate within feminism — discussion and disagreement about emphases, explanations, strategies and interpretation — we have succumbed to the idea of liberal pluralism so dear to the intellectual culture of our society. This suggests that we can have any number of different brands of feminism on the supermarket shelf — something to suit every woman, so that we have a proliferation of trade marks qualifying the brand: liberal feminism, radical feminism, cultural feminism, revolutionary feminism, marxist feminism, socialist feminism, christian feminism, Jewish feminism, spiritual feminism, Black feminism, lesbian feminism, s/m feminism, and post-feminism. The list could go on, of course, according to specific identity definitions, or by implication (e.g. heterosexual feminism, white feminism). From a spectrum of political orientations we have come right through to identity politics, with the ultimate horizon being 'whatever a woman says, goes' and good-bye to feminism altogether.

The emergence of formations like lesbian feminism or Black feminism are due, of course, to the identification of particular political issues which had been neglected by feminist theory. If Black feminists have called 'feminism' white, it is to highlight its implicit racism, just as lesbians have called for recognition of heterosexist bias. These issues having been raised, however, it is inconceivable to argue for the continued existence of a theoretical political feminist position which is racist or heterosexist, a 'white' or a 'heterosexual' feminism which deliberately continues to ignore the issues of race and sexuality. Rather, feminism (unmodified)[2] has expanded in political sophistication and complexity and awareness.

This is not to say, of course, that racist, heterosexist, middle-class and other biases have ceased to exist, or to be articulated once they have been theoretically recognised; what it does mean, however, is that we would not continue to call them feminist or acceptable to feminism. The recognition and theoretical incorporation of these issues has meant an expansion of the feminist agenda and hence of feminist criteria by which we make political (and editorial) judgements.

In our liberal pluralist climate, however, there is an apparent anxiety not to be seen to judge or 'legislate' what is feminism. That would smack of trotskyism, party line and dogma. No doubt it also derives in part from a legitimate desire not to judge, attack, condemn or criticise other women or, in the case of editors, not to exercise editorial power. I suspect, however, that it equally derives from a fear of conflict and from defensiveness, i.e. a fear of having one's own position examined and criticised, and hence a willingness to abstain from criticism of others and to seek safety in a pluralism of tolerance.

I do not think that tolerance is politically despicable, on the contrary, I think it is essential to feminist politics. Indeed, I would count it as part of a feminist *method*, as relevant to editors as to reviewers and feminists in general. But I understand by it a tolerance of understanding, understanding the positions of other women and how they come to hold them. This is very different from a tolerance of acceptance, of letting anything pass without challenge. For how can feminist theory develop if whatever women say goes, if we don't engage in political analysis of the implications of a particular position? How can our own ideas develop and change if we don't examine them critically and exercise political judgement? We seem to associate 'judgement' with sentencing and condemnation, rather than seeing it as an essential part of thinking and of politics.

Judging an article in terms of feminist politics is not, of course, as easy as recognising a label or a stated identity. Often, we do not know what position to take in relation to a new issue, or what would be a *feminist* position. That is just where we need debate and analysis. As editors of a feminist publication where such debate takes place, we can therefore not decide whether to accept or reject a contribution to that debate on the grounds of the position it takes. We would have to judge the article in terms of a feminist method and commitment and the agenda of feminist theory.

Despite the disagreements and debates within feminism, it is possible to arrive at a base line definition of what 'feminist' means. Liz Kelly suggests the following definition of a feminist position: a recognition that 'men, collectively and as individuals, have an interest in maintaining women's oppression, [and] ... a call to action to change the world'.[3] A recognition, in other words, that women are oppressed, and oppressed by men, and a commitment to liberation from that oppression. It is difficult to see how any feminist could disagree with such a definition, or why, if she thinks that, say, capitalism rather than men causes the oppression of women, she would wish to call herself a feminist rather than a marxist. That this base line definition of the meaning of 'feminist' doesn't amount to a full-blown *theory and explanation* of our oppression in its diversity should also be obvious.

Regardless of our theoretical explanations, however, we can derive a feminist practice from this definition. As editors, readers or reviewers of other women's positions we would look for a commitment to social change in the interest of *all* women; but we would also look for a method of criticising other women's positions which showed a tolerance of understanding, a tolerance, in other words, of the woman who holds the position, without necessarily accepting the politics of her views.

In editorial policy as well as in reviewing and in our interactions with each other, our feminist practice has often veered between two extremes: either a pluralist tolerance of anything any woman says, inspired by a well-intentioned but politically misguided principle of 'not judging women', or else a form of trashing, of personal attack in reviewing, which seems the reverse. But in fact, the two practices are part of the same coin, the result of not distinguishing sharply between 'woman' on the one hand and 'feminist' or feminist politics on the other, a confusion, in other words, of identity with politics.

In practice, feminist editing is of course a great deal more complex, and there are many more issues to consider than the theoretical meaning of 'feminist'. An actual magazine or press is not just 'feminist' in the theoretical sense, but an instance of political organising. Through its policy it defines a community, of readers and contributors, and a focus. It is here that identity definitions have their justification, and that, say, working class or Black feminists may decide to organise a magazine specifically around issues of race and class, and to provide the space for working-class or Black women to write. The necessity of specific organising arises out of practical politics and realities, i.e. the fact that many groups of women did and do not have the same access to publishing and expression of their views as white, middle-class, educated women who tend to dominate, even in the feminist media. Since the early magazines 'by and for women' we have come to understand that 'women' aren't a homogeneous group, a happy sisterhood of equals, and that we need to take positive steps, both in feminist theory and in feminist political organising, if we want feminism to reflect the interests of *all* women. No *one* feminist magazine is going to fulfil that brief, every magazine chooses its priority and therefore also excludes, but they still are, if they are feminist, part of the same feminism: a politics for the liberation of *all women*.

Notes:

1. Andrea Dworkin, 'Against the Male Flood: Censorship, Pornography, and Equality', *Trivia* 7 (Summer 1985), pp. 12–13.
2. Catharine MacKinnon, 'Feminism, Marxism, Method, and the State: Toward Feminist Jurisprudence', *Signs* 8, no. 4 (Summer 1983), p. 639.
3. Liz Kelly, 'The New Defeatism', *Trouble & Strife* 11 (Summer 1987), p. 24.

LIBEL — A FEMINIST WEAPON?

Barbara Rogers

The libel laws in this country are perhaps the main means of censorship of criticism — but also, I would argue, a vital means of protection for people who are being viciously attacked in the media — as 'loony lefties', lesbian mothers, gay men, hysterical feminists, and so on and on. The libel laws are a mess, but until we can reform them we need to understand how they work and not be afraid to use them in our defence. As things stand at the moment, it's open season for defamation. And it *is* doing us a lot of damage.

Feminists, and radical people in general, seem to believe that we are powerless to act in the face of libel. It is often stated that it is only the rich and powerful who can sue the capitalist media without risking total bankruptcy, since there is no legal aid for libel cases. I would argue with this position as someone who has experienced libel myself, not as a lawyer but as both defendant and plaintiff. You need steady nerves but not necessarily a lot of money. A majority of libel actions are settled before they go for trial. It is the huge court costs that everyone is afraid of, not the damages, which is why there's such a rush to settle if they believe you really might pursue it. It's all a bit like a poker game.

If you are the person who has been attacked in print, once the other side know you're not going to challenge them, they can do whatever they like. As a potential defendant who wants to be free to criticise others, if you've got any sense (or a background in publishing) you know you can't be nasty about people gratuitously and get away with it every time. But you need to know enough to assess the risks, and much of the time it becomes more a matter of knowing who you're dealing with than the finer points of the law.

For example, I was involved in a lot of work against Rio Tinto Zinc. We attacked them constantly and widely — with impunity, since it was clear from the start that they would not challenge us. (We were of course doing no more than telling the truth, but we could easily have been sued for libel.) The reason they did nothing is simple: if you challenge an alleged libel you risk making it worse, because everyone repeats the original statements. A company like RTZ likes to keep up great barriers of anonymity and secrecy, so we felt able to attack it as much as we liked. However much we provoked them they would not react — rather, they hoped we would simply go away if ignored.

From the perspective of the individual being attacked by the media, it's not usually a question of prosecution, of actually going to court. It's whether or not to issue a warning. This most usefully comes in the form of a letter from a specialist solicitor. If the national media backs down on many occasions over highly defensible statements, on the basis of a solicitor's letter, there's no reason why we should not be prepared to use this simple challenge. The reason that publishers usually settle so quickly — generally for an apology and damages of a few hundred pounds — is not that they can't afford to proceed, but because it looks extremely bad if they have a libel suit pending against them.

This is what happened with a book publisher I was involved with, who completely crumbled under a challenge based on what those of us involved in producing the book considered to be frivolous claims. Although the publisher thought the complainant would probably go no further than a solicitor's letter, he was very worried about how it would look to his bank manager, to people doing company searches on him, and so on. He didn't want to have this problem outstanding at a time when he was seeking finance. It all becomes a game of nerves. This book was about South African propaganda: a connection was made between South Africa and a certain college. A well-known liberal associated with the college threatened all manner of things if the book wasn't withdrawn, damages paid and an apology made. They seemed likely to get an injunction at the least, so the book *was* withdrawn. It finally appeared a year later with a small publisher, but received nothing like the publicity it could have if the original publisher had had the courage to stand up to the threats. But the risk had just seemed too great.

However, in another case I was involved in, the outcome was different. I suggested in a book published by the Africa Bureau that a magazine called *To The Point International*, based in Antwerp, was a South African government propaganda front. The magazine sent a solicitor's letter threatening a libel action, and the Africa Bureau trustees became extremely nervous, because as a voluntary organisation without limited liability, they would have been personally liable for damages for costs. However we persuaded them to hold fast until the other side had to go through a process called 'discovery', that is, disclose who they were and how they were funded. Obviously they were reluctant to do this and a few weeks later the magazine disbanded and the journalists left in disgust saying it *was* a propaganda front. Basically we called their bluff and won.

The case of the media coverage of Peter Tatchell's parliamentary candidacy for Bermondsey was instructive. After the first tentative attacks on him, Peter made it clear that he was not going to threaten any action, and thus he laid himself open for more and more scurrilous and demonstrably untrue allegations. He could have learned a lesson from Randolph Churchill, who is said to have made a lot of money between the wars by threatening to sue everyone who said anything about him in print that was not totally favourable — the result being that in the end no-one would say anything even remotely critical of him. Libel solicitors are less interested in what has actually been said, incidentally, than in how likely the other side are to pursue the case.

It is important that feminists, and the left, challenge the media's assumption that we will never confront them. Libel laws *are* stacked on their side but we must be prepared to use them too. At the time of writing *Everywoman* magazine is suing both the *Islington Gazette* and the *Evening Standard* for some vicious and false claims about us: 'about as libellous as you can possibly get' was our legal advice. This allegation is completely untrue but very damaging to us. Within a week we sent a solicitor's letter, to which they both replied promptly but unsatisfactorily. Our solicitor has now issued a writ and we are ourselves now in the process of 'discovery', where they can examine our records. We are aiming for an apology and damages.

Of course, in being prepared to bring a libel suit, you risk the original allegations being repeated. But if you wish to enter public life, you must expect attacks from the media and be prepared to answer back. If people's fear of this stops them from being in the public sphere, then this is the most pernicious form of censorship of all.

The libel laws, to me, incorporate an important element of the right to reply. They are the reason for the many apologies you see in the papers (or after *That's Life* on TV). If we are viciously attacked we should defend ourselves. It's not just for us, it's for all the others who will be the next targets if we don't act. Perhaps most important of all, we should be having a wide-ranging debate on what *we* want for the future as a defence for ordinary people against those who own and control the media, and use it as a personal weapon against us.

WHO WATCHES THE WATCHDOGS?

Kate Holman

What do the existing structures set up to supervise media standards offer to women? For an answer we must examine the record of two main bodies: the Press Council, which covers newspapers, national and local, and magazines; and the Broadcasting Complaints Commission with the same role in radio and TV.

The Press Council

The Press Council was set up in 1953 by the newspaper industry itself, adapting a form of self-regulation in a bid to avoid tougher, statutory controls. It has been characterised by barrister Geoffrey Robertson as a 'blind watchdog which barks retrospectively and then only when someone steps on its tail'. According to Fleet Street commentator Tom Baistow it is 'a eunuch, impotent in the face of the crime and crumpet brigade'.

These critics highlight failings which are by now well catalogued. First of all, the council is operated and funded by the very people it sets out to regulate. It draws 98 per cent of its funding, and over a third of its members, from management organisations. The National Union of Journalists pulled out in 1980, complaining that it had just four seats out of 36 to represent its 30,000 plus members. Depending as it does on the voluntary co-operation of newspaper editors, it has no authority to enforce its rulings. Indeed there have been many examples of the tabloid press demonstrating its disdain for the Press Council by reprinting the offending article or picture alongside the council's criticism.

The *Sun* republished photographs of 'Princess Di' in a bikini on holiday, when she was five months pregnant, with the council's objection that 'Personal consent would have been required for the publication of pictures in these circumstances of any woman who was pregnant'. The ruling sounds a fair one, but reflects the council's obsequious attitude to the Royal Family rather than a general respect for women.

Judging by the ferocity of insults poured on the organisation by newspapers managements, one might believe for a moment that it is genuinely hitting home. But *Sunday Express* editor Sir John Junor's description of the 'po-faced, pompous, pin-striped, humourless twits who sit on the Press Council', or Sir James Goldsmith's assessment of a 'shameful and farcical organisation' turning out 'the usual blend of perfidy, sanctimony and humbug', are designed to belittle and discredit the council so that any of its findings lack credibility.

The Press Council is indeed a fig leaf, designed to cover up the worst excesses of the British Press, but not to make any changes. It rejects public scrutiny: the complaints committee meets in secret and no transcript of proceedings is published.

It is opposed to statutory controls on the press of any sort, and to the Right of Reply. It attacked printworkers for taking action to secure a fairer representation for other trade unionists. 'The council condemns equally any union, chapel (newspaper union branch) or any other group exerting pressure to force a newspaper to publish material agaist the will of its editor,' it declared. Yet it has remained noticeably quiet on the scandal of growing monopoly ownership of the press. And it believes newspapers have a right to be politically partisan, even if that means a massive bias in favour of the Right. Many groups, including the TUC, have put forward proposals for reforming the Press Council. But others, including members of the NUJ, believe it to be 'constitutionally incapable of reform'.

For the ordinary individual seeking redress for press abuse or misrepresentation, the Press Council is a poor bet. It is notoriously slow, taking months to reach a verdict. The 'Fast Track' procedure introduced in 1984 applies only to factual innacuracies, and can be simply vetoed by an editor. No help is offered to complainants, and indeed a series of obstacles stand in the way of a 'successful' outcome. All complaints are forwarded automatically to the editor concerned, and everything stands still until a response is received. Complainants must agree in advance not to take any legal action whatever the result. And the Press Council keeps all documents relating to the case. Nonetheless — not surprisingly in view of the continuing decline in press standards — the number of complaints to the council has multiplied dramatically in recent years. In 1986 out of 1136 complaints received, a mere five per cent were upheld.

The percentage is smaller than 11 years ago, when 32 complaints out of 440 were upheld.

The Press Council can be perceived already to have a predominantly male profile, what with watchdogs and pin stripes — albeit an impotent masculinity. And this impression is reinforced on closer analysis. The Press Council's characteristics: white, middle class, male, pro-establishment, and anti-trade union, reflect its members and the way they are selected. Chaired until October 1988 by an Oxford don, Sir Zelman Cowen, it is dominated by the members from newspaper management, who are exclusively male. Its structure is a mirror image of the British press. After all, newspapers are still run by men, for men: less than 10 per cent of Fleet Street journalists are female, and, despite recent promotions, most of those are in the more junior positions. In the provincial press too, women remain in the lower-paid, less responsible posts. And even in magazines, men tend to occupy the top jobs.

There are six women on the council out of a total of 32 members, with a further seven men having consultative status. All are lay members chosen by a five-strong Appointments Commission including just one woman: a Tory councillor from pastoral Sussex. How representative are the women? Anyone can put their name forward to the Press Council, but participation depends on being able to attend meetings in central London, during weekday working hours. In other words only those without problems of time off work or loss of earnings, or the demands of young or school age children, need apply. Those that do apply, are more likely to be successful, professional women who have come to terms with a masculine environment.

One noticeable aspect of the council's report for 1985 is the tiny minority of cases relating to women. Those that there are are sometimes revealing. For example, a complaint by a woman reported in the *Sun* to have taken part in a 'drunken brawl' in Iceland, in which 'British girls tore the clothes off one married man' and 'used their bodies as tempting bait' was rejected. To the Press Council it was merely a 'colourful report'. To the woman involved, who claimed the reporter lied, it must have been a degrading piece of sexual stereotyping with untold consequences in her own life.

Another complaint highlighted a 'robust and hostile' (the council's own description) article in the *Sunday Times* about Islington Council, in which the main targets selected for vilification were Islington Women's Signing-on Campaign, self-defence courses for lesbians, and Islington Under-Fives Action Group. The report was not found to be 'misleading or distorted', although the Press Council believed Islington itself should have had some opportunity to reply. The women's groups, apparently, were fair game.

The only case relating to a rape report was also unsuccessful. An article in which a rape victim was said to have suffered 'no actual violence' was not condemned by the council, on the grounds that the comment was made by a police officer. Even after what has since become known as the 'Ealing Vicarage Rape' case in 1986 — one of the most appalling illustrations of the press's attitude to rape, in which a photograph of the victim was published by the *Sun* — it took the Press Council a year to complete its investigation, although this was launched by the council itself the day the picture appeared.

The council's attitude to privacy is particularly unfair to women. The council's policy declares that 'entry into public life does not disqualify an individual from his [sic] right to privacy about his private affairs'. It has been keen — as shown — to defend Royals like Princess Diana and Prince Andrew from press harassment. Yet when former Labour MP Maureen Colquhoun complained about the *Daily Mail*'s outrageous persecution of herself and her woman lover, the council declared that she had forfeited her right to personal privacy because she had 'taken a very strong stand on feminist issues'. Would an MP who had taken an equally strong stand on housing issues, or health issues, be similarly penalised?

The Press Council's approach to the Women's Movement is perhaps most clearly shown by rulings relating to the Greenham Common Peace Camp. It rejected eye witness accounts by two Greenham Women of a demonstration against the then Defence Secretary Michael Heseltine, in favour of the testimony of a *Daily Telegraph* reporter (male), who claimed the Minister was punched and kicked.

And in a more notorious case, it rejected a complaint against the *Daily Express* who used a woman reporter, Sarah Bond, to infiltrate the Peace Camp. Her reports, *The Inside Story of Greenham*, were given sensational prominence in the paper at a time when the women were being evicted and the peace protest was receiving a lot of public attention. Her brief, stated the complainants, was to act as an *agent provocateur* among the women, and to put together a lurid and damaging account of life at Greenham Common.

The Press Council decided that the 'use of subterfuge' was

justified on the grounds that Sarah Bond would not have been able to gain entry to the camp, or get the 'inside story', if she had disclosed that she was a journalist from the *Daily Express*. That statement in itself should have led the council to examine why the peace women, who needed public notice if their campaign was to succeed, wanted nothing to do with some sections of the Press. But the council preferred to overlook Fleet Street's vicious propaganda campaign against the women.

The picture that emerges is of an organisation sharing the male values and viewpoint of the industry it serves; an organisation overwhelmingly ignorant of the way women live. Furthermore it appears that women already recognise this, for out of 139 complaints heard by the council in 1985, only 15 of the complainants were women — among them Lady Mosley, wife of the pre-war Fascist leader, and Victoria Gillick. Only *one* of the complaints which could be said to relate specifically to women was upheld.

Broadcasting

The broadcasting equivalent of the Press Council is the Broadcasting Complaints Commission (the BCC), which started work in 1981, replacing the BBC Programmes Complaints Commission and the IBA Complaints Review Board. The BCC was set up by the Government. It has five members, appointed by the Home Secretary. They include two women: one of them, the 'Chairman' [sic], the titled Lady Anglesey. Modelled on the Press Council, its powers are perhaps even more limited, hardly extending the controls over content, standards and 'balance' which are already exercised by the BBC and IBA under the Broadcasting Acts. The BCC can adjudicate only on questions of 'unjust or unfair treatment' or 'unwarranted infringement of privacy'. Complaints can be brought only by those directly affected.

In 1986–7, the Commission dismissed 174 of the 222 complaints it received as being outside its terms of reference. Another 32 (including some left over from the previous year) were thrown out without an adjudication. Most were judged 'inappropriate' or not directly relevant to the complainant. Under section 55 of the Broadcasting Act the BCC has discretion over which complaints it entertains. Only 12 (5 per cent of the complaints received) were upheld.

The means of redress consist of publication of the adjudication in

TV Times, the *Listener* or *Radio Times*, or on some occasions a broadcast summary of the finding. The latter may seem impressive, affording access to a huge audience. But the terse, official statements which flash by in a break between programmes are unlikely to make the same impact as the original broadcast.

The BCC's procedures are slow and complicated. It has no trained fact-finding staff, and cannot rule on matters subject to libel proceedings. Its members have no special knowledge of the media, and form an even more undemocratic and unaccountable elite than the Press Council. It is true that broadcasting is less outrageously biased than the press. As a newer industry, it has integrated women better in some areas, with the marked exception of technical departments. Nevertheless it has a long way to go to achieve a really positive and fair presentation of women.

After the Hungerford massacre in August 1987, and the questions about film and TV violence that followed it, the Tory Government announced the setting up of a further 'Broadcasting Standards Council'. According to the Home Secretary, it will be a statutory body able to initiate research and consider individual complaints. Companies may be required to broadcast its findings. It is not expected to be in operation before Summer 1989. No mention has been made of any sort of democratic structure, nor what powers it will have to enforce its standards. The appointment of Sir William Rees-Mogg as its chairman is indicative of its probable future role.

Not only does this new committee also look remarkably like the Press Council; it will sit alongside all the other existing bodies who will continue to operate as before. This suggests the most futile duplication of purpose, likely to leave the average viewer totally confused. Rather than take on a serious examination of the impact of violence on television, the Government has proposed the new council as an empty gesture, to appease public concern.

Alternatives

Facing such poor odds in the battle for a fairer deal from the media, what changes should women be looking for? Let us canter swiftly through the alternatives.

Following the National Union of Journalists' withdrawal from the Press Council, the union opened up its own disciplinary procedure to complaints from members of the public. The first successful case involving sexist bias was against freelance Terry Lovell for an article in the *Sun* headlined *The Sexiest Bits of a Woman*. But whereas he

suffered no penalty, Annie Bachini, the woman who complained, was publicly vilified by Bernard Levin in his *Times* column. It was not a precedent calculated to encourage other women to turn to the NUJ.

In 1986 the union established an Ethics Council to promote professional standards, based on its Code of Conduct, and consider complaints. However the difficulty which bedevils the NUJ is the contradiction in punishing the very members it exists to defend, and the problem of enforcing its rulings.

In 1986, the *London Standard* published the address of a women's refuge, in defiance of earlier advice from the union. The endangering of women's lives through breaches of privacy is an issue of continual concern, which has received little sympathy from the Press Council. The council has rejected complaints over the publication of a picture of a policewoman who was receiving harassing telephone calls, and the name and address of a pensioner attacked in her home.

A group of women, heeding union advice not to approach the Press Council, turned to the NUJ for help. Their appeal was heard sympathetically, and another letter went to the *Standard*. But the women observed ruefully: 'The current code of practice governing such reporting is weak and contains no enforceable sanctions against those who break it.'

Another alternative centres on the Right of Reply campaign, initiated by the Campaign for Press and Broadcasting Freedom, with the support of all the media trade unions. The CPBF has acted as an advice unit, helping individuals and groups to win redress. Around 1984, particularly during the miners' dispute, the campaign achieved some notable victories when NGA and SOGAT members working in Fleet Street refused to work on pages maligning Arthur Scargill and the NUM. Action on women's behalf has come more slowly, although the Association for Improvement in Maternity Services (AIMS) won a Right of Reply from the *Daily Mail* in 1984. The following year the CPBF published a Code of Conduct on Sexism in the Media, with the aim of raising awareness among media workers and encouraging them not to process sexist material.

The Right of Reply campaign has been extremely successful in focusing attention on media abuse. But as a means of individual redress it too has drawbacks. It is arbitrary, depending on the attitudes of individual editors or groups of workers. It is understandable that male print union members have been quickest to act on behalf of *fellow* trade unionists.

Secondly it becomes untenable when taken to its logical conclusion. For so much of tabloid newspaper output is offensive or inaccurate, that if every aggrieved party won redress the volume of 'Reply' would outstrip the original matter. More importantly, the Right of Reply campaign has suffered a harsh setback through the defeats inflicted on the media unions, especially at Wapping. The destruction of industrial power has brought with it the loss of influence over newspaper content on everyone's behalf.

One alternative to the Press Council that has achieved considerable support is the appointment of a Press Ombudsman or men [sic]. This could either be a statutory post with responsibility for all newspapers, as in Sweden; or an internal appointment made by individual papers as in Canada and the United States. Robert Maxwell has promised to implement the idea on the *Daily Mirror*. In all cases, the Ombudsman's job would be to take up complaints from members of the public.

One drawback from women's point of view is rather obvious. Is there such a thing as an Ombudswoman? If the post were statutory, it has been suggested that an appropriate appointee would be a judge. In this country there are only three female High Court judges among a total of 79, and given the attitude of most male judges to rape, for instance, there is precious little evidence that such an appointment would benefit women in any way.

Even an Ombudsman appointed internally from the ranks of respected 'experienced journalists' would invariably be a man, because of the preponderance of men in senior positions; and almost by definition would be someone who accepted and worked within established press values.

The same argument applies to panels of the 'great and the good' to supervise standards, such as newspaper trustees. Even if such bodies were prepared to challenge the status quo — which is doubtful — women would always be in the minority because of the nature of the industry, and would never achieve the power necessary to overturn media values. The question of power is crucial. Any organisation which claims to exercise it and yet is shown to be impotent, discredits itself, as is demonstrated by the Press Council.

The Campaign for Press and Broadcasting Freedom has formulated an ambitious plan for a Media Complaints Board: a statutory body which would take over the functions of the Press

Council and the Broadcasting Complaints Commission, which would have much wider powers to enforce a right of reply and impose sanctions against offenders. Members could be elected, possibly through a link up with local authorities, or the establishment of local media councils with responsibility for supervising media outlets and their relationship with the community. Such a structure, if it were effective, would mark a revolutionary transformation in media accountability. But it would require on the part of government a willingness to tackle media bias that has never existed up to now. Furthermore, safeguards would be needed to guarantee repesentation for women and minority groups, and to bar any one political tendency from seizing control.

More modestly, the Labour Party and the TUC have backed the establishment of a 'Communications Council', with 'the right to demand air time or column space for the correction of errors of fact or redress of grievances'. How would this right be achieved? For this is the heart of the problem of censorship. How can a regulatory body be effective in curbing the media without being accused of attacking the 'freedom' of the press and broadcasting? Where should the balance be struck between safeguarding genuine media freedom, and controlling the vicious abuses that appear so frequently?

It seems clear that any organisation relying on the voluntary co-operation of the media — particularly the press — may as well pack up and go home. The answer must be a combination of statutory controls, plus a long-term transformation of the way the industry works. Legislation is required in some areas: to abolish 'Page Three' pictures as proposed by Clare Short's Bill, for instance; to create much tougher restrictions on monopoly ownership; and probably to provide a right of reply to factual errors and wilful misrepresentation.

If this brings accusations of censorship, then it is time to move off the defensive. It is the *press* that is guilty of censorship, in consistently falsifying and narrowing women's lives. Moves to adjust this imbalance should be seen as a liberation, not a restriction. Women have declared — in the *Woman* survey — that they hate Page Three pictures. Now *they* need freedom from this abuse.

Under current circumstances, to implement much wider legislation than that proposed above, might provoke a backlash, masquerading under the banner of 'press freedom' but really concerned with power and profit. There would also be a risk of it being misused. In the final analysis, women will not get a fair deal from the media without sweeping reforms which can only take place alongside much broader changes in society. These will bring not only restrictions on individual ownership of the media, greater democracy, improved access, and freedom from sexual and racial abuse; but will also overturn the power of advertisers and the state to dictate what can be said, and who can say it.

In the meantime, existing 'news values' must be changed, and that means a transformation in journalists' training, plus the employment of more women in the industry and particularly in Fleet Street, providing support to one another in challenging the current ethos. Many positive stories about women are currently confined to 'Women's pages' or 'spiked' (not used). For women, the unfettered 'Right to Report' means putting those stories onto the news or feature pages, or into the main news bulletins, where they should be.

At present, working conditions ensure that women reaching senior positions have to be even more dedicated to their careers than men. Shorter working hours, childcare: these things would bring in a broader range of women. Women at all levels in the industry, like other workers, need a bigger say. This could best be organised through existing trade unions — but only if those unions, particularly in print, purge themselves of the discriminatory practices and attitudes that have proved so divisive. Greater democracy and accountability would benefit women consumers, such as the election of the BBC Board of Governors to be accountable to the public. Liaison between workers and consumers must be built up.

Finally, women need more confidence in challenging the media; and this is where campaigns like the Right to Reply are so useful. The steady pressure of consumer complaints can be supplemented by direct action — such as the picket by Asian women of the *Daily Mail* in Manchester in 1985, following the 'Brides for Sale' allegations.

Access to information also breeds confidence, and if more women acquire the skills of sub-editing, or typesetting, or film-making; if more women use them to 'roll their own' and create alternative sources of information, the media will cease to be so intimidating.

Perhaps the most ambitious proposal for women's intervention in the media has come from a grouping of Scottish women, in a report for the end of the UN Decade for Women in 1985. They proposed a national women's Media Council, bringing together representatives from the press and broadcasting, advertising, media groups and women's organisations, and unions. The report did not envisage any statutory powers. The Council's work would be more gradual. 'A programme or programmes which a national Media Council might initiate would be far-reaching and possibly long term.' They would include educating media workers about sexism; bringing women forward, particularly to policy-making positions, through training and positive action; and pressing for a more positive image of women. The report added: 'Experiences and information shared can lead to real progress.'

Would not such a broad church run the risk of submerging in political differences? The answer is yes. The crucial question is whether women would identify their common interests closely enough to form a united front, recognising that media discrimination applies to us all.

THE NATIONAL UNION OF JOURNALISTS' ATTITUDE TO CONTROLLING MEDIA SEXISM

Denise Searle

Clause 10 of the NUJ code of conduct states:

> A journalist shall only mention a person's race, colour, creed, illegitimacy, marital status (or lack of it), gender or sexual orientation if this information is strictly relevant. A journalist shall neither originate nor process material which encourages discrimination on any of the above-mentioned grounds.

Sexism in the media is a tricky area for the National Union of Journalists, which represents the vast majority of journalists in the UK and Republic of Ireland. The union spends tens of thousands of pounds a year on attempts to improve the ethical standards of its members, has an elaborate equality structure and a code of conduct prohibiting the production of material likely to cause sex discrimination. Yet NUJ members are responsible for a lot of the exploitative articles and photographs appearing daily in national tabloid newspapers and numerous other media outlets.

A reasonably accurate picture of the NUJ would be feminist activists initiating anti-sexist campaigns and highlighting bad practice, confronted by a loose group of reactionaries centred on the national press. These people view the campaigns as an attack on the 'right to report' and disregard the activists as 'extremists'.

This vociferous minority, which includes some of the leadership and full-time officials, often obstructs and complains about activities aimed at improving standards, crying 'censorship' if the union ever attempts to discipline a journalist for producing discriminatory or exploitative material.

The NUJ is committed to tackling sexism and other forms of bias by upholding its code of conduct. Current policy is to work through chapels (the printing industry term for workplace branches or shops), emphasising journalists' responsibilities to avoid causing discrimination. The aim is to create a climate of high ethical standards. In such an atmosphere, the argument runs, individual journalists would be less inclined to generate sexist, racist and other forms of prejudicial articles and photographs. The chapel would take on anyone that steps out of line.

The problem is that the NUJ has never decided how far it should go to stop journalists producing sexist material. The union would like to stop the denigration of women and minority groups by the media, but is scared of being labelled 'censor'. For example the leadership has shunned campaigns to end tabloid newspapers' use of photographs of scantily clad women on the grounds that the efforts conflict with the NUJ's support for press and broadcasting freedom.

This stance has resulted in an uncomfortable compromise between a rule book requiring members to abide by the code of conduct and a leadership which puts less than its full weight into enforcing the code. The situation satisfies neither activists who are concerned about ethical standards nor those who think the NUJ has no business telling journalists what to write or process.

The code of conduct is not a weak liberal set of good intentions, it encompasses stringent guidelines which are clearly at odds with the working practices of many journalists on tabloid newspapers. The NUJ is therefore open to accusations of manipulating the media whether or not the code is applied with any force.

Champions of ethical standards in the NUJ, like myself, accept that the guidelines are an attempt at control, but most argue that they do not amount to censorship. We are increasingly using civil liberties arguments, emphasising that the code of conduct is a means of safeguarding the freedom of journalists' subjects. The axis of our case is that sexist material discriminates against women by perpetuating stereotypes such as sex-crazed housewife, dolly-bird secretary or battling granny. These false images can lead to women being undervalued at work, condescending treatment, sexual harassment and even violence, when some men find that women deviate from the submissive role they have been ascribed.

The central question then becomes: What leads to the greatest infringement of civil liberties — a demand on some journalists to change their style of working, or sexist journalism which denigrates and, in extreme cases, potentially endangers half the population?

This latter reasoning is likely to play a major role in future NUJ debates, but its proponents have a long way to go. There is still a significant minority who think maintaining ethical standards is secondary to the union's 'main functions' of defending and improving members' pay and conditions. Many chapels would not dream of using the code of conduct to improve practices at their newspaper, magazine or broadcasting station.

An example was the rapid and dramatic move down market of the *Daily Star* (renamed the *Star*) during the six weeks in September and October 1987 that it was edited by former *Sunday Sport* editorial director, Michael Gabbert.

The NUJ chapel at the *Star* was 'dismayed' and 'disgusted' by the change in the paper, which they felt had deteriorated into a 'porn sheet'. Yet they made no attempt to rescue standards industrially by refusing collectively to generate or handle the high proportion of sex-based stories and numerous exploitative photographs of semi-naked women included in every issue. According to NUJ chapel representatives at the *Star*, the journalists felt the paper's content was a matter for the editor and did not want to interfere.

The chapel's position was particularly ironic given that a third of the 61 London-based staff had no work to do after the change in editorship. These had been senior writers responsible for features and important news stories. Chapel officers complained to management that the change in content of the *Star* had made these journalists redundant and demanded large pay offs to leave the company. Management refused. Several journalists left because of the decline in standards, and one was sacked after voicing his opinion at a Labour party conference fringe meeting organised by the Campaign for Press and Broadcasting Freedom.

Pressure to clean up the 'tits, bums and bonking' image of the *Star* eventually came from major advertisers instead of from the NUJ chapel. Gabbert was removed by the paper's owners, Express Newspapers, and the *Star* returned to its former market position, somewhere between the *Sun* and the *Daily Mirror*.

Feminists in the NUJ have been pushing the union to take sexism seriously since the 1960s. On the surface there has been considerable success. All branches and chapels must elect an equality officer responsible for promoting equal opportunities at work and providing a focus for questions and complaints connected with clause 10 of the code of conduct. Several large branches have women's committees which are active in their own right. London Magazine Branch women's committee, for example, recently monitored its own members' publications for sexism and published a report on the findings containing recommendations for improvement. The union appointed its first equality organiser in 1985.

At national level, anti-sexist initiatives come largely from the equality council which was set up in 1983. The council is also responsible for campaigns to tackle discrimination against lesbians and gays, disabled people and ethnic minorities, the latter in co-operation with the NUJ's race relations working party.

The equality council played a central role in setting up the NUJ's ethics council in 1986 to promote and enforce the code of conduct and ethical standards generally, taking these issues out of the NUJ's central disciplinary machinery. Members of the public may appeal directly to the ethics council as an alternative to the toothless, employer-dominated Press Council. One aim of the ethics council is to win a right of reply through chapel action for people who feel they have been misrepresented by the media.

The ethics council's main success has been as a mechanism by which the general public, concerned about low standards in journalism, can approach NUJ members directly. The council has been snowed under with complaints from inside and outside the union. However sexism has barely featured. The bulk of the ethics council's work has concerned objections about the media's ill-treatment of lesbians, gays, ethnic minorities and disabled people.

Out of 132 cases dealt with in the first 18 months, only four were connected with discriminatory images of women. Two of these concerned *Sunday Sport*, the bottom of the market colour Sunday tabloid, one was over a condescending story in the *Mail on Sunday* about one of the founders of the Greenham Common peace camp, and the other criticised the sexist treatment by the *Croydon Post* of Brenda Dean, general secretary of the printworkers' union, SOGAT. All four protests ran out of the six month time limit set for processing code of conduct complaints, largely due to lack of co-operation from the chapels concerned, so none of the plaintiffs received any retribution.

Women appear to be sceptical about the worth of complaining. Hardly surprising given the low rate of success of even seemingly cast iron complaints. In 1983, London Magazine Branch's women's committee complained about a *Sunday Express* article on Dr Sally Ride, the first US woman in space. The committee said the story, headlined 'In orbit — with no lipstick', paid more attention to whether Ride took lipstick or perfume into space than to her achievements as a scientist. Reference to her qualifications and role did not appear until the last four paragraphs, whereas accompanying male astronauts' professional attributes and functions were clearly described at a much earlier stage. Ride, an astrophysicist, was also quoted as saying that the space flight was like a roller coaster ride at Disneyworld. The committee felt the article trivialised and glamourised the image of women and would therefore lead to discrimination.

The *Express* and *Sunday Express* chapels took the complaint seriously, in contrast to the reception normally given by Fleet Street. Ross Mark, the author, could not be present at the branch hearing as he was based in Washington, but he submitted a written plea and two colleagues gave evidence on his behalf. The branch panel decided there was a prima facie case to answer and referred the matter to the NUJ National Executive Council for a formal inquiry. The NEC, however, decided that the complaint was 'trivial' and threw it out, by seven votes to six.

Not all efforts end so fruitlessly. Many examples of sexism are caused by carelessness and chapels outside national newspapers are often keen to help the ethics council improve standards. Several cases have been settled informally, such as the complaint against the Chatham News over the denigratory use of the term 'spinster'. The chapel and the paper's management apologised and said the description would not be used again.

The NUJ's effectiveness in tackling sexism and getting the code of conduct taken seriously usually depends on the percentage of women journalists at a workplace. Sexism is often reduced when significant numbers of women are present in the newsroom or on the subs desk, disturbing the 'men-only' vacuum. Feminists on the staff will then hopefully be able to dispel the myth that promoting the code amounts to censorship.

Improvements in ethical standards go hand in hand with equality in the workplace. Currently women are concentrated in the lower paid, less prestigious areas of journalism, such as magazines, books and provincial newspapers, which tend to be less discriminatory. Once the NUJ ensures that women are equally represented in all sectors of the media, there will be a much greater chance of wiping out sexism in high profile areas such as national newspapers.

APPENDIX I: Excerpts from the Minneapolis Ordinance

(1) *Special Findings on Pornography*: The council finds that pornography is central in creating and maintaining the civil inequality of the sexes. Pornography is a systematic practice of exploitation and subordination based on sex which differentially harms women. The bigotry and contempt it promotes, with the acts of aggression it fosters, harm women's opportunities for equality of rights in employment, education, property rights, public accommodations and public services; create public harassment and private denigration; promote injury and degradation such as rape, battery and prostitution and inhibit just enforcement of laws against these acts; contribute significantly to restricting women from full exercise of citizenship and participation in public life, including in neighborhoods; damage relations between the sexes; and undermine women's equal exercise of rights to speech and action guaranteed to all citizens under the constitutions and laws of the United States and the State of Minnesota.

(gg) *Pornography*. Pornography is a form of discrimination on the basis of sex.
(1) Pornography is the sexually explicit subordination of women, graphically depicted, whether in pictures or in words, that also includes one or more of the following.

    (i) women are presented as dehumanized sexual objects, things or commodities; or

    (ii) women are presented as sexual objects who enjoy pain or humiliation; or

    (iii) women are presented as sexual objects who experience sexual pleasure in being raped; or

    (iv) women are presented as sexual objects tied up or cut up or mutilated or bruised or physically hurt; or

    (v) women are presented in postures of sexual submission; [or sexual servility, including by inviting penetration] or

    (vi) women's body parts — including but not limited to vaginas, breasts, and buttocks — are exhibited, such that women are reduced to those parts; or

    (vii) women are presented as whores by nature; or

    (viii) women are presented being penetrated by objects or animals; or

    (ix) women are presented in scenarios of degradation, injury, abasement, torture, shown as filthy or inferior, bleeding, bruised, or hurt in a context that makes these conditions sexual.

(2)The use of men, children, or transsexuals in the place of women . . . is pornography for purposes of . . . this statute.

(1) *Discrimination by trafficking in pornography.*

The production, sale, exhibition, or distribution of pornography is discrimination against women by means of trafficking in pornography:

(1) City, state, and federally funded public libraries or private and public university and college libraries in which pornography is available for study, including on open shelves shall not be construed to be trafficking in pornography but special display presentations of pornography in said places is sex discrimination.

(2) The formation of private clubs or associations for purposes of trafficking in pornography is illegal and shall be considered a conspiracy to violate the civil rights of women.

(3) Any woman has a cause of action hereunder as a woman acting against the subordination of women. Any man or transsexual who alleges injury by pornography in the way women are injured by it shall also have a cause of action.

(m) *Coercion into pornography performances.* Any person, including transsexual, who is coerced, intimidated, or fraudulently induced (hereafter, "coerced") into performing for pornography shall have a cause of action against the maker(s), seller(s), exhibitor(s) or distributor(s) of said pornography for damages and for the elimination of the products of the performance(s) from the public view.

(1)*Limitation of action.* This claim shall not expire before five years have elapsed from the date of the coerced performance(s) or from the last appearance or sale of any product of the performance(s); whichever date is later;

(2) Proof of one or more of the following facts or conditions shall not, without more, negate a finding of coercion:

(aa) that the person is a woman; or

(bb) that the person is or has been a prostitute; or

(cc) that the person has attained the age of majority; or

(dd) that the person is connected by blood or marriage to anyone involved in or related to the making of the pornography; or

(ee) that the person has previously had, or been thought to have had, sexual relations with anyone including anyone involved in or related to the making of the pornography; or

(ff) that the person has previously posed for sexually explicit pictures for or with anyone, including anyone involved in or related to the making of the pornography; or

(gg) that anyone else, including a spouse or other relative, has given permission on the person's behalf; or

(hh) that the person actually consented to a use of the performance that is changed into pornography; or (ii) that the person knew that the purpose of the acts or events in question was to make pornography; or

(jj) that the person showed no resistance or appeared to cooperate actively in the photographic sessions or in the sexual events that produced the pornography; or (kk) that the person signed a contract, or made statements affirming a willingness to cooperate; or

    (ll) that no physical force, threats, or weapons were used in the making of the pornography; or

    (mm) that the person was paid or otherwise compensated.

(n) *Forcing pornography on a person.* Any woman, man, child or transsexual who has pornography forced on them in any place of employment, in education, in a home, or in a public place has a cause of action against the perpetrator and/or institution.

(o) *Assault or physical attack due to pornography.* Any woman, man, child or transsexual who is assaulted, physically attacked or injured in a way that is directly caused by specific pornography has a claim for damages against the perpetrator, the maker(s), distributor(s), seller(s), and/or exhibitor(s), and for an injunction against the specific pornography's further exhibition, distribution, or sale. No damages shall be assessed (A) against maker(s) for pornography made, (B) against distributor(s) for pornography distributed, (C) against seller(s) for pornography sold, or (D) against exhibitors for pornography exhibited prior to the effective date of this act.

(p) *Defenses.* Where the materials which are the subject matter of a cause of action under subsections (l), (m), (n), or (o) of this section are pornography, it shall not be a defense that the defendant did not know or intend that the materials are pornography or sex discrimination.

APPENDIX II: Excerpts from The Public Order Act 1986

Part III
Racial Hatred

General Note

In this part, all the former offences relating to racial hatred have been brought together and rationalised to incorporate improved and common features in conjunction with a number of new offences. This followed some extremely cooperative debate in Parliament during which many constructive criticisms from the Opposition were acted upon by the Government.

The principal provision in the old law was s.5A, Public Order Act 1936. An offence would be committed if threatening, abusive or insulting words or written matter were used, published or distributed in a case where, in all the circumstances, hatred was likely to be stirred up against a racial group in Great Britain. This offence has been extended in ss.18 and 19 to include behaviour and the display of written material; it applies to private as well as public places and includes the private circulation of material; and it now applies to such conduct where the intention is to stir up racial hatred. In addition, a new offence of possessing racially inflammatory material has been created with related powers of entry, search and forfeiture in ss.23–25. By s.5, Theatres Act 1968, the presenter or director of a play which involved the use of threatening, abusive or insulting words would be guilty of an offence if he intended to stir up racial hatred and that was a likely consequence. This is now incorporated into s.20 which includes, however, the strict liability element as an alternative base for conduct. In addition, s.20 contains the extension mentioned above, together with provisions modelled upon s.27, Cable and Broadcasting Act 1984. That offence is also modified to create consistency and is brought into this Act as s.22. For completeness, a new offence of distributing, playing or showing a recording is created in s.21.

These reforms are a response to continued criticism that racial harmony remains as elusive as ever and that racial discrimination is being actively fostered by individuals and political groups who appear to be untouched by any attempts by the law to suppress their activities. For examples of the latter, see Standing Committee, pp. 880–4. For a critical review, see P. Gordon, *Incitement to Racial Hatred* (1982) Runnymede Trust. Part of the problem has been that a narrow scope was selected as suitable for legal intervention because of concern about interference with free speech. In addition, there have been difficulties in proving offences, either because evidence has been hard to find or because courts have been reluctant or unwilling to convict.

The measures contained in this Part do have greater potential for success than the offences which they replace. The ambit of behaviour is wider; intentional conduct, regardless of the result, is punishable; racialist propaganda will be subject to control. Nevertheless, obstacles remain. The use of threatening, abusive or insulting conduct remains as the criminal threshold and will not extend to "less blatantly bigoted ... more apparently rational and moderate" messages (former Government's White Paper prior to the Race Relations Act 1976: Cmnd. 6234, para. 126). The object of the conduct still must be to stir up racial "hatred," a strong expression which may be difficult to establish. An attempt to couch the offence in terms of intimidation was rejected in debate: Standing Committee, col. 835ff. Furthermore, the action or consent of the Attorney-General is still required in order to mount a prosecution. On the other hand, these obstacles represent sensitivity to the dangers of encroaching upon free expression however unacceptable the content. "It is arguable that false and evil publications of this kind may well be more effectively defeated by public education and debate than by prosecution and that in practice the criminal law would be ineffective to deal with such material": *ibid.* Yet it may be that such arguments are most persuasive only when new moral orthodoxies are in the process of being created; such inhibitions have not noticeably influenced the prohibition of obscenity, blasphemy or defamation, for example. Possibly, Part III marks another stage in establishing such consensus against discriminating attitudes, although its effectiveness will remain open to doubt.

For the restriction on prosecutions without Attorney-General's permission, and for sentences, see s.27.

By s.42(2), this section applied to Scotland.

Meaning of "racial hatred"

Meaning of "racial hatred"

17. In this Part "racial hatred" means hatred against a group of persons in Great Britain defined by reference to colour, race, nationality (including citizenship) or ethnic or national origins.

General Note

By s.29, racial hatred in Part III has the meaning given in this section. It is based upon the definition of racial group in s.3, Race Relations Act 1976. That definition has been discussed in *Mandla* v. *Lee* [1983] 2 A.C. 548. The House of Lords explained the nature of ethnic origins in terms of a group's regarding itself and being regarded by others as a distinct community by virtue of certain characteristics such as: a long shared history, a cultural tradition of its own, a common ancestry, a common language and literature, a common religion, and being a minority. On that basis, Sikhs were held to be a racial group by reference to ethnic origins. On the same basis, Jews and Romany gypsies can be defined as such. The Attorney-General indicated that he will consider prosecutions for offences under Part III against such gypsies in exactly the same way as in respect of other ethnic groups: *Hansard*, H.C., Vol. 481, col. 463.

"Hatred" is not defined but connotes intense dislike, animosity. It implies sufficient dislike to be manifested in active demonstration of ill-will. Such hatred must be manifested against a group living in Great Britain but it can be the result of threatening, abusive or insulting conduct directed at persons outside Great Britain.

Acts intended or likely to stir up racial hatred

Use of words or behaviour or display of written material

18..—(1) A person who uses threatening, abusive or insulting words or behaviour, or displays any written material which is threatening, abusive or insulting, is guilty of an offence if—

(*a*) he intends thereby to stir up racial hatred, or

(*b*) having regard to all the circumstances racial hatred is likely to be stirred up thereby.

(2) An offence under this section may be committed in a public or a private place, except that no offence is committed where the words or behaviour are used, or the written material is displayed, by a person inside a dwelling and are not heard or seen except by other persons in that or another dwelling.

(3) A constable may arrest without warrant anyone he reasonably suspects is committing an offence under this section.

(4) In proceedings for an offence under this section it is a defence for the accused to prove that he was inside a dwelling and had no reason to believe that the words or behaviour used, or the written material displayed, would be heard or seen by a person outside that or any other dwelling.

(5) A person who is not shown to have intended to stir up racial hatred is not guilty of an offence under this section if he did not intend his words or behaviour, or the written material, to be, and was not aware that it might be, threatening, abusive or insulting.

(6) This section does not apply to words or behaviour used, or written material displayed, solely for the purpose of being included in a programme broadcast or included in a cable programme service.

Publishing or distributing written material

19.—(1) a person who publishes or distributes written material which is threatening, abusive or insulting is guilty of an offence if—

(*a*) he intends thereby to stir up racial hatred, or

(*b*) having regard to all the circumstances racial hatred is likely to be stirred up thereby.

(2) In proceedings for an offence under this section it is a defence for an accused who is not shown to have intended to stir up racial hatred to prove that he was not aware of the content of the material and did not suspect,and had no reason to suspect, that it was threatening, abusive or insulting.

(3) References in this Part to the publication or distribution of written material are to its publication or distribution to the public or a section of the public.

General Note

This section replaces part of s.5A, Public Order Act 1936 which is repealed by s.40(3) and Sch. 3. Graffiti, including swastikas, is included. Written material, as defined in s.29 was originally envisaged as covering video and film but s.21 was introduced to put the matter beyond doubt.

Public performance of play

20.—(1) If a public performance of a play is given which involves the use of threatening, abusive or insulting words or behaviour, any person who presents or directs the performance is guilty of an offence if—

(*a*) he intends thereby to stir up racial hatred, or

(*b*) having regard to all the circumstances (and, in particular, taking the performance as a whole) racial hatred is likely to be stirred up thereby.

(2) If a person presenting or directing the performance is not shown to have intended to stir up racial hatred, it is a defence for him to prove—

(a) that he did not know and had no reason to suspect that the performance would involve the use of the offending words or behaviour, or

(*b*) that he did not know and had no reason to suspect that the offending words or behaviour were threatening, abusive or insulting, or

(*c*) that he did not know and had no reason to suspect that the circumstances in which the performance would be given would be such that racial hatred would be likely to be stirred up.

(3) This section does not apply to a performance given solely or primarily for one or more of the following purposes—

(*a*) rehearsal,

(*b*) making a recording of the performance, or

(*c*) enabling the performance to be broadcast or included in a cable programme service;

but if it is proved that the performance was attended by persons other than those directly connected with the giving of the performance or the doing in relation to it of the things mentioned in paragraph (*b*) or (*c*), the performance shall, unless the contrary is shown, be taken not to have been given solely or primarily for the purposes mentioned above.

(4) For the purposes of this section—

(*a*) a person shall not be treated as presenting a performance of a play by reason only of his taking part in it as a performer,

(*b*) a person taking part as a performer in a performance directed by another shall be treated as a person who directed the performance if without reasonable excuse he performs otherwise than in accordance with that person's direction, and

(*c*) a person shall be taken to have directed a performance of a play given under his direction notwithstanding that he was not present during the performance;

and a person shall not be treated as aiding and abetting the commission of an offence under this section by reason only of his taking part in a performance as a performer.

(5) In this section "play" and "public performance" have the same meaning as in the Theatres Act 1968.

(6) The following provisions of the Theatres Act 1968 apply in relation to an offence under this section as they apply to an offence under section 2 of that Act —

>   section 9 (script as evidence of what was performed),
>   section 10 (power to make copies of script),
>   section 15 (powers of entry and inspection).

Distributing, showing or playing a recording

21.—(1) A person who distributes, or shows or plays, a recording of visual images or sounds which are threatening, abusive or insulting is guilty of an offence if—

>   (*a*) he intends thereby to stir up racial hatred, or
>   (*b*) having regard to all the circumstances racial hatred is likely to be stirred up thereby.

(2) In this Part "recording" means any record from which visual images or sounds may, by any means, be reproduced; and references to the distribution, showing or playing of a recording are to its distribution, showing or playing to the public or a section of the public.

(3) In proceedings for an offence under this section it is a defence for an accused who is not shown to have intended to stir up racial hatred to prove that he was not aware of the content of the recording and did not suspect, and had no reason to suspect, that it was threatening, abusive or insulting.

(4) This section does not apply to the showing or playing of a recording solely for the purpose of enabling the recording to be broadcast or included in cable programme service.

General Note

This section is concerned with the effects of video and film, although it was conceded in Parliament that a particular problem of racial hatred has not yet arisen in respect of such materials. The broad pattern of this Part is again followed. See generally, notes to s.18(1), (5), (6).

Broadcasting or including programme in cable programme service

22.—(1) If a programme involving threatening, abusive or insulting visual images or sounds is broadcast, or included in a cable programme service, each of the persons mentioned in subsection (2) is guilty of an offence if—

>   (*a*) he intends thereby to stir up racial hatred, or
>   (*b*) The persons are—
>
>>   (*a*) the person providing the broadcasting or cable programme service,
>>   (*b*) any person by whom the programme is produced or directed, and
>>   (*c*) any person by whom offending words or behaviour are used.

(3) If the person providing the service, or a person by whom the programme was produced or directed, is not shown to have intended to stir up racial hatred, it is a defence for him to prove that—

(*a*) he did not know and had no reason to suspect that the programme would involve the offending material, and

(*b*) having regard to the circumstances in which the programme was broadcast, or included in a cable programme service, it was not reasonably practicable for him to secure the removal of the material.

(4) It is a defence for a person by whom the programme was produced or directed who is not shown to have intended to stir up racial hatred to prove that he did not know and had not reason to suspect—

(*a*) that the programme would be broadcast or included in a cable programme service, or

(*b*) that the circumstances in which the programme would be broadcast or so included would be such that racial hatred would be likely to stirred up.

(5) It is a defence for a person by whom offending words or behaviour were used and who is not shown to have intended to stir up racial hatred to pove that he did not know and had no reason to suspect—

(*a*) that a programme involving the use of the offending material would be broadcast or included in a cable programme service, or

(*b*) that the circmstances in which a programme involving the use of the offending material would be broadcast, or so included, or in which a programme broadcast or so included would involve the use of the offending material, would be such that racial hatred would be likely to be stirred up.

(6) A person who is not shown to have intended to stir up racial hatred is not guilty of an offence under this section if he did not know, and had no reason to suspect, that the offending material was threatening, abusive or insulting.

(7) This section does not apply—

(*a*) to the broadcasting of a programme by the British Broadcasting Corporation or the Independent Broadcasting Authority, or

(*b*) to the inclusion of a programme in a cable programme service by the reception and immediate retransmission of a broadcast by either of those authorities.

(8) The following provisions of the Cable and Broadcasting Act 1984 apply to an offence under this section as they apply to a "relevant offence" as defined in section 33(2) of that Act—

section 33 (scripts as evidence),

section 34 (power to make copies of scripts and records),

section 35 (availability of visual and sound records);

and sections 33 and 34 of that Act apply to an offence under this section in connection with the broadcasting of a programme as they apply to an offence in connection with the inclusion of a programme in a cable programme service.

Possession of racially inflammatory material

23.—(1) A person who has in his possession written material which is threatening, abusive or insulting, or a recording of visual images or sounds which are threatening, abusive or insulting, with a view to—

(*a*) in the case of written material, its being displayed, published, distributed, broadcast or included in a cable programme service, whether by himself or another, or

(*b*) in the case of a recording, its being distributed, shown, played, broadcast or included in a cable programme service, whether by himself or another,

is guilty of an offence if he intends racial hatred to be stirred up thereby or, having regard to all the circumstances, racial hatred is likely to be stirred up thereby.

(2) For this purpose regard shall be had to such display, publication, distribution, showing, playing, broadcasting or inclusion in a cable programme service as he has, or it may reasonably be inferred that he has, in view.

(3) In proceedings for an offence under this section it is a defence for an accused who is not shown to have intended to stir up racial hatred to prove that he was not aware of the content of the written material or recording and did not suspect, and had no reason to suspect, that it was threatening, abusive or insulting.

(4) This section does not apply to the possession of written material or a recording by or on behalf of the British Broadcasting Corporation or the Independent Broadcasting Authority or with a view to its being broadcast by either of those authorities.

General Note

In this section, a new offence is created to deal with the accumulation and storing of materials which are to be used to foment racial hatred. The possessor of the materials does not need to be the one who disseminates it. Possession appears to involve both a degree of control over the material and knowledge that such control is being exercised: see *Warner* v. *Metropolitan Police Commissioner* [1969] 2 A.C. 256. Knowledge about the threatening, abusive or insulting nature of the material is irrelevant but there is a defence for innocent possession in sub. (3), following the general approach adopted in this Part. The BBC and IBA are exempted by subs. (4); their duties under the BBC's Licence and the Independent Broadcasting Act 1981 are considered to be adequate to deal with any problem which might be likely to arise.

The section is not intended to stifle the genuine pursuit of research. However, the risk that dissemination of research findings will stimulate racial hatred must be borne by the person storing the material, for example, the researcher or a library. Persons engaging upon race-related research will have a difficult burden to discharge when raising any defence under subs. (3); for a library it may be a little easier.

Powers of entry and search

24.—(1) If in England and Wales a justice of the peace is satisfied by information on oath laid by a constable that there are reasonable grounds for suspecting that a person has possession of written material or a recording in contravention of section 23, the justice may issue a warrant under his hand authorising any constable to enter and search the premises where it is suspected the material or recording is situated.

(2) If in Scotland a sheriff or justice of the peace is satisfied by evidence on oath that there are reasonable grounds for suspecting that a person has possession of written material or a recording in contravention of section 23, the sheriff or justice may issue a warrant authorising any constable to enter and search the premises where it is suspected the material or recording is situated.

(3) A constable entering or searching premises in pursuance of a warrant issued under this section may use reasonable force if necessary.

(4) In this section "premises" means any place and, in particular, includes—

(*a*) any vehicle, vessel, aircraft or hovercraft,

(*b*) any offshore installation as defined in section 1(3)(*b*) of the Mineral Workings (Offshore Installations) Act 1971, and

(*c*) any tent or movable structure.

Power to order forfeiture

25.—(1) A court by or before which a person is convicted of—

(*a*) an offence under section 18 relating to the display of written material, or

(*b*) an offence under section 19, 21 or 23,

shall order to be forfeited any written material or recording produced to the court and shown to its satisfaction to be written material or a recording to which the offence relates.

(2) An order made under this section shall not take effect—

(*a*) in the case of an order made in proceedings in England and Wales, until the expiry of the ordinary time within which an appeal may be instituted or, where an appeal is duly instituted, until it is finally decided or abandoned;

(*b*) in the case of an order made in proceedings in Scotland, until the expiration of the time within which, by virtue of any statute, an appeal may be instituted or, where such an appeal is duly instituted, until the appeal is finally decided or abandoned.

(3) For the purposes of subsection (2)(*a*)—

(*a*) an application for a case stated or for leave to appeal shall be treated as the institution of an appeal, and

(*b*) where a decision on appeal is subject to a further appeal, the appeal is not finally determined until the expiry of the ordinary time within which a further appeal may be instituted or, where a further appeal is duly instituted, until the further appeal is finally decided or abandoned.

(4) For the purposes of subsection (2)(*b*) the lodging of an application for a stated case or note of appeal against sentence shall be treated as the institution of an appeal.

Procedure and punishment

27.—(1) No proceedings for an offence under this Part may be instituted in England and Wales except by or with the consent of the Attorney General.

(2) For the purposes of the rules in England and Wales against charging more than one offence in the same count or information, each of sections 18 to 23 creates one offence.

(3) A person guilty of an offence under this Part is liable—

(*a*) on conviction on indictment to imprisonment for a term not exceeding two years or a fine or both;

(*b*) on summary conviction to imprisonment for a term not exceeding six months or a fine not exceeding the statutory maximum or both.

Subs. (1)

The Attorney-General's approval was considered necessary to protect against mischievous, frivolous or unsupported prosecutions, whether they are used in order to harass individuals or to bring discredit to the legislation. Counter-principles of free expression, including free elections and a free media, were also considered to be more appropriate for the Attorney-General. It was indicated in Standing Committee, however, that if the new Crown Prosecution Service were to establish a reputation for probity and action, then this constraint upon prosecutions might be reconsidered. In practice, in any event, the Director of Public Prosecutions will already be closely involved in any such decisions.

Offences by corporations

28.—(1) Where a body corporate is guilty of an offence under this Part and it is shown that the offence was committed with the consent or connivance of a director, manager, secretary or other similar officer of the body, or a person purporting to act in any such capacity, he as well as the body corporate is guilty of the offence and liable to be proceeded against and punished accordingly.

(2) Where the affairs of a body corporate are managed by its members, subsection (1) applies in relation to the acts and defaults of a member in connection with his functions of management as it applies to a director.

APPENDIX III: Campaign against Pornography and Censorship Policy Statement

June 1988

1. SEXISM

We believe that women are oppressed, as women, within a system of sexism in which men as a group have access to power and privilege that women do not have. Within this system, women are discriminated against in employment (low-pay, low-status jobs), in exclusion from employment, in every aspect of public and private life (differential treatment in sports and social clubs, restaurants, in access to credit and similar facilities), and by the fact that women's work as wives, mother and carers is undervalued and unrewarded.

We believe that women are victims of violence, sexual violence and sexual harassment, at home, at work, on the streets and in public places. Women are not only discriminated against, but regarded as 'inferior' (less intelligent, less important, less able). On the one hand, women are trivialized, treated as sex objects and even treated with contempt, while on the other hand, they are idealized and sentimentalized.

We believe that discrimination against women is perpetuated by these negative attitudes and that these attitudes and the behaviour and practices that result from them are at the core of sex discrimination.

Further, we believe that although men have power and privilege within the system of sexism, both women and men are conditioned to accept the role of 'subordinate' and 'dominant' respectively, and that both sexist conditioning and the system of sexism are damaging to women and men.

We believe in the right of women to be free from discrmination, to be treated equally in education, training and employment and every other aspect of their lives. In addition, their work as wives, mothers and carers should be valued, rewarded and supported. Women should have freedom of movement without danger of violence or harassment and women should be regarded, represented and treated with complete respect as human beings.

2. PORNOGRAPHY AND SEXISM

We believe that images which represent women in sex stereotyped ways (such as 'Janet and John' children's books, soap powder 'housewives', Oxo 'mums', Mills and Boon and 'Jackie' magazine heroines) are an essential part of creating and maintaining the system of sexism.

We believe that the portrayal of women as sex objects (in pin-ups, car and other adverts, 'Miss World Competitions', Page 3) is one of the most powerful and visible expressions of the negative attitudes of sexism and is central to the sex objectification, and therefore dehumanisation and degradation, of women.

We believe that pornography is the most extreme portrayal of women as less than human and less than equal. We believe that pornography reinforces women's unequal status by presenting them only as sexual and 'sexualized' objects for men's titillation and gratification and perpetuates their unequal status). We therefore believe that pornography sexualises inequality.

Further, we believe that pornography relentlessly communicates one message only: "this is what women are, this is what women want, this is how women deserve to be treated", i.e. with contempt, humiliation and as apparently 'willing' victims of sexual exploitation and violence. We believe therefore that pornography is propaganda against women which perpetuates sexism, sex discrimination and sexual violence.

WHAT PORNOGRAPHY IS:
We believe that pornography includes what is called 'softcore' pornography (portrayals of women with their legs splayed, vaginas and anuses gaping and exposed to the camera, posed 'provocatively' inviting sexual arousal and penetration, subjected to bondage, coercion and even violence).

We also believe that pornography includes what is called 'hardcore' pornography (torture, flaying, cannibalism, crushing of breasts in vices, exploding vaginas packed with hand-grenades, eyes gouged out, beatings, dismemberings, and burnings, multiple rape, women engaged in sexual intercourse with dogs, pigs and monkeys, the actual killing of women on screen in 'snuff' films, the filming of real rapes by rapists.

We believe that the distinction between soft and hardcore pornography is misleading because pornography is a continuum of the representation of women as sex objects, sexually available, inviting sexual access, violated, victims of sexual violence, frequently portrayed as 'enjoying' their treatment as 'sex objects' or being raped, tortured or assaulted.

WE DEFINE PORNOGRAPHY AS:
"The graphic, sexually explicit subordination of women through pictures and/or words, that also includes **one or more** of the following: women portrayed as sexual objects, things or commodities, enjoying pain or humiliation or rape, being tied up, cut up, mutilated, bruised or physically hurt, in postures of sexual submission or servility or display, reduced to body parts, penetrated by objects or animals, or presented in scenarios of degradation, injury, torture, shown as filthy or inferior, bleeding, bruised or hurt in a context which is sexual.

Pornography does not include erotica (defined as sexually explicit materials premised on equality) and it does not include bona fide sex education materials, or medical or forensic literature." In short we define pornography as depicting a combination of sexual objectification, violence and subordination.

4. PORNOGRAPHY AND CENSORSHIP
We believe that pornography should be eliminated on the grounds that it

contributes to sex discrimination, sexual inequality, sexual violence and sexism. We believe that pornography should be eliminated through correct information, education, persuasion, legislation and lawful direct action on the grounds that it harms women.

We believe in free speech free expression and freedom of information. We are totally against censorship in every form. Censorship is about the limitation of freedom: eliminating pornography is about promoting the freedom of women. We believe in human rights and the rights of women.

Further, we believe that pornography silences women and censors the freedom of women. There are some so-called 'freedoms' that society agrees to limit because of the harm and the damage that they do to other people: i.e. the 'freedom' to murder, the 'freedom' to steal, the 'freedom' to rape, the 'freedom' to incite racial hatred.

We therefore believe that the 'freedom' to manufacture and distribute pornography should be limited for the same reasons, i.e. because it causes harm and damage to women. Pornography acts as an 'incitement to sexual hatred and violence' in the same way that racist and fascist literature acts as an 'incitement to racial hatred' (and which is unlawful under the Race Relations Act 1976).

We believe that pornography should be legislated against on the same grounds, i.e. that it incites sexual hatred and violence against women. We also believe that in pursuit of their own civil liberties, women should have the right to take legal action (a civil suit as a civil right) against the manufacturers and distributors of pornography for the damage and harm done to them.

We believe that freedom for women (i.e. women's civil rights and civil liberties) depends on the elimination of pornography as well as the elimination of sex discrimination. We firmly believe that the two must go hand in hand.

5. PORNOGRAPHY AND OBSCENITY

We believe that the obscenity legislation which is currently used to control the circulation of pornography actually contributes to its continued use and abuse. The obscenity legislation keeps pornography accessible to men, but limits its 'display', thereby keeping it 'out of sight' of women and children.

We believe that it is men's use of pornography that influences their 'negative' attitudes and 'damaging' behaviour towards women and therefore that obscenity legislation does nothing to solve the real problem of men's use of pornography, which is the source and cause of identifiable harm to women.

The obscenity legislation defines pornography subjectively, in terms of what is 'likely to deprave and corrupt' and what is 'offensive'. We believe that pornography is concrete and objective and can be described and defined specifically and should be eliminated on the grounds of what it is and what it does: perpetuating the oppression of women denying women's rights and the human rights of women.

We believe that the obscenity legislation does not 'protect' women from harm, but keeps them vulnerable and ignorant. Rather than protecting women, the obscenity legislation maintains the *pretence* of protecting public morality and has been used repressively to censor art, literature and free speech and to suppress the freedoms of gay men and lesbian women.

We therefore believe that all the obscenity legislation relating to pornography should be repealed and replaced by legislation against pornography which defines pornography specifically in terms of sex plus violence plus subordination, the grounds that it maintains sex discrimination and incites sexual hatred and violence.

THE PORNOGRAPHY INDUSTRY
We believe pornography is big business. In the USA it grosses $10 billion a year — more than the music and film industries combined. We believe this industry exploits the poorest and most vulnerable women, whose opportunities to earn a living are limited by sexism and sex discrimination.

We believe that it takes advantage of the existing cycle of abuse and sexual abuse (e.g. a majority of prostitutes have been found to be the victims of childhood sexual abuse, in which pornography played a part).

We believe that it particularly exploits Black and third world women who are forced by poverty and racial discrimination into the pornography industry, which also perpetuates racist as well as sexist stereotypes.

7. WOMEN AND PORNOGRAPHY
We believe that women are conditioned by sexism to conform to the stereotyped images of femininity and womanhood. This means that women are often unaware of the ways that they are misrepresented and mistreated, often willingly agree to participate in the misrepresentation and mistreatment and feel that they 'enjoy it' or 'don't mind it'. This applies to pornography as well as to other forms of sexism. We believe that women are also forced to go along with their exploitation by sexism (in pornography as well as in employment) for economic reasons and are often coerced into pornography.

We understand the reasons for women's participation in pornography, but believe, nevertheless, that it is damaging to them as individuals as well as to women as a group. We believe that equal opportunities for women in employment and the elimination of sex discrimination would give women the real freedom of choice, diminishing the attraction that the pornography industry now holds as a form of well-paid employment.

For further information contact Campaign Against Pornography and Censorship (CPC), P.O. Box 844, London SE5 9QP.

APPENDIX IV: CPBF Manifesto 1986

A Manifesto for the Media

Fundamental to any democracy is the right to know and the right to self-expression. Consequently the few wealthy individuals, multi-national media conglomerates and unaccountable public corporations that own and control our communications systems have tremendous power.

Their business is to represent our lives as a means of supplying us with information and entertainment. In doing so they profoundly influence our ideas and opinions.

In an age of instant world-wide communication, those who control the flow of information, and the images and interpretations used in its communication, can enslave every society to which they have access. There is little correlaton between the bias in their analysis of world affairs towards the technologically more advanced, capitalist nations, and the cultural diversity of their markets, including contemporary Britain.

Nor do their commercial aims encompass the varied aspirations of the electorate. Racism, sexism and other forms of stereotyping in the media further obscure the contribution that large sections of the community make to society.

The invisibility of those who do not conform to the world-view of multi-national media companies adds a special kind of censorship to the more obvious forms that surround nuclear power, the arms race and the security services, or the situation in the north of Ireland.

In this country, despite the recommendations of several Royal Commissions and Parliamentary Reports, the public still has few rights in respect of the media, unless people can afford to go to court. Yet our ability to communicate, to learn and to organise freely, is a test of the openness of our democracy. Anti-trades union legislation, the Public Order Act, the sale of British Telecom and other privatisation measures introduced by the present government, along with interference with the BBC and plans to deregulate the airwaves have reduced these rights dramatically.

This Manifesto has been devised to stimulate public discussion about the crucial role the media plays in democracy, and to influence policy-makers. The CPBF is keen to receive comments, and suggestions about policies and legislation that will make the media more accessible and accountable to the people it is meant to serve.

The Right to Know

We can only enjoy democracy if we are free to make up our own minds. That requires a free flow of informaton and the right to demand accurate answers of those in positions of responsibility and power.

They are riddled with the "British Disease" of obsessive secrecy, and invoke commercial confidentiality and national security to avoid scrutiny and smother criticism.

More and more information is being compiled on computers controlled by private firms, the police and other government agencies. We need Freedom of Information legislation covering policy issues and personal files, to ensure that public and private sectors are obliged to explain the decisions they take on our behalf as voters and consumers.

Such legislation must be linked to the repeal of Section 2 of the Official Secrets Act and the Prevention of Terrorism Act; reform of the Contempt of Court Act to allow full coverage of the administration of justice; an end to security vetting of broadcasting staff; and the abolition of the notorious D-notice and Parliamentary Lobby systems.

Too often the vested interests of proprietors and politicians forbid coverage of "sensitive" issues.

Journalists should have the right to investigate stories on our behalf and make public their findings. In return we have the right to demand that they are accountable for their actions within the terms of a well publicised Code of Conduct.

The Right to Fair Representation

The majority of the population are robbed of the right to self-expression in the media, because journalism is dominated by white, able-bodied, heterosexual and middle class males who attempt to represent the lives and attitudes of others.

This situation will not change unless pressure is put on managements and unions to take positive action, and open up the media to those who are currently under or mis-represented — the working class, women, black people, lesbian and gay men, people with disabilities, young and old.

It means integrated casting policies, and acknowledging those for whom English is not a first language.

Advisory bodies representing and accountable to those groups worst served by the media would assist this process but a broader range of publications and programmes is also vital.

The creation of greater diversity cannot be left to market forces.

VAT on newspaper and magazine advertising could be invested in equipment, cheap loan finance and direct subsidy to help give a voice to those whose lives currently remain hidden, managed by regional Media Enterprise Boards.

Access and Accountability

We have no right of access to the media, nor is it any direct sense accountable to the public.

Our rights are supposed to be protected by the "great and the good" on the BBC Board of Governors, the Independent Broadcasting Authority, the Press Council, the Advertising Standards Authority, and the British Board of Film Censors.

Their world is a far cry from the poverty of the inner cities, the experience of most women, the varied culture of Britain's black communities, the isolation of the unemployed or the alienation of many young people, just as being based in a few large cities limits the perspectives of the media.

Present arrangements must be replaced by democratic, systems of regulation to combine the functions of the Press Council and the Broadcasting Complaints Commission.

Media monopolies must be broken up, and government plans to deregulate broadcasting and sell off licences must be scrapped.

Locally elected bodies with powers to ensure that all sections of the community have access and the right to fair representation in the media could be co-ordinated at national level.

Media organisations must recognise their special responsibility and ensure that consumers are guaranteed redress if they are unfairly abused.

Workers' Participation

The freedom of workers to organise is essential to democracy. Interference with the independence of media unions is a direct threat to press and broadcasting freedom.

Cynical use of the law by proprietors like Shah and Murdoch in an attempt to coerce printworkers is not just a means of shedding jobs or introducing new technologies. It represents an assault on the ability of print unions to apply sanctions in pursuit of the Right of Reply, as an antidote to the power of publishers to attack the weak and protect the strong.

Media unions should establish procedures through which aggrieved parties can approach them to seek redress, and work for a single media union.

Existing anti-union legislation should be repealed. There should be greater emphasis on industrial democracy within the media, with opportunities for workers to elect representatives onto editorial boards and boards of management to counter commercial influence on editorial decisions and monitor employers' practices, as an added safeguard against illicit activities by multi-nationals.

The Right to Make Contact

Electronic communication systems give the appearance of an exclusive and expensive business-oriented technology. Yet to gain access to them all people need is the facility to plug in a phone or a TV set.

The present government has allowed the development of telecommunications to be determined by market forces. An integrated approach based on public need rather than private greed is required, under a Ministry responsible for the press, broadcasting, the arts and telecommunications.

The latest technologies have the potential to extend and enhance the democratic process. They could provide easy two-way access to public services for pensioners, the house-bound, people with disabilities and the geographically isolated.

Tower blocks lend themselves to communal aerials and satellite dish transmission, telephone lines and cable links can be automatically installed in new housing — but local authorities are hesitant and British Telecom is restructuring towards commercial not public service goals.

The right to make contact involves extending the public call box system; ensuring that all households have a phone installed free; cheap rental and call charges; and increased access to cable and satellite transmission.

It means bringing British Telecom under public control, continuing state ownership of postal services, and the creation of a Communications Council to plan, monitor and regulate uses of electronic communications.

International co-operation, firm domestic legislation and public investment are the only way to ensure that the new technologies benefit the widest number of people.

Freedom of the Airwaves

Radio and TV currently offer a narrow range of options in terms of entertainment, information and opinion. Opportunities to air alternative views are rare.

Small wonder there are calls for freedom of the airwaves.

For some this means freedom to broadcast legitimate views and aspirations without having to battle with unaccountable organisations.

For others it means running radio and TV on "free market" principles, and lifting public controls — the thinking behind the government's Peacock Inquiry into BBC funding, the ill-fated Community Radio "experiment", and its Green Paper to review the structure of broadcasting.

American and European experiences show that the commercial approach further limits consumer choice and access, through cost cutting and the pursuit of profits. Community stations would be squeezed out of existence as they competed for audiences and advertising with the conglomerates that aleady dominate Fleet Street.

A democratically accountable agency able to allocate TV, radio, cable and satellite franchises with commitment to public service broadcasting, would ensure diversity in the media.

As a first step towards consumer participation and choice, it would need to be supplemented at local level by bodies with powers to share out air-time in a way that reflects the communities to be served.

Freedom of the airwaves does not mean a free for all — it means ensuring that all sections of society and all shades of legitimate opinion have the right of expression on air.

Facilities for All

If communications are to be in any sense representative, restrictions on monopoly control of the media must go hand in hand with the provision of publishing facilities open to everyone and under democratic control.

Publishing brings with it the opportunity to amass huge profits, and directly influence others. This linkage of commercial and political aims is unlikely to work in favour of the poor, the oppressed or those whose politics challenge the status quo.

The occasional opportunity to express an opinion by marking a cross on a ballot paper is no substitute for the ability to broadcast ideas.

The cost of publishing, distributing and promoting newspapers, magazines, or TV programmes is a major reason why the media remains in the hands of the elite. The cost of a national printing corporation and a network of broadcasting facilities could be met from a levy on advertising revenue or profits. Local management, in conjunction with Media Enterprise Boards must be linked to improved training in communication technologies at school and non-vocational level to encourage greater media literacy.

Media distribution systems are also controlled by a handful of companies whose policies act as a form of censorship. We need the legislation that exists in France, to guarantee all lawful publications the right to distribution and display.

The Right of Reply

Since we have no rights of redress unless we can afford to go to law, we are entirely at the mercy of the media. That is why we need a legal Right of Reply.

Everyone has a favourite example of abuses of media power — sensationalising stories, trivialising events, intruding on people's private grief, misrepresentation and plain lies.

The Press Council, financed by newspaper proprietors and largely ignored by Editors, with its cumbersome procedures and lack-lustre record is shunned by the journalists' union as a "toothless watchdog". The Broadcasting Complaints Commission is little better.

Only through organised campaigns, often supported by the CPBF and backed by the print unions, have people been able to gain adequate redress.

A legally enforceable Right of Reply, administered by an independent body able to respond rapidly to complaints about media errors, excesses and bias, and with the power to impose sanctions against offending companies should not interfere with the option of industrial action to obtain redress against recalcitrant editors or proprietors.

BIBLIOGRAPHY

Article 19, *Information, Freedom and Censorship — the Article 19 World Report*, Longmans 1988.

Baker, Bob and Harvey, Neil (eds), *Publishing for People and Fighting Censorship*, London Labour Library, 1985.

Barker, Martin, *The Video Nasties: Freedom and Censorship in the Media*, Pluto 1984.

Betterton, Rosemary, *Looking On*, Pandora 1987

Burstyn, Varda (ed), *Women Against Censorship*, Toronto, Douglas & McIntyre 1985.

Calvoceressi, Peter, *Freedom to Publish*, Index on Censorship 1980.

Carter, Angela, *The Sadeian Woman*, Virago 1979.

Christians, C.G., Potzoll, K.B. & Fackler, M., *Ethics: Cases and Moral Reasoning*, Longmans 1987.

Cline, Victor (ed), *Where Do You Draw the Line? An Exploration into Media Violence, Pornography and Censorship*, Provo (Utah), Brigham Young University Press, 1974.

Curran, James et al, *Bending Reality: the State of the Media*, Pluto/CPBF 1986.

Curran, James and Seaton, Jean, *Power Without Responsibility: The Press and Broadcasting in Britain* (2nd ed), Methuen 1985.

Davies, Kath, Dickey, Julienne and Stratford, Teresa, *Out of Focus: Writings on Women and the Media*, Women's Press 1987.

Dick, Eddie and McLean, Brian, *Open to Question: Mary Whitehouse*, The Scottish Film Council, 1988.

Dickey, Julienne & CPBF Women's Group, *Women in Focus: Guidelines for Eliminating Media Sexism*, CPBF 1985.

Donnerstein, Edward, Linz, David and Penrod, Steven, *The Question of Pornography: Research Findings and Policy Implications*, Macmillan 1987.

Dworkin, Andrea, *Pornography: Men Possessing Women*, Women's Press 1981.

Everywoman Magazine, *Pornography and Sexual Violence: Evidence of the Links*, Everywoman 1988.

Eysenck, H.J. and Nias, D.K.B., *Sex, Violence and the Media*, Paladin 1980.

Findlater, Richard, *Banned: A Review of Theatrical Censorship in Britain*, McGibbon & Kee, 1967.

Foucault, Michael, *The History of Sexuality. Vol. 1: an Introduction*, Allen Lane 1979.

Griffin, Susan, *Pornography and Silence*, Women's Press, 1981.

Haskell, Molly, *From Reverence to Rape*, NY, Penguin 1974.

Lederer, Laura, *Take Back the Night: Women on Pornography*, NY, William Morrow 1980.

Kappeler, Susanne, *The Pornography of Representation*, Polity Press 1986.

Olsen, Tillie, *Silences*, Virago 1980.

Robertson, Geoffrey & Nicol, Andrew, *Media Law*, Sage 1984.

Russ, Joanna, *How to Suppress Women's Writing*, Women's Press, 1984.

Snitow, Ann, Stansell, Christine and Thompson, Sharon, *Desire: The politics of Sexuality*, Virago 1984.

Suleiman, Susan Rubin (ed), *The Female Body in Western Culture*, Harvard University Press 1986.

Tomkinson, Martin, *The Pornbrokers: The Rise of the Soho Sex Barons*, Virgin 1982.

Williams, Bernard, *Report of the Committee on Obscenity and Film Censorship*, HMSO 1979.

NOTES ON CONTRIBUTORS

Melissa Benn is a journalist and writer. She currently works on *City Limits* magazine, and is a regular contributor to *The Guardian*, *Spare Rib*, *New Statesman* and *Marxism Today*. Her book *Death in the City* was published in 1986.

Diane Biondo is a white American lesbian, author of three plays (*Slipstream*, *Hitting Home*, *Penance*). She has worked in the book trade for nine years, and is currently working at Sisterwrite. **Florence Hamilton** is a Scottish lesbian who has lived in London for 15 years. She has worked at Sisterwrite for two years, and is currently writing a book on colonial feminists in India. **Debbie Licorish** is a 24-year-old black woman. She was the buyer of UK books for Sisterwrite, and now works at the Women's Press.

Annie Blue Radical Feminist/Lesbian Mother/White/Working Class. Born Lancashire, England . . . surviving in Hackney, London.

Elizabeth Carola I am a radical feminist lesbian, active for many years in feminist campaigning against violence against women, particularly incest and pornography. I write fiction as well as theory and generally try hard to reconcile the political and creative, in myself and in the world.

Anne Conway lives and works in Dublin. She is involved in the women's trade union and anti-imperialist movements. She presently works in the Dublin Well Woman Centre.

Lisa Duggan is a lesbian feminist writer and historian working on a dissertation on the history of American sexology.

Berta Freistadt is a Londoner. Born British of Austro-Hungarian/Scottish-Irish parents, she is half Jewish. She lives with her cat and likes most of all to mess about in the garden with plants and worms and things. She writes plays, stories and poetry.

Sue George I'm 31 and live in London with my 4-year-old son. Currently I work for the Women's Film, TV and Video Network, and my first novel will be published by Century Hutchinson in January 1988.

Kirsten Hearn I am a 32-year-old fat proud blind lesbian, an activist in the disability and lesbian and gay communities, and a tactile sculptor, writer and sometimes singer. I enjoy swimming, eating and listening to 'The Archers'.

Alice Henry has been a member of the *off our backs* collective for 10 years. She is a resident alien in Britain and enjoys doing practical work for Women in Manual Trades.

Kate Holman is a freelance journalist and former member of the NUJ Equality Working Party. She is now working in Brussels.

Nan Hunter is a feminist lawyer and activist in New York. She works with the Reproductive Freedom Project of the American Civil Liberties Union.

Catherine Itzin is the mother of two teenagers. Author of *Stages in the Revolution* (1982) and other books. Currently Senior Research Officer, Dept of Sociology, University of Essex, and Women's Officer, London Borough of Brent. Member of the Women's Rights and Executive Committees of the National Council of Civil Liberties.

Sheila Jeffreys: I am a lesbian and a revolutionary feminist who has been active since 1977 in campaigning against pornography and male violence. I write and teach on the history of sexuality. I am the author of *The Spinster and her Enemies: Feminism and Sexuality 1880–1930*, Pandora 1985. I am on the collective of the Lesbian Archive and Information Centre and involved in the Lesbian History Group.

Susanne Kappeler teaches in English and American Studies at the University of East Anglia. She has published articles in feminist and other publications, and is the author of books including *The Pornography of Representation*. She was a founding member of the Cambridge Women's Resources Centre, is on the editorial collective of *Trouble and Strife*, and is a member of Norwich Consultants on Sexual Violence.

Liz Kelly has been active in the women's liberation movement since 1973, working mainly on the issue of sexual violence. She is currently working with Mary MacLeod and Esther Sarager at the Child Abuse Studies Unit, Polytechnic of North London, to develop feminist theory and practice in relation to child sexual abuse. Her book *Surviving Sexual Violence* will be published in 1988 by Polity Press.

Mandy Merck is a journalist, lecturer and editor of the media studies quarterly *Screen*. She is currently working on a lesbian and gay series for Channel 4.

Wendy Moore is a journalist. She is also secretary of the Campaign for Press and Broadcasting Freedom and former co-chair of the NUJ Equality Council — but is writing in a personal capacity.

Sigrid Nielsen was born in 1948. She has published short stories, reviews and articles. With Gail Chester, she edited *In Other Words: Writing as a Feminist* (Hutchinson 1987). She co-founded Lavender Menace (now West & Wilde), Scotland, lesbian and gay bookshop, and was a founding member of Scotland's feminist publisher, Stramullion.

Noreen O'Donoghue has worked for the Women's Community Press in Dublin since 1983. Her interest is in encouraging women to write their own stories, and to broaden the definition of history and of literature.

Sona Osman I am a socialist feminist lawyer; I used to work on *Spare Rib* and have written articles for various publications. I like eating too.

Pratibha Pramar is a writer, film-maker and a political activist. She has co-edited several books, including *The Empire Strikes Back* (Hutchinson, 1982), *Through the Break* (Sheba, 1987), *Charting the Journey: Writings by Black and Third World Women* (Sheba, 1988), and has written for *Marxism Today, Women's Review, City Limits* and other periodicals. Her films and videos include *Emergence* (1986) and *Reframing AIDS* (1988).

Barbara Rogers is a founder member of *Everywoman* magazine and is responsible for editorial work. She has written books on women, and on Southern Africa, which include *52%: Getting Women's Power into Politics*, *The Domestication of Women* and *Men Only: An investigation of Men's Organisations*.

Ros Schwartz is a freelance translator from French and Italian, and a sporadic writer of articles on the subject. She contributed to and co-edited *Reviewing the Reviews* (Journeyman Press, 1987), and is one of the editors of the first anthology of writing by Jewish feminists in Britain, to be published by The Women's Press in 1989.

Denise Searle has been a journalist since 1979 and has worked on a variety of weekly and monthly magazines in Britain. She is currently a sub-editor for the Sofia Press Agency in Bulgaria. She was a member of the National Executive Council of the National Union of Journalists 1985–7, and was secretary of the Shelve it! campaign to confine *Sunday Sport* to the top shelf of newsagents' shops.

Elizabeth Sidney is a past president of the Women's Liberal Federation and past chairman of the Liberal party's policy panel on employment. She is presently a member of the Interim Committee of Women Democrats in the SLD, and Chair of the Green Alliance. She co-wrote *The Future Woman* with Shirley Conran.

Barbara Smith is a right-off feminist dyke who has contributed to various lesbian, gay and feminist publications including *Square Peg*, *Spare Rib*, *Gay Times*, *Gay Scotland* and *The Pink Paper*. She is presently researching an M.Phil. thesis on the anthropology of Ancient Greek drama, and lives, studies and fucks in North London.

Teresa Stratford is a vice-chair of the Campaign for Press and Broadcasting Freedom, and chairs its legislation group. She works at St Thomas' Hospital, where she is Senior Occupational Therapist, and writes a regular column on health for *City Limits*.

Carole S. Vance is an athropologist at Columbia University in New York. She writes about sex, gender, politics and the body. She is the editor of *Pleasure and Danger: Exploring Female Sexuality* (1984), and is currently completing a book on the Meese Commission.

Melba Wilson is a freelance journalist who writes on health and issues affecting black people.